ARABIC SECOND LANGUAGE ACQUISITION OF MORPHOSYNTAX

D1595881

ARABIC SECOND LANGUAGE ACQUISITION OF MORPHOSYNTAX

MOHAMMAD T. ALHAWARY
The University of Oklahoma

Yale University Press
New Haven and London

Publisher: Mary Jane Peluso

Editorial Assistant: Elise Panza

Project Editor: Timothy Shea

Production Editor: Ann-Marie Imbornoni

Production Controller: Karen Stickler

Printed in the United States of America.

ISBN: 978-0-300-14129-0
Library of Congress Control Number: 2008943948

A catalogue record for this book is available from the British Library.

This paper meets the requirements of ANSI/NISO Z39.48-1992 (Permanence of Paper).

10 9 8 7 6 5 4 3 2 1

To
Abu 'Amr Ibn Al-'Alaa'
(70–154 H./689–771 C.E.),
the first Arab linguist who did field linguistics,
eliciting data from the tribes of Arabia

Contents

Preface

The transcription of all Arabic texts in the body of the book follows the International Phonetic Alphabet or standard equivalents as in marking vowel length. A list of all transliteration symbols used is provided. For the citation of Arabic titles and names of Arab authors in the references section, a simplified transliteration system based on standard usage in Arabic and Middle Eastern Studies journals has been adopted. The symbol ' represents the *hamza* (glottal stop) and ' represents the *'ayn* (voiced pharyngeal fricative consonant). In addition, following standard practice, the definite article {ʔal-} is fully stated (without assimilating any part) in all of the Arabic examples except in cited utterances of the L2 learners.

Acknowledgments

This book and the research upon which it is based would not have been possible without the effort and help of many people. My gratitude goes first to all the participants in this research, who volunteered on campuses in the United States, France, Japan, and Spain. I owe sincere gratitude to all those who generously gave their time to help recruit the participants, including Professor Peter Abboud, Professor Aman Attieh, Professor Amin Bonnah, Professor Margaret Nydell, Professor Jean Tardy, Professor Abdelghani Benali, Professor Georgine Ayoub, Professor Robert Ratcliffe, Tominaga Masato, Professor Ignacio Gutiérrez de Terán, and Professor Waleed Saleh Alkhalifa.

I would like to thank the external reviewers for their careful reading and insightful comments: Professor Adel Suleiman Gamal of the University of Arizona, Professor Ahmed Fakhri of West Virginia University, Dr. Shukri Abed of the Middle East Institute, and Professor Solomon Sara of Georgetown University.

I would also like to thank Mary Jane Peluso of Yale University Press for all her efforts in bringing this book to publication and for her vision in publishing much-needed resource books for the less commonly taught languages. I would also like to thank Elise Panza for her diligent work and all the prompt assistance which she provided during the different preperartion stages of the book. Many thanks go to Ann-Marie Imbornoni for proofreading the book and for her invaluable editorial comments and suggestions. I thank all other Yale University Press staff including: Timothy Shea and Karen Stickler, for their work during the final production stage. I thank Shayna Woidke for redrawing some of the illustrations and Pearson Education, Inc., for granting permission to reprint the copyrighted illustrations.

I am especially indebted to my wife, Jennifer, and our four children, for their love and moral support, and for putting up with what seemed to be endless hours of work which I spent on the different stages of the data, the checking and re-checking of the data, and the writing of this book. In addition, I greatly benefited from Jennifer's invaluable editing and proofreading remarks. Her expert advice stems from her training in linguistics and from having been herself a learner of Arabic as a foreign language.

Finally, I would like to gratefully acknowledge the funding provided for parts of this research by the Research Council, College of Arts and Sciences, School of International and Area Studies, and Department of Modern Languages, Literatures, and Linguistics at the University of Oklahoma.

Introduction

The objectives of this book are to provide data-driven findings as well as systematic analysis of second language acquisition (SLA) of Arabic. Little has been published on Arabic second language acquisition. Studies that have appeared so far either focus on a limited set of structures or suffer from methodological limitations related mostly to elicitation techniques and small data samples. This book aims at exploring a broad range of structures and acquisition issues based on large data samples collected longitudinally (from 9 participants over a school year) and cross-sectionally (over the past ten years from 109 participants with three different lengths of formal exposure to Arabic as a second/foreign language (L2): first year, second year, and third year). The data were collected from Arabic L2 learners with different native languages (L1s), specifically, from adult native English, French, Spanish, and Japanese speakers learning Arabic as an L2 at the university level at their home institutions in the United States, France, Spain, and Japan, respectively. Parts of the data have been published or presented at national and international conferences. However, the book includes significant additional amounts of data that have not previously appeared elsewhere in order to provide a larger picture of the acquisition issues and questions explored.

Focus here is on the analysis of the different processes, hypotheses, stages, and acquisition patterns of the participants. An attempt will be made to relate the findings to a range of observations, some of which have been established as truisms, as well as to hypotheses in the field of SLA, although little has been reported on Arabic SLA. The point of departure for the underlying methodology of the present work assumes avoidance of the limitations of earlier second language acquisition approaches, from contrastive and error analysis to the present. In essence, this means the following aspects are taken into account:

- The overall L2 performance of the participants rather than solely errors
- Rule application in non-contexts and the full scope of Interlanguage rule use
- The (formal) input of the participants in the classroom
- Qualitative and quantitative analyses of the data
- Inclusion of both longitudinal and cross-sectional data
- L2 learners with different L1s
- Accurate description and analysis of the target forms
- Large data samples from a large number of participants

Doubtless, accounting for the process of second language acquisition is not without limitations. For example, to date and despite technological breakthroughs, a whole host of variables such as external acquisition variables (age, aptitude, attitude, anxiety, motivation, learning environment, social distance, ethnicity, etc.) are still not possible to quantify and therefore SLA is constrained from being able to fully account for second language acquisition phenomenon (for example, Pienemann and Johnston 1987). Hence, to date the field lacks a comprehensive theory of acquisition (Klein 1991). Notwithstanding the unavoidable limitations of present inquiries into SLA research, the data here are significant not only for shedding light on the production abilities of Arabic L2ers with different L1s from an explanatory perspective but also for contributing to predictive issues of current theories and models of SLA, especially those to do with second language processing and L1 transfer.

Thus, two main research objectives are of particular interest to the present work. The first is to document and explain generally how Arabic second language morphosyntactic knowledge develops over time. This includes identifying forms that are acquired before others, forms that are acquired upon exposure, and forms that resist acquisition even after long exposure. This also includes explaining and identifying intermediate stages during the acquisition process. The second objective is to speculate on second language knowledge representation and internal learning and processing mechanisms. In essence, the book aims at providing answers to the following questions, among others:

- How do Arabic L2 learners come to know about the combinatorial properties of morphemes, words, phrases, and clauses? (see Hawkins 2001)
- Do they develop L2 knowledge representation systematically or randomly?
- Can they acquire the same range of syntactic and morphological knowledge as native speakers and to what extent?
- What are the developmental paths or stages, if any, along which Arabic L2 learners progress?
- What is the role of L1 in learning Arabic as an L2?
- What are other factors that have a bearing on learning Arabic as a second language?

The book is organized as follows:

- Chapter 1: Description of Target Morphosyntactic Structures
- Chapter 2: Existing Arabic SLA Studies
- Chapter 3: The Acquisition of Gender Agreement
- Chapter 4: The Acquisition of Tense/Aspect and Verbal Agreement
- Chapter 5: The Acquisition of Null Subjects
- Chapter 6: The Acquisition of Negation, Mood, and Case
- Chapter 7: Theoretical Implications
- Chapter 8: Pedagogical and Applied Implications

Chapter 1 gives a brief description of the target structures and other relevant aspects of the language related to the data reported on in chapters 3-6. Chapter 2 provides a survey of all Arabic SLA studies conducted to date. Explanation of the findings is kept to a minimum, with summary boxes added to help further capture the main findings and methods of each study. Chapters 3-6 constitute the data and findings sections of the book. In these chapters, the book adopts a descriptive style in reporting about the various methods (including the demographic details of the participants, elicitation techniques, coding, and data analysis, etc.) and the findings yielded. In addition, an attempt is made at providing an account of the formal input which the participants received, in particular those in the longitudinal study. To preserve the usability of the data and to allow the reader to readily access the nature and extent of the success of the Arabic L2 learners/participants, the data are analyzed qualitatively and quantitatively and the findings are briefly and descriptively stated, avoiding speculative discussion of factors and issues not immediately evident to the reader. The latter is reserved for Chapter 7, which aims at connecting the reported observations and findings of the Arabic data with recent and current proposals in the SLA literature. Chapter 8 aims at providing suggested implications and practical applications of the findings to the subfields of Arabic applied linguistics. The glossary is intended to help make the text more accessible to the general reader and the non-specialist.

The book will be particularly useful for second language acquisition practitioners seeking cross-linguistic evidence, Arabic textbook writers, Arabic testing experts, teachers-in-training of Arabic as a second/foreign language, and teachers and Arabists seeking to know how Arabic is learned from the learner's perspective. The book will also be useful in the contexts of foreign language learning of Arabic by English, French, Spanish, and Japanese speakers in classrooms around the world or in the respective countries where these languages are spoken as L1s.

Transliteration Symbols

Below is a list of transliteration symbols used to represent the Arabic sound system.

Consonants:

Arabic Symbol	Transliteration Symbol	
ب	b	voiced bilabial stop
ت	t	voiceless alveolar stop
ث	θ	voiceless inter-dental fricative
ج	dʒ	voiced palato-alveolar fricative
ح	ħ	voiceless pharyngeal fricative
خ	x	voiceless velar fricative
د	d	voiced alveolar stop
ذ	ð	voiced inter-dental fricative
ر	r	voiced alveolar trill
ز	z	voiced alveolar fricative
س	s	voiceless alveolar fricative
ش	š	voiceless palato-alveolor fricative
ص	sˤ	voiceless alveolar fricative emphatic
ض	dˤ	voiced alveolar stop emphatic
ط	tˤ	voiceless alveolar stop emphatic
ظ	ðˤ	voiced inter-dental fricative emphatic
ع	ʕ	voiced pharyngeal fricative
غ	γ	voiced velar fricative
ف	f	voiceless labio-dental fricative
ق	q	voiceless uvular stop
ك	k	voiceless velar stop

ل	l	voiced alveolar lateral
م	m	voiced bilabial nasal
ن	n	voiced alveolar nasal
هـ	h	voiceless glottal fricative
و	w	voiced bilabial velar glide
ي	y	voiced palatal glide
ء	ʔ	(voiceless) glottal stop
يّ	yy	geminate of y
وّ	ww	geminate of w

Vowels:

Arabic Symbol	Transliteration Symbol	
◌َ	a	short front/back low
ا	ā	long front/back low
◌ُ	u	short high back rounded
و	ū	long high back rounded
◌ِ	i	short high front unrounded
ي	ī	long high front unrounded

Abbreviations

Symbol	Meaning
1	First person
2	Second person
3	Third person
A	Adjective
acc	Accusative Case
AGR	Grammatical Agreement
ANOVA	Analysis of Variance
A-P	Active Participle
CA	Classical Arabic
CP	Complementizer Phrase
d	Dual
Dem	Demonstrative Pronoun
Det	Determiner
dip	Diptote
DP	Determiner Phrase
f	Feminine
gen	Genitive Case
h	Human
IL	Interlanguage
impera	Imperative
imperf	Imperfective
indef	Indefinite

indic	Indicative Mood
juss	Jussive Mood
L1	First/native language
L2	Second/foreign language
L2er	Second language learner
LFG	Lexical Functional Grammar
m	Masculine
MANOVA	Multivariate Analysis of Variance
MSA	Modern Standard Arabic
N	Noun
N-A	Noun-Adjective
nom	Nominative Case
NP	Noun Phrase
OVS	Object-Verb-Subject
p	Plural
perf	Perfective
P-P	Passive participle
s	Singular
SLA	Second Language Acquisition
subjunc	Subjunctive Mood
S-V	Subject-Verb
SVO	Subject-Verb-Object
t	Time/session of data collection
TL	Target Language
V	Verb
VP	Verb Phrase
VSO	Verb-Subject-Object
UG	Universal Grammar

CHAPTER 1

Description of Target Morphosyntactic Structures

The description provided here relates primarily to Modern Standard Arabic (MSA), which is essentially the same as Classical Arabic (CA), though the former is somewhat more simplified syntactically and generally more restricted in optional rule use. Significant differences between the two will be pointed out in the course of this chapter to indicate that both versions are acceptable grammatically. Indeed, current Arabic textbooks in use—which constitute the learners' language input—seem to follow the MSA tendency. The description is not intended to be exhaustive but rather focuses on aspects of the language relevant to the data investigated and on basic features which are characterized by a great degree of regularity and which Arabic learners are exposed to in the first years of their learning.

1.1 Arabic Word Structure

1.1.1 *Root and base form*

As in other Semitic languages, words in Arabic have a unique underlying form-meaning relationship. Arabic words are derived from combining patterns and core root consonants. The former usually consist of vowels and auxiliary consonants and the latter carries the core semantic meaning. The complete meaning of a given word obtains only from combining both, since the pattern also carry the meaning related to the affixation form. The main point here is that a given word can have a large number of related words sharing the same semantic core meaning. Thus, as Table 1.1 shows, from the root *d-r-s* "that to do with studying" a large number of related words can be derived. The derivation is carried out by different types of affixation, including prefixes, suffixes, and infixes or circumfixes. Infixing takes place word internally, as illustrated in Figure 1.1 (following O'Grady et al. 2001), where the perfective infix *a-a* is affixed to the root *d-r-s* "that to do with studying" to form the past tense.

Table 1.1

Root **d-r-s**	Derived Form	Lexical Category	Gloss
	darasa	V	"he studied"
	yadrus	V	"he studies"
	darrasa	V	"he taught"
	tadārasa	V	"they both (2.p.d) studied"
	dirāsa	N	"studying"
	dars	N	"a lesson"
	darsān	N	"two lessons"
	durūs	N	"lessons"
	madrasa	N	"a school/a study place"
	madāris	N	"schools/study places"

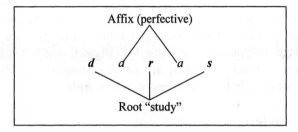

Figure 1.1

As pointed out by traditional Arab grammarians, the vast majority of words (nouns and verbs) have three root consonants; some (nouns and verbs) have four; and some (nouns) five. Table 1.2 displays examples of this phenomenon in nouns and verbs. Additionally, such words can be base forms from which other forms can be derived, or what is referred to in traditional Arabic grammar as *mudʒarrada* and *mazīda* forms, respectively. Thus, from the base form *darasa* "he studied" another verb, for example, *darrasa* "he taught" can be derived by duplicating the second consonant to add a causative meaning (see Tables 1.1-1.2).

Table 1.2

Number of Root Consonants	Root	Derived Form	Lexical Category	Gloss
3	**d-r-s**	*darasa*	V	"he studied"
3	**r-dʒ-l**	*radʒul*	N	"a man"
4	**d-ħ-r-dʒ**	*daħradʒa*	V	"he rolled"
4	**d-r-h-m**	*dirham*	N	"a penny"
5	**s-f-r-dʒ-l**	*safardʒal*	N	"quince"

The tables above illustrate basic Arabic derivational morphology in nouns and verbs. Adjectives are similarly derived, mostly from three root consonants or trilateral (that is, consisting of three root consonants) base forms and, like verbs and nouns, have many different patterns, as illustrated in Table 1.3. The examples include real adjectives and active and passive participles derived from verbs. All listed examples appear in the masculine form.

Table 1.3

Root	Derived Form	Lexical Category	Gender	Gloss
k-b-r	*kabīr*	A	M	"big"
q-l-q	*qaliq*	A	M	"worried"
ʕ- tˤ-š	*ʕatˤšān*	A	M	"thirsty"
ħ-m-r	*ʔaħmar*	A	M	"red"
d-r-s	*dāris*	A-P	M	"studier/researcher"
d-r-s	*madrūs*	P-P	M	"studied"

The foregoing description offers only a brief account of the working of the root system in the Arabic language. Whether or not it may have implications for L2 learning, it is worth mentioning here that many studies have provided evidence in support of the psychological reality of the root system (in Arabic and Semitic languages) based on slips of the tongue data (for example, Abd El-Jawad and Abu-Salim 1987; Berg and Abd El-Jawad

1996), aphasic data (for example, Prunet et al. 2000), hypocoristic data (Davis and Zawaydeh 2001; Frisch and Zawaydeh 2001), and first language development data (Berman 1985, 1999; Badry 2005; see also McCarthy 1981). Others have claimed that the processes of derivation in Arabic rely on the word as a base form rather than on the root (for example, Ratcliffe 1997; Benmamoun 1999). Whatever the case (for first language development), it is more crucial to note here that not all patterns have productive uniformity and that L2ers are not usually introduced to the notion of root and pattern from the beginning. The derived forms illustrated in the tables above are usually introduced as base forms for other forms, such as past versus present and singular versus dual and plural, with the notion of roots and patterns introduced later mainly to develop the skill of looking up words in Arabic dictionaries.

1.1.2 *Gender of nouns and adjectives*

Arabic nouns are marked by either natural gender or grammatical gender. Natural gender refers to natural or biological assignment of gender (masculine and feminine) to words according to the natural distinction of human and animal referents, as in (1) below; whereas grammatical gender refers to the arbitrary assignment of gender (masculine or feminine) to words whose referents often do not exhibit any apparent reason for the distinction, as in (2). Additionally, Arabic does not exhibit neutral gender.

(1)	Natural gender:	*ʔinsān*	"a male human being"
		ʔinsān-a	"a female human being"
		qitˤtˤ	"a male cat"
		qitˤtˤ-a	"a female cat"
(2)	Grammatical gender:	*kursī*	"chair.m"
		tˤāwil-a	"table-f"

The words listed in (1) and (2) illustrate that the masculine form is marked by a zero morpheme {-0}, the masculine form being usually the default base form. The examples also show that the feminine form is marked by the suffix {-a}.[1] However, the natural feminine forms need not be derived from the masculine forms, as in (3)—not unlike grammatical gender, as illustrated in (2).

(3) *radʒul*   "a man"

    ʔimraʔ-a   "a woman"

    dʒamal   "a he-camel"

    nāq-a   "a she-camel"

In addition, there are three small subclasses of nouns that violate the above distinction: nouns, such as *ħayy-a* "snake," that end with the feminine ending {-a} but can be used as feminine or masculine depending on the intended (natural) gender of an animal; nouns, such as *faras* "horse," that do not end with the gender suffix {-a} but can be used as feminine or masculine depending on the intended gender; and nouns, such as those listed in (4) below, that involve grammatical gender but do not exhibit a feminine gender suffix. This third subclass of words can be used as either feminine or masculine in CA. In MSA, however, they are mostly used as masculine as part of a simplifying trend.

(4) *tˁarīq*   "road"

    sabīl   "path, road"

    sūq   "market"

    dalū   "bucket"

    sikkīn   "knife"

    xamr   "wine"

The feminine suffix {-a} is not the only feminine gender marker in Arabic. There are two other feminine suffixes not quite different in principle from {-a}. These are {-ā} and {-āʔ}, as in the words listed in (5).

(5) *ʔunθā*   "female"

    ʕasˁā   "a stick-f"

    sˁaħrāʔ "a desert-f"

    samāʔ   "a sky-f"[2]

The vast majority of Arabic feminine singular nouns exhibit these three endings (see Ṣaydāwī 1999:297). However, there are some exceptions that can be termed as crypto feminine (to use Whorf's terminology), where, for example, a small subclass of words is marked for feminine (grammatical) gender by a zero morpheme (that is, by having the same ending as the masculine form), as in (6).

(6) *nafs* "self.f"
ħarb "war.f"
ʔardˤ "earth.f"
šams "sun.f"
kaʔs "a glass.f"
dār "a house.f"[3]

In addition, there are some proper names that have the masculine (zero) ending and are used as female names and some proper names that end with a feminine suffix and are used as male names, as in (7) below.

(7) *zaynab* = a female name
suʕād = a female name
ħamza = a male name
yaħyā = a male name

Proper names, however, should not present the same degree of difficulty as crypto feminine terms, since proper names are usually learned as unanalyzed chunks. Notwithstanding the few irregular cases of gender markings on nouns (especially the feminine nouns that do not end with a feminine suffix), nouns are characterized by a great deal of regularity in MSA.[4]

Adjectives are characterized by even more regularity in MSA, exhibiting the same gender suffixes as nouns: {*-a*}, {*-ā*}, and {*-āʔ*}. Table 1.4 (cf. Table 1.3 above) lists adjectives inflected for both masculine and feminine gender distinctions. The table illustrates the three feminine endings, the most prevalent of which is the {*-a*} suffix. The table also illustrates that the choice of the ending depends on the particular pattern of adjectives, setting aside their semantic triggers as observed by traditional Arab grammarians (for example, see Al-Hulwānī 1972:270-271). Given that it is permissible in MSA to supply the suffix {*-a*} where CA would require the suffix {*-ā*}, as in *ʕatˤšān* and *ʕatˤšā*/*ʕatˤšān-a* "thirsty" for masculine and feminine respectively, this means that the feminine affix can in fact be restricted to two rather than three suffixes (see Majma' Al-lugha Al-'Arabiyya 1984:126, 131-132). Hence this makes it an easier task for the

L2er to supply the feminine ending on adjectives. In other words, except when the masculine form (ending with a zero morpheme) has the pattern of *ʔafʕal* with the corresponding feminine pattern being *faʕlā*, which is specific to color adjectives and body deformities, the only other option is the feminine ending {-*a*}.

Table 1.4

Masculine	Feminine	Gloss	Reasons for Type of Suffix
dāris	*dāris-a*	"studying/student"	due to pattern/derived A-P
madrūs	*madrūs-a*	"studied"	due to pattern/derived P-P
qaliq	*qaliq-a*	"worried"	due to pattern
kabīr	*kabīr-a*	"big"	due to pattern
ʕatˤšān	*ʕatˤšā/ ʕatˤšān-a**	"thirsty"	due to pattern
ʔahmar	*hamrāʔ*	"red"	color adjective/due to pattern
ʔaʕradʒ	*ʕardʒāʔ*	"limping"	due to pattern

* = The {-*a*} suffix is allowed in MSA instead of CA's feminine pattern *faʕlā*.

In addition, there is a class of adjectives of certain patterns, such as *mifʕal, mifʕāl, mifʕīl,* or *faʕūl* (when they carry the meaning of an active participle) and *faʕīl, fiʕl,* or *faʕl* (when they carry the meaning of the passive participle), that do not require a feminine suffix in CA (that is, the masculine and feminine form are identical, ending with a zero morpheme), as in (8) below (see Al-Ghalayyīnī 2000:100-101).

(8)   *radʒul dʒarīh*   *ʔimraʔa dʒarīh*
        man   wounded.m   woman   wounded.m
        "a wounded man"   "a wounded woman"[5]

However, the simplification tendency in MSA has been to mark the adjective with the feminine referent by means of the {-*a*} suffix as acknowledged by the Egyptian Arabic Language Academy to be grammatically correct (see Majma' Al-Lugha Al-'Arabiyya 1984). The CA examples in (8) are rewritten in (9) as sanctioned MSA use.

(9)   *radʒul dʒarīh*   *ʔimraʔa dʒarīh-a*
       man   wounded.m   woman wounded.f
       "a wounded man"   "a wounded woman"

Similarly, there are words in CA that do not exhibit a feminine ending, as they refer to an exclusively female quality, such as *ħāmil* "pregnant," *ħāʔidˤ* "menstruating," and *θayyib* "a female who is not virgin." Such words follow the regular rule in MSA, exhibiting the feminine suffix {-a}. Thus, it is grammatically correct in MSA to have *ħāmil-a* "pregnant," *ħāʔidˤ-a* "menstruating," and *θayyib-a* "a female who is not virgin" (Majmaʿ Al-Lugha Al-ʿArabiyya 1984:126, 131-133). Thus, gender markings (feminine or masculine) for adjectives, as for nouns, are quite regular in MSA.

It is worthwhile to note here that current Arabic L2 textbooks follow the simplification tendencies and rules of MSA. Furthermore, the highly regular feminine gender suffix {-a} in nouns and adjectives is the most prevalent of the three suffixes and almost exclusively used during the first year of Arabic L2 instruction.

1. 2 Nominal Inflectional Agreement Features
1.2.1 *Agreement within NPs*
In Arabic, NPs consisting of a head noun and an attributive adjective involve agreement between these two elements in gender (masculine or feminine), number (singular, dual, or plural), definiteness, and case (nominative, accusative, or genitive). Examples (10)-(13) illustrate the Arabic agreement phenomenon between the head noun and the attributive adjective with respect to number (singular), gender (singular masculine and singular feminine), and case (nominative, accusative, and genitive).

10(a) *tˤālib-u-n*   *qasˤīr-u-n*
       student.s.m-nom-indef   short.s.m-nom-indef
       "a short (male) student"

10(b) *tˤālib-a-n*   *qasˤīr-a-n*
       student.s.m-acc-indef   short.s.m-acc-indef
       "a short (male) student"

10(c) *tˤālib-i-n*   *qasˤīr-i-n*
       student.s.m-gen-indef   short.s.m-gen-indef
       "a short (male) student"

11(a)   *t^{ʕ}ālib-at-u-n*   *qas^{ʕ}īr-at-u-n*
        student-s.f-nom-indef   short-s.f-nom-indef
        "a short (female) student"

11(b)   *t^{ʕ}ālib-at-a-n*   *qas^{ʕ}īr-at-a-n*
        student-s.f-acc-indef   short-s.f-acc-indef
        "a short (female) student"

11(c)   *t^{ʕ}ālib-at-i-n*   *qas^{ʕ}īr-at-i-n*
        student-s.f-gen-indef short-s.f-gen-indef
        "a short (female) student"

12(a)   *ʔal-maqʕad-u*   *ʔal-s^{ʕ}aɣīr-u*
        the-desk.s.m-nom   the-small.s.m-nom
        "the small desk"

12(b)   *ʔal-maqʕad-a*   *ʔal-s^{ʕ}aɣīr-a*
        the-desk.s.m-acc   the-small.s.m-acc
        "the small desk"

12(c)   *ʔal-maqʕad-i*   *ʔal-s^{ʕ}aɣīr-i*
        the-desk.s.m-gen   the-small.s.m-gen
        "the small desk"

13(a)   *ʔal-t^{ʕ}āwil-at-u*   *ʔal-s^{ʕ}aɣīr-at-u*
        the-table-s.f-nom   the-small-s.f-nom
        "the small table"

13(b)   *ʔal-t^{ʕ}āwil-at-a*   *ʔal-s^{ʕ}aɣīr-at-a*
        the-table-s.f-acc   the-small-s.f-acc
        "the small table"

13(c)   *ʔal-t^{ʕ}āwil-at-i*   *ʔal-s^{ʕ}aɣīr-at-i*
        the-table-s.f-gen   the-small-s.f-gen
        "the small table"

Examples (10)-(11) show that the indefinite (in the singular) is signaled by *nunation* "an ending marker," or {*-n*}. As explained above, when case is produced on words inflected for a feminine ending {*-a*}, then the feminine ending that is realized is {*-at*}, with [t] surfacing in formal MSA, as in (11) and (13). However, it is quite possible to not produce case endings without affecting the meaning, so long as a straightforward SVO word order (see Section 1.3 below) is maintained, corresponding to pause forms in CA and MSA, as is often observed in casual MSA, semiformal speech, and spoken Arabic.[6] Thus, the corresponding pause, but regularly attested, forms in MSA of (10)-(13) are given below as (14)-(17).

(14) $t^ʕālib$ $qasʕīr$
       student.s.m   short.s.m
       "a short (male) student"

(15) $t^ʕālib$-a $qasʕīr$-a
       student-s.f   short-s.f
       "a short (female) student"

(16) $ʔal$-$maqʕad$ $ʔal$-$sʕaɣīr$
       the-desk.s.m   the-small.s.m
       "the small desk"

(17) $ʔal$-$t^ʕāwil$-a $ʔal$-$sʕaɣīr$-a
       the-table-s.f   the-small-s.f
       "the small table"

1.3   Equational (Verbless) Sentence Structure

Equational or verbless sentences consist of two main constituent phrase structures without a copular lexical verb surfacing and are marked in the imperfective/present tense. The first phrase is usually referred to as *mubtadaʔ* "starter" (or topic/subject) and the second as *xabar* "news" (or comment/predicate). Both constituent structures agree in number, gender, and case but not in definiteness. The first constituent occurs usually in the definite while the second occurs in the indefinite.[7] Sentences (18)-(26) illustrate the structure of equational sentences.

(18) $ʔal$-$t^ʕālib$-u $dʒadīd$-u-n
       the-student.s.m-nom   new.s.m-nom-indef
       "The (male) student is new."

(19) $ʔal$-$t^ʕālib$-at-u $dʒadīd$-at-u-n
       the-student-s.f-nom   new-s.f-nom-indef
       "The (female) student is new."

(20)   huwa $dʒadīd$-u-n
       he   new.s.m-nom-indef
       "He is new."

(21)   hiya $dʒadīd$-at-u-n
       she   new-s.f-nom-indef
       "She is new."

(22) $wālid$-at-ī $sūriyy$-at-u-n
       mother-s.f-my   Syrian-s.f-nom-indef
       "My mother is Syrian."

(23) *hāðā*   *tˤālib-u-n*
this.s.m   student.s.m-nom-indef
"This is a (male) student."

(24) *hāðihi*   *tˤālib-at-u-n*
this.s.f   student-s.f-nom-indef
"This is a (female) student."

(25) *hāðā*   *tˤālib-u-n*   *dʒadīd-u-n*
this.s.m   student.s.m-nom-indef   new.s.m-nom-indef
"This is a new (male) student."

(26) *hāðā*   *ʔal-tˤālib-u*   *dʒadīd-u-n*
this.s.m   the-student.s.m-nom   new.s.m-nom-indef
"This (male) student is new."

Sentences (18)-(26) above indicate that the first constituent phrase must be definite whether by means of the definite article as in (18)-(19), personal pronoun as in (20)-(21), possessive pronoun as in (22), or demonstrative pronoun as in (23)-(24). Sentences (25)-(26) show that either constituent phrase may consist of more than one word. As discussed above, it is quite possible to produce such sentences without case endings, as is generally attested in casual and semiformal speech, without disrupting the meaning, since case does not carry crucial meaning as long as an SVO or VSO word order is strictly observed. However, both constituent phrases must be inflected for the feature agreement of number and gender. Accordingly, the pause form without case markings of (18)-(19), for example, can be reproduced as (27)-(28) below.

(27) *ʔal-tˤālib*   *dʒadīd*
the-student.s.m   new.s.m
"The (male) student is new."

(28) *ʔal-tˤālib-a*   *dʒadīd-a*
the-student-s.f   new-s.f
"The (female) student is new."

Sentences (25)-(26) show the distinction between sentences containing a demonstrative pronoun as subject of a verbless sentence and NPs containing a demonstrative modifying a head noun, respectively. In the latter, the noun modified by the demonstrative pronoun is always definite. Demonstrative pronouns are inflected for gender, number, animacy, and case and match the head nouns with respect to these features. In such a phrase, a head noun, together with the demonstrative, serves as any argument type, including subject, object, and object of a preposition, etc., as in sentences (29)-(31), respectively.

(29)   *hāðihi*   *ʔal-sayyār-a(t-u)*   *kabīr-a(t-u-n)*[8]
       this.s.f   the-car-s.f-nom   big-s.f-nom-indef
       "This car is big."

(30)   *ʔu-ḥibb(-u)*   *hāðihi*   *ʔal-sayyār-a(t-a)*
       1.s-like-indic   this.s.f   the-car-s.f-acc
       "I like this car."

(31)   *ʔa-nðˤur(-u)*   *ʔilā*   *hāðihi*   *ʔal-sayyār-a(t-i)*
       1.s-look-indic   at   this.s.f   the-car-s.f-gen
       "I (am) look(ing) at this car."

However, if the head noun or (predicative) adjective occurs in the indefinite following a demonstrative pronoun, then both elements would constitute two (phrasal) constituents of an equational (verbless copular) sentence with the noun or adjective functioning as a predicate argument and the demonstrative pronoun as the subject, as in (23)-(25).

1.3.1 *Past tense of equational (verbless) sentences*

For equational sentences to be expressed in the past (or the future) tense, the copular verb *kāna* "was" surfaces.[9] In this case, of course, the structure is no longer equational in nature (that is, verbless), equational sentences occurring restrictively in the imperfective/present tense. The verb *kāna* is inflected for person, gender, and number to agree with the subject as any other verb in Arabic. In addition, the predicate exhibits agreement with the subject (in gender and number) and is in the accusative case, as in (32)-(37).

(32)   *kāna*   *ʔal-tˤālib(-u)*   *mubakkir(-a-n)*[10]
       be.perf.3.s.m   the-student.s.m-nom   early.s.m-acc-indef
       "The (male) student was early."

(33)   *kāna*   *ʔal-tˤullāb(-u)*   *mubakkir-īna*[11]
       be.perf.3.s.m   the-student.p.m-nom   early-p.m.acc
       "The (male) students were early."

(34)   *ʔal-tˤullāb(-u)*   *kān-ū*   *mubakkir-īna*
         the-student.p.m-nom   be.perf-3.p.m   early-p.m.acc
         "The (male) students were early."

(35)   *kān-at*   *ʔal-tˤālib-a(t-u)*   *mubakkir-a(t-a-n)*
         be.perf-3.s.f   the-student-s.f-nom   early-s.f-acc-indef
         "The (female) student was early."

(36)   *kān-at*   *ʔal-tˤālib-āt(-u)*   *mubakkir-āt(-i-n)*
         be.perf-3.s.f   the-student-p.f-nom   early-p.f-acc-indef
         "The (female) students were early."

(37)   *ʔal-tˤālib-āt(-u)*   *kun-na*   *mubakkir-āt(-i-n)*
         the-student-p.f-nom   be.perf-3.p.f   early-p.f-acc-indef
         "The (female) students were early."

Additionally, sentences (33)-(34) and (36)-(37) show that the copular verb *kāna* may precede the subject or follow it with the consequence that *kāna* in the former is only inflected for person and gender and in the latter fully inflected for person, gender, and number (see Section 1.4 below for more on agreement within SV or VSO order). In addition to the above agreement pattern between *kāna* and the subject, the predicate exhibits agreement with the subject (in gender and number) and is in the accusative case.

1.3.2 *Negation of equational (verbless) sentences*

Negation of equational sentences can be expressed, though not exclusively,[12] by use of *laysa* "is not," which is inflected for person, gender, and number, as in sentences (38)-(42).[13]

(38)   *laysa*   *ʔal-tˤālib(-u)*   *mubakkir(-a-n)*[14]
         not.3.s.m   the-student.s.m-nom   early.s.m-acc
         "The (male) student is not early."

(39)   *laysa*   *ʔal-tˤullāb(-u)*   *mubakkir-īna*
         not.3.s.m   the-student.p.m-nom   early-p.m.acc
         "The (male) students are not early."

(40)   *ʔal-tˤullāb(-u)*   *lays-ū*   *mubakkir-īna*
         the-student.p.m-nom   not-3.p.m   early-p.m.acc
         "The (male) students are not early."

(41)   *lays-at*   *ʔal-tˤālib-a(t-u)*   *mubakkir-a(t-a-n)*
         not-3.s.f   the-student-s.f-nom   early-s.f-acc-indef
         "The (female) student is not early."

(42)   *lays-at*   *ʔal-t⁵ālib-āt(-u)*   *mubakkir-āt(-i-n)*
       not-3.s.f   the-student-p.f-nom   early-p.f-acc-indef
       "The (female) students are not early."

(43)   *ʔal-t⁵ālib-āt(-u)*   *las-na*   *mubakkir-āt(-i-n)*
       the-student-p.f-nom   not-3.p.f   early-p.f-acc-indef
       "The (female) students are not early."

Like the copular *kāna* verb, *laysa* may precede the subject of the negated construction as in (38)-(39) and (41)-(42) or follow it as in (40) and (43) with the consequence that the negator *laysa*, in the former, is only inflected for person and gender and is fully inflected for person, gender, and number in the latter (see Section 1.4 below for more details on agreement within SV or VSO order).

1.4   Verbal Inflectional Agreement Features
1.4.1   *Verbal agreement, tense, and null subjects*
A single lexical verb in Arabic is usually inflected for the features tense (past/perfective or present/imperfective), person, number, and gender.[15] In addition, imperfective verbs are inflected for mood (indicative, subjunctive, and jussive). As Arabic is a pro-drop/null-subject language, a verb with a pronoun suffix attached to it can be the only word in a sentence, as in (44)-(46).

(44)   *daras-ū*
       study.perf-3.p.m
       "They studied."

(45)   *ya-drus-ū-na*
       3-study.imperf-p.m-indic
       "They study."

(46)   *ʔu-drus-ū-0*
       2-study.impera-p.m-jussive
       "Study!"

The distinction between the past/perfective and present/imperfective is readily established by the presence (imperfective) or absence (perfective) of the prefix; that is, past tense is marked with a suffix only and present tense is marked with a prefix or a prefix and a suffix. Agreement features contained in the prefix include person and gender information, whereas agreement features contained in the suffix include number and gender information.

When an explicit subject is involved, two types of agreement hold between the subject and the verb, depending on whether the subject is pre-verbal or post-verbal. In a pre-verbal subject construction (in both the perfective and imperfective), the subject and the verb share full agreement features of person, gender, and number, as in (47)-(50) below.

47(a) *Ɂal-tˤālib(-u)*[16]   *darasa*
        the-student.s.m-nom   study.perf.3.s.m
        "The (male) student studied."

47(b) *Ɂal-tˤālib(-u)*   *ya-drus(-u)*
        the-student.s.m-nom   3.s.m-study.imperf-indic
        "The (male) student studies."

48(a) *Ɂal-tˤālib-a(t-u)*   *daras-at*
        the-student-s.f-nom   study.perf-3.s.f
        "The (female) student studied."

48(b) *Ɂal-tˤālib-a(t-u)*   *ta-drus(-u)*
        the-student-s.f-nom   3.s.f-study.imperf-indic
        "The (female) student studies."

49(a) *Ɂal-tˤullāb(-u)*   *daras-ū*
        the-student.p.m-nom   study.perf-3.p.m
        "The (male) students studied."

49(b) *Ɂal-tˤullāb(-u)*   *ya-drus-ū-na*
        the-student.p.m-nom   3-study.imperf-p.m-indic
        "The (male) students study."

50(a) *Ɂal-tˤālib-āt(-u)*   *daras-na*
        the-student-p.f-nom   study.perf-3.p.f
        "The (female) students studied."

50(b) *Ɂal-tˤālib-āt(-u)*   *ya-drus-na*
        the-student-p.f-nom   3-study.imperf-p.f
        "The (female) students study."

However, in a post-verbal subject construction, the subject and the verb agree only in person and gender, as in (51)-(54).

51(a)   *darasa*   *ʔal-tˤālib(-u)*
        study.perf.3.s.m   the-student.s.m-nom
        "The (male) student studied."

51(b)   *ya-drus(-u)*   *ʔal-tˤālib(-u)*
        3.s.m-study.imperf-indic   the-student.s.m-nom
        "The (male) student studies."

52(a)   *daras-at*   *ʔal-tˤālib-a(t-u)*
        study.perf-3.s.f   the-student-s.f-nom
        "The (female) student studied."

52(b)   *ta-drus(-u)*   *ʔal-tˤālib-a(t-u)*
        3.s.f-study.imperf-indic   the-student-s.f-nom
        "The (female) student studies."

53(a)   *darasa*   *ʔal-tˤullāb(-u)*
        study.perf.3.s.m   the-student.p.m-nom
        "The (male) students studied."

53(b)   *ya-drus(-u)*   *ʔal-tˤullāb(-u)*
        3.s.m-study.imperf-indic   the-student.p.m-nom
        "The (male) students study."

54(a)   *daras-at*   *ʔal-tˤālib-āt(-u)*
        study.perf-3.s.f   the-student-p.f-nom
        "The (female) students studied."

54(b)   *ta-drus(-u)*   *ʔal-tˤālib-āt(-u)*
        3.s.f-study.imperf-indic   the-student-p.f-nom
        "The (female) students study."

1.4.2 *Verbal negation*

Arabic negation markers seem to interact more with Arabic morphology than they do with syntax. As will be evident below, Arabic negation markers follow a straightforward usage. They occur in a sentence-initial position before the verb (in a VSO order) or after the subject (in an SVO order) and do not involve complicated word order rules as do English negation markers, for example. The focus here is mainly on *mā*, *lā*, *lam*, and *lan* and their basic contexts (for a more detailed typological description of Arabic negation markers, see Fassi Fehri 1993:163-174).

The negation marker *lā* negates the imperfective/present tense, while *mā* negates the perfective/past tense, as in sentences (55)-(58) below.

(55) lā   ya-drus(-u)   Ɂal-tˤālib(-u)
      not 3.s.m-study.imperf-indic   the-student.s.m-nom
      "The (male) student does not study."

(56) Ɂal-tˤullāb(-u)   lā   ya-drus-ū-na
      the-student.p.m-nom   not 3-study.imperf-p.m-indic
      "The (male) students do not study."

(57) mā   darasa   Ɂal-tˤālib(-u)
      not study.perf.3.s.m   the-student.s.m-nom
      "The (male) student did not study."

(58) Ɂal-tˤullāb(-u)   mā   daras-ū
      the-student.p.m-nom   not study.perf-3.p.m
      "The (male) students did not study."

As sentences (55)-(58) show, neither negative particle exhibits any further exchange of grammatical information with the verb irrespective of word order. The verbs in sentences (56) and (58) would be identical to those in (55) and (57), respectively, since the verb in a VSO order agrees with the subject only in person and gender.

In addition to negating the past tense, mā negates equational sentences, usually more often when expressing possessive meaning, as in (59)-(60) below.[17]

(59) mā   ʕind-ī   sayyār-a(t-un)
      not at-me   car-s.f-nom
      "I do not have a car."

(60) mā   Ɂanā   bi-dʒāɁiʕ(-in)
      not I   with-hungry.s.m-gen
      "I am not really hungry."

The negation marker lam is specialized in negating the perfective/past tense (and as an optional variant rule of mā in MSA). However, lam shares some feature specification with the verb following it. The verb receives a "default tense specification," occurring in the imperfective with a jussive mood feature due to the occurrence of the negation marker (see Fassi Fehri 1993:163). Thus, sentences (57)-(58), listed above, are negated with lam in (61)-(62) below.

(61)   *lam   ya-drus-0*   *ʔal-tˤālib(-u)*
not   3.s.m-study.imperf-juss   the-student.s.m-nom
"The (male) student did not study."

(62)   *ʔal-tˤullāb(-u)*   *lam   ya-drus-ū-0*
the-student.p.m-nom   not   3-study.imperf-p.m-juss
"The (male) students did not study."

In a VSO word order the verb in (62) would be identical to that in (61), since the verb in a VSO order agrees with the subject only in person and gender.

The negation marker *lan* is specialized in negating the future tense. However, it assigns the subjunctive case to the verb (in the imperfective) following it, as illustrated in sentences (63)-(64).

(63)   *lan   ya-drus(-a)*   *ʔal-tˤālib(-u)*
not   3.s.m-study.imperf-subjunc   the-student.s.m-nom
"The (male) student will not study."

(64)   *ʔal-tˤullāb(-u)*   *lan   ya-drus-ū-0*
the-student.p.m-nom   not   3-study.imperf-p.m-subjunc
"The (male) students will not study."

Negating the future tense usually requires dropping the independent future (morpheme) particle *sawfa* or the bound future marker {-*sa*} that is attached to the verb as a prefix to signal the future. Thus, sentences (63)-(64) above are negative counterparts of sentences (65)-(66) below.

(65)   *sawfa/ sa-ya-drus(-u)*   *ʔal-tˤālib(-u)*
will/   will-3.s.m-study.imperf-indic the-student.s.m-nom
"The (male) student will study."

(66)   *ʔal-tˤullāb(-u)*   *sawfa/ sa-ya-drus-ū-na*
the-student.p.m-nom   will   will-3-study.imperf-p.m-indic
"The (male) students will study."

However, it is possible to retain the particle *sawfa* for emphasis, as in (67)-(68) below.

(67)   *sawfa   lan   ya-drus(-a)*   *ʔal-tˤālib(-u)*
       will   not   3.s.m-study.imperf-subjunc   the-student.s.m-nom
       "The (male) student will NOT study."

(68)   *ʔal-tˤullāb(-u)*   *sawfa   lan   ya-drus-ū-0*
       the-student.p.m-nom   will   not   3-study.imperf-p.m-subjunc
       "The (male) students will NOT study."

1.5   Summary

The foregoing account is not intended to be an exhaustive description but rather to elucidate the most relevant aspects of the target morphosyntactic structures. In particular, the focus here is on some of the most basic and regular features that Arabic L2 learners are exposed to in their first years of learning. The morphosyntactic features focused on here involve:

(1) word structure
(2) gender
(3) phrasal structure and agreement
(4) equational (verbless) sentence structure
(5) negation of equational (verbless) sentence structure
(6) verbal structure and agreement
(7) negation of verbal structure

The findings and conclusions take into account the degree of form-function complexity and the learning task involved, which is one of the most important L2 learning factors. Attempts will also be made whenever possible to analyze the distribution of these forms in the formal input which the participants received.

CHAPTER 2

Existing Arabic Second Language Acquisition Research

Before presenting an overview of second language acquisition (SLA) studies conducted on Arabic as a second language (L2), it is necessary to offer a definition of what second language acquisition is and how it differs from foreign language pedagogy. Whereas foreign language pedagogy is concerned with the various approaches, methods, and techniques of how a foreign/second language should be taught, the field of second language acquisition is concerned with how a language is learned. In other words, while foreign language pedagogy reflects the teacher's perspective, SLA instead focuses on the learner, including the nature of the learner's developing language or what is referred to as the "Interlanguage" (IL) system. The IL system is considered a natural language constituting a continuum, subject to systematic development towards approximation of the target language or towards a fossilized non-target-like state. The scope of SLA investigation includes internal and external factors as well as the learning processes, stages, and strategies involved.

During the early days of applied linguistics and SLA research, SLA was heavily focused on informing foreign language pedagogy. Over the years this emphasis has gradually shifted, however, so that now SLA research not only examines pedagogical issues but also investigates various language phenomena not directly related to pedagogy. SLA studies have been influenced by different competing approaches to language and language learning, including the behaviorist, the nativist/rationalist, the cognitive constructivist, the functionalist, and the connectionist, among others.

Arabic SLA studies can best be characterized as sporadic and, until only very recently, parsimonious. The overview of the studies described below proceeds chronologically and according to the various approaches

that have been the landmarks of the SLA research field in general since its
earliest inception to the present.

2.1   Contrastive and Error Analysis Studies

The earliest types of studies conducted in the field of applied
linguistics in general and SLA in particular were Contrastive Analysis
(1940s-1950s) and Error Analysis (1960s-1970s). One of the main concerns
of Error Analysis was to identify—based on the output production (written
and verbal) of the L2 learner (L2er)—errors according to different categories
and to speculate on their sources or causes. Error categories included
interlingual errors (caused by L1 interference), *intralingual* errors (made by
L2ers regardless of their L1), *developmental* errors (caused by the L2er's
constructed hypotheses of the L2 system according to the extent of exposure
to L2), *overgeneralization* errors, *simplification* errors, and *induced* errors
(caused by instructional lapses or errors) (see Richards 1974; Stenson 1974;
Larsen-Freeman and Long 1991).

Perhaps the earliest adult Arabic SLA studies are Al-Ani (1972-1973)
and Rammuny (1976), both of which were conducted within the Error
Analysis framework. Al-Ani (1972-1973) analyzed "a limited" number of
written compositions for "major" errors. (See Box 2.1.) The exact number of
written samples was not reported; there was no attempt to analyze all written
errors in the students' compositions and no attempt to offer any statistical
figures of the errors found, apart from the tokens listed as examples of the
speculated sources of errors. Errors identified were roughly categorized
along three levels: orthographic and phonological, diction and dictionary
usage, and grammatical errors. Al-Ani attributed most errors to interference
from L1 (such as errors resulting from undersuppliance of the definite article
with nouns and from gender and number agreement mismatches), while
others were identified as examples of overgeneralization (for example,
affixing the definite article on proper names) and performance errors (for
example, affixing the article on the head noun in *idafa* constructions).
However, some errors were attributed as performance errors (such as the
gender agreement error in *ʔal-ḥarb* [feminine] *ʔal-qāsī* [masculine] → *ʔal-
ḥarb* [feminine] *ʔal-qāsiya* [feminine] "the severe war") rather than as
competence errors. Al-Ani concluded that it was not always easy to

categorize an error and to identify its source, thus echoing one of the drawbacks of Error Analysis.

Box 2.1 Features of interference/errors (Al-Ani 1972-1973)

Languages: L1 = English, L2 = Arabic

Proficiency level of L2: Advanced
n = "a limited number"

Task: Written compositions

Results:
1. Orthographic and phonological
   • Spelling errors
2. Diction and dictionary usage
   • Word choice errors
3. Grammatical
   • Definite article errors
   • Agreement errors
   • Preposition errors

Rammuny's study (1976) investigated L2 learners' errors more extensively. (See Box 2.2.) The study analyzed data from written Arabic proficiency tests. Unlike Al-Ani's study, all learners' errors were analyzed, except those occurring less than five times. Rammuny identified four main categories of errors similar to those in Al-Ani's study: orthographic and phonological, lexical, structural (including noun-adjective and verb-subject agreement, preposition use, definiteness, referent pronouns, demonstrative constructions, plural forms, noun clauses introduced by the complementizers *ʔan* and *ʔin*, case and mood, relative pronouns, interrogatives, negation, conditionals, numerals, and comparison of adjectives), and stylistic errors. Each of the four categories was then subdivided according to four causes, including inefficient "teaching-learning strategies" (or *induced* errors, in Error Analysis's terms), "interference" of L1, "unfamiliarity" (or competence), and "socio-psychological" (or performance). Thus, for example, of the 578 errors identified as structural errors, 406 were attributed as induced, 145 as L1 interference, 4 as competence, and 23 as performance errors. The ratios of the causes of errors, with respect to the total of number of errors (1,520) in the entire data set and along the four main categories of errors, are as follows: induced errors at 49 percent, L1 interference errors at 27.9 percent, competence errors at 16.9 percent, and performance errors at 6.2 percent.

Box 2.2 Statistical study of errors (Rammuny 1976)						
Languages: L1 = English, L2 = Arabic						
Proficiency levels of L2:						
Literary Arabic	2 years	3 years	4 years	5 years	6 years	Total
	n = 62	n = 27	n = 16	n = 8	n = 2	n = 115

Task: Written Arabic proficiency tests (APT)

Results:
1. Orthographic and phonological errors (222)
2. Lexical errors (455)
3. Structural errors (578)
4. Stylistic errors (265)

    Although the two foregoing studies document significant Arabic L2ers' errors and shed light on them, the numbers of correct rule application tokens are not provided along with the errors. Hence, only a partial account of the Interlanguage systems of the learners and not a full account of the L2ers' performance is provided. However, this is a characteristic limitation of Error Analysis methodology in the period in general.[1]

2.2   Performance/Developmental Studies
    The trend of detecting L2 learners' errors gave way to another approach which became known as Performance or Developmental Analysis and which was concerned with detecting consistent patterns in the production of the L2 learner. The developmental approach gave rise to three

areas of investigation: *morpheme order, developmental sequence*, and *communication strategies* (see also Larsen-Freeman and Long 1991).

Fakhri (1984) investigated the notion of communication strategies as methods of "achieving communication" and of "encoding meaning" by L2ers given their limited knowledge of the target language (Brown 1980:83). Communication strategies examined in other languages as L2s had been found to include strategies such as transfer from L1, generalizations, avoidance of form, circumlocution, message adjustment, prefabricated patterns, code switching, etc. (see, for example, Tarone 1977, 1980; Faerch and Kasper 1983; O'Malley and Chamot 1990).

Fakhri's study (1984) was based on recorded spontaneous data that consisted of 12 narratives elicited over a month from a female adult English speaker learning Moroccan Arabic as an L2. (See Box 2.3.) The participant had lived in Morocco for three years. Fakhri identified the "most frequent" communication strategies used by the participant as similar to those reported in the literature, including circumlocution, lexical borrowing from L1 (to compensate for lexical deficiency), elicitation of vocabulary (by asking the interlocutor for words in the TL), expanded use of formulaic expression (by using learned phrases or expressions in contexts not used by L1 speakers; for example, *meskīna!* "Poor girl" → **meskīna bezāf!* "Very poor girl!") and morphosyntactic innovation (that is, IL forms). The latter is explained in terms of supplying the subject (free morpheme) pronoun in contexts of incorrect (agreement) inflection on the verb in an attempt to compensate for the deficiency and avoid confusing the listener. Another reason provided for this strategy is that the production of the redundant pronoun is related to whether or not a character in a narrative is in focus. For example, if the character is in focus, as in the case of stories with one character, the pronoun is used in the first reference and then dropped in subsequent clauses even though the inflections on the verbs are incorrect; but if more than one character is involved, the pronoun is not dropped even though the inflections are sometimes correct and sufficient to keep the references straight. Fakhri indicates that the participant of the study did drop the pronoun in other contexts where subject (agreement) inflections were incorrect. Fakhri seems to rule out L1 transfer.

Box 2.3 Use of communication strategies (Fakhri 1984)

Languages: L1 = English, L2 = Moroccan Arabic

Proficiency level of L2: 3rd year
n = 1

Task: Elicited production on narrative tasks

Results: Major communication strategies and occurrence % within genre components

Communication Strategies	Orientation	Episodic	Evaluation
Circumlocution	39%	18%	25%
Lexical Borrowing from L1	33%	73%	6%
Elicitation of Vocabulary	28%	9%	6%
Expanded Formulaic Expression	0%	0%	63%

The study also revealed that communication strategies are constrained by the specific narrative genre components. For example, the data revealed that the participant resorted to lexical borrowing (73 percent) during the episodic part of the narrative more often than she did in the orientation part (33 percent), whereas she resorted to circumlocution (18 percent) and vocabulary elicitations (9 percent) in the episodic part far less than she did in the orientation part (39 and 28 percent, respectively). Fakhri points out that because of the urgent need in the episodic part to convey meanings/events to an intrigued listener, his subject resorted more to lexical borrowings and relied less on vocabulary elicitations and circumlocution to make the narration more effective; similarly, by resorting to vocabulary elicitations and circumlocution strategies in the orientation part (where there was no urgency to convey information to do with the time and place of the events), she made sure the listener did not miss essential information.

Notwithstanding the limited scope of the data, Fakhri's study indicates that communication strategies not only seem to be systematic but also are likely to be constrained by the features of the specific genre in which they occur (here, narrative discourse); therefore, different strategies may be employed in different discourse genres.

The *strategies* approach, in general, has been criticized mainly due to vagueness of definitions and concepts and for lack of independently motivated explanation as to whether such strategies are dissimilar from adjustments in normal language use to maintain real-time language processing and communication in response to the limited IL system (see, for example, Oxford and Cohen 1992, Bialystok 1990).

Al-Buainain (1986, 1991) was conducted within the *developmental* framework to account for the overall performance of the L2er, including the identification of developmental sequences/stages and processes which, in mastering a given structure, an L2er goes through from the pre-target-like stage to target-like mastery with possible individual variations (see, for example, Wode 1978; Huebner 1979; Meisel et al. 1981). Developmental investigations were triggered by L1 acquisition studies to examine whether or not the sequences in L1 and L2 acquisition were the same. Structures investigated include wh-questions, negation, relative clauses, word order, etc. For example, English negation was examined in L2ers with different L1s and was found to be acquired along predictable stages similar to those found in L1. The acquisition stages reported include 1) use of *No* in utterance-initial position, 2) use of *no/not* in utterance-internal preverbal position, 3) use of *no* with modals and auxiliaries as unanalyzed chunks, and 4) differential use of the negative particle from auxiliaries and models (see, for example, Schumann 1979).

Similarly, the acquisition of wh-questions was reported to take place along predictable steps not unlike those in L1: 1) with rising intonation without inversion, 2) with wh-word fronting without subject-verb inversion, 3) with inversion with modals and overinversion, and 4) with correct use and proper inversion with auxiliary verbs (see, for example, Cancino et al. 1978).

Al-Buainain (1986, 1991) investigated the acquisition of negation and interrogation based on cross-sectional data from 53 adult native (British) English speakers learning Arabic as an L2. The participants were university students from five different universities and were enrolled in Arabic courses at five different proficiency/length of exposure levels ranging from one to five years. (See Box 2.4.) The analyzed cross-sectional data consisted of the participants' written performance on translation and manipulation tasks.

Box 2.4 Development of negation and interrogation (Al-Buainain 1986)

Languages: L1 = (British) English, L2 = Arabic

Proficiency levels of L2:

MSA	1 year	2 years	3 years	4 years	5 years	Total
	n = 10	n = 11	n = 11	n = 12	n = 9	n = 53

Tasks:
i. Translation: interrogation (84 items), negation (64 items)
ii. Manipulation: interrogation (84 scrambled ordered items), negation (32 items with negative particle, 32 without negative particle)

Sample stimuli:
    (a) Translate into Arabic: *Why are they here?*
    (b) Translate into Arabic: *Ahmad is not going to come.*
    (c) Arrange in correct order to make a question: لماذا هم هنا "Here they why."
    (d) Change into negative: (لن) أحمد سوف يأتي. "Ahmad will come. (will not)"
    (e) Change into negative: سوف يأتي. "He will come."

Results: Findings of acquisition hierarchy of stages based on tasks and measures

Structure	Translation Task (Guttmann)	Manipulation Task (Guttmann)	Translation & Manipulation Tasks (ANOVA)
Negation	*lā → lam → lan → laysa*	*lā & lam → lan & laysa*	*lā & lam → lan & laysa*
Interrogation	positive wh → positive inter → total inter → positive Yes/No → negative wh → negative inter	positive Yes/No → positive inter → positive wh → total inter → negative wh → negative inter	*which → how → when/where/why → what → who*

Quantitative analysis of the data revealed 1) improvement and gradual progression of group performance with respect to both structures along all the five levels, 2) performance difference with respect to task type, and 3) better performance on interrogation than on negation with respect to group proficiency levels 1-3 but not so with respect to group levels 4-5. However, the analysis also showed that there were significant interactions among the three variables investigated (that is, effect of length/time of exposure on learning, effect of task on group performance, and effect of structure type on performance). In other words, none of the three variables could be claimed to have a main effect separately. For example, it could not be determined whether the manipulation task worked better or was easier than the translation task alone without also attributing the difference to levels; similarly, it could not be determined whether the difference in performance between the two structures was due to structure-type variable alone without also attributing the difference in performance to group and time variables. Hence, the evidence of Arabic negation being more difficult than interrogation is inconclusive. The reason is also probably due to the disparity and the skewed nature of tasks used. It is not clear how the tasks would yield reliable findings, since the tasks recycled the same vocabulary and the translation tasks preceded the manipulation tasks.

Given the limitations to do with tasks and the finding that main effect of structure-type variable is overridden by interaction effect between variables, the study does not offer conclusive evidence as to whether negation is more difficult than interrogation. Al-Buainain speculated that negation was more difficult, because it interacts with more grammar elements that also need to be acquired (for example, word order, tense, person, number, and gender inflection on the particle *laysa* "not"), unlike interrogation, which involves mainly word order. However, this remains to be empirically observed.

Other findings reported in Al-Buainain (1986, 1991) are related to the acquisition sub-stages of each of the two structures separately, although here too the findings are affected by the limitations of the elicitation tasks. With respect to negation, different statistical measures showed at least two different orders of acquisition involving the different negative particles. One of these resulted in the acquisition of the implicational hierarchy *lā* → *lam* → *lan* → *laysa* and another yielded the hierarchy *lā* & *lam* → *lan* & *laysa*. With respect to interrogation, the analysis resulted in three different orders of acquisition based on statistical measures and performance on tasks. One such order is: positive Yes/No questions → positive wh-questions → positive interrogatives → total interrogatives → negative wh-questions → negative interrogatives.

Al-Buainain offers a brief qualitative analysis of the participants' acquisition of negation based on translation data alone. For example, the acquisition of negation involving the negative particle *lā* is explained to proceed, with possible overlapping, along the following sub-stages: 1) suppliance of *lā* but not in the appropriate position, 2) its correct placement but with the incorrect order of the remainder of the sentence, 3) redundant production of the subject pronoun, and 4) correct production and placement of *lā* and the verb with the proper (agreement) inflection on the verb following it. Although stages 3-4 are not related to negation forms per se, Al-Buainain's findings with respect to Arabic negation in particular somewhat support the general observation (about any given structure) in developmental sequence studies (Zobl 1984) that L2 acquisition (universally) progresses over time along intermediate stages, starting from highly deviant and simple IL forms to more acceptable variants as the IL system of the L2ers approximates more to the target language. However, it has also been generally attested in L2 (and L1) acquisition that L2ers may 1) start with producing target-like (TL) forms, then 2) go through a stage where they may overgeneralize a given form, and finally 3) they apply the rules correctly and produce TL forms. This is usually referred to in the literature as U-shaped learning behavior (see Gass and Selinker 1994:158).

Al-Buainain does not offer any qualitative analysis of the participants' acquisition of interrogation in the order mentioned above apart from offering further speculation as to the emergence of interrogative forms in relation to negation. Al-Buainain suggests that since negative interrogative was the last type of interrogative to be acquired, this would support the (inconclusive) finding that negation was more difficult than interrogation. However, the difficulty may be due to the fact that negative interrogatives combine two structures (not one) or it may be due to the author's claim that negative interrogatives are "semantically problematic" (or not intuitively transparent), following Langendoen (1970) (see also Al-Buainain 1986:242).

2.3   Developmental, Interlanguage, and Current Models

The Performance or Developmental framework later triggered more Interlanguage studies that were similarly concerned with developmental stages, but from a speech processing perspective. Four Arabic SLA studies were conducted during the last decade: three focused on production (Nielsen

1997; Alhawary 1999, 2003; and Mansouri 2000) and one on comprehension (Abu Radwan 2002).

The first three studies examined Pienemann's (1992, 1998) Processability Theory (PT) which claims that grammatical development in L2 proceeds according to a set implicational sequence. PT is one of the most recent refined attempts aimed at explaining L2 grammatical development from a cognitive-interactionist perspective. The approach relies heavily on the recourse of the L2er to general cognitive processes rather than to a specific innate universal linguistic component. PT's main assumption is that L2ers are able to utilize the same general cognitive resources as adult native speakers, but they need to create their own language-specific processing prerequisites or procedures for the L2. These procedures are claimed to emerge in L2 acquisition constrained by a speech-processing prerequisite hierarchy. Thus, with respect to morphology, processing prerequisite procedures is explained in terms of three types of morphemes: 1) lexical morphemes, 2) phrasal (that is, "phrasal" as in phrase structure) morphemes, and 3) inter-phrasal morphemes. These are assumed to be processable by the L2er along five main distinct stages in an implicational set sequence as follows:

Stage 1	Absence of any language-specific procedures
Stage 2	Development of "category procedures" where lexical morphemes (for example, the {-ed} tense marker in English) emerge
Stage 3	Development of "phrasal procedures" where exchange of grammatical agreement within a constituent phrase emerges (for example, noun-adjective agreement)
Stage 4	Development of "inter-phrasal morphemes" where exchange of grammatical agreement across two constituent phrases emerges (for example, subject-verb agreement)
Stage 5	Development of "subordinate clause procedures" which allow for emergence of the distinctive features of subordinate clauses or the distinction between a main and a subordinate clause (for example, object complement clauses, adverbial complement clauses, and relative clauses).

The implicational nature of the above hierarchy "derives from the assumption that the processing resources developed at one stage are necessary prerequisites for the following stage" (Pienemann 1998:87). Hence, the claim that "stages cannot be skipped through formal instruction" (Pienemann 1998:250).

Nielsen (1997) was the first Arabic SLA study which attempted to examine the predictions made by PT. (See Box 2.5.) The data consisted of longitudinal data collected during 9 sessions over a 15-month period from 2 adult Danish speakers learning Arabic as an L2. Elicitation tasks consisted of oral interviews, role play, and presentations. The most significant finding of the study relates to acquisition of noun-adjective (N-A) agreement (a stage 3 structure) and subject-verb (S-V) agreement (a stage 4 structure) as well as gender agreement between demonstrative pronouns and a head noun (a stage 3 structure). The analysis focused on singular masculine and singular feminine agreement in both structures. The results revealed that while neither S-V nor N-A agreement emerged in learner B's Interlanguage system, both forms emerged at the same time in learner A's Interlanguage system (in recording 4). PT would predict that one form would emerge before the other. The results also revealed that gender agreement between demonstrative pronouns and a head noun (a stage 3 structure) emerged in neither of the two participants' Interlanguage systems (including that of learner A, although this learner was able to process structures at stage 3 and stage 4). Accordingly, PT's prediction is disconfirmed by these two findings.

Other findings reported in Nielsen's study (1997) are related to production of the definite article with a noun (a stage 2 structure) as well as definiteness agreement (a stage 3 structure) in three NP types, as illustrated in 1-3 below.

(1) Definite noun-adjective phrase: (Ɂal-Noun + Ɂal-Adjective)
   Ɂal-bin-t   *Ɂal-kabīr-a*
   the-girl-s.f   the-big-s.f
   "the big girl"

(2) Demonstrative phrase: (Demonstrative + Ɂal-Noun)
   hāðā   *Ɂal-walad*
   this.s.m   the-boy.s.m
   "this boy"

(3) *Ɂidˤāfa* construction: (Noun + (Ɂal-)-Noun)
   makān   *Ɂal-ḥarb*
   place   the-war
   "the place of the war"

The observational findings show that while only one of the two participants was able to acquire the definite noun-adjective phrase (a stage 3 structure) in recording 5 (that is, only after having already, in recording 4, acquired S-V agreement, a stage 4 structure), neither of them acquired the other constructions during the entire period of the observation. Thus, these findings provide further counterevidence to PT. The only finding in support of PT comes from emergence of the definite article on nouns (a stage 2 structure). The findings show that the definite article on nouns emerged in recordings 2 and 3 in the Interlanguage systems of learners B and A, respectively.[2]

Box 2.5 Acquisition order of agreement procedures (Nielsen 1997)				
Languages: L1 = Danish, L2 = Arabic				
Proficiency level of L2: 1st year (first 15 months) **n** = 2 (longitudinal)				
Task: Elicited production				
Results: Emergence of agreement procedures				
Structures	**L2ers**	**Stage**	**Recording/ Time**	**Emerged**
Definite Article on Nouns	A	2	3	+
	B	2	2	+
Definite Noun-Definite Adjective	A	3	5	+
	B	3	0	-
Noun-Adjective Agreement	A	3	4	+
	B	3	0	-
Demonstrative Gender Agreement	A	3	0	-
	B	3	0	-
Subject-Verb Agreement	A	4	4	+
	B	4	0	-

Alhawary (1999, 2003) also investigated the predictions of the speech-processing hierarchy claimed by PT. (See Box 2.6.) The study was conducted within a longitudinal setting that followed closely nine participants learning Arabic as an L2 over a school year. Eight of the nine participants were native (American) English speakers who were zero beginners at the time. Data elicitation sessions were held every two weeks, using different tasks including picture description, picture differences, picture sequencing, video story retelling, and informal interviews. The study investigated a number of structures, but the most unambiguous findings are related to acquisition of Arabic N-A and S-V agreement. According to PT, the former is predicted to be acquired before the latter.[3] The study focused

---

Box 2.6 PT: Counterevidence from Arabic SLA (Alhawary 1999, 2003)

Languages: L1 = (American) English, L2 = Arabic

Proficiency level of L2: 1st year
n = 9 (longitudinal)

Task: Elicited production

Results: Emergence of N-A and S-V agreement in the L2ers using two criteria

Emergence Criterion (2 minimal tokens)		90% Correct Criterion	
L2ers	**N-A Agreement**	**S-V Agreement**	**N-A Agreement**	**S-V Agreement**
Beth	1	2	2	4
Mark	1	2	1	2
Adam	1	2	0	0
Ann	2	1	2	2
Kay	3	1	0	2
Viola	4	2	3	2
John	6	2	5	4
Jeff	0	2	1	4
Mary	0	3	0	3

Figures = chronological data sessions

on third person singular feminine and masculine (for S-V agreement) and singular masculine and feminine (for N-A agreement). Alhawary (1999, 2003) relied on the same emergence criterion used in Nielsen (1997): rule application of both singular masculine and feminine on the same lexical (verb/noun) item within the same data set. Based on this emergence criterion, the findings showed that the majority (six) of the participants, including Ann, Kay, Viola, John, Jeff, and Mary, acquired S-V agreement before they did N-A agreement. An examining of the formal input which the participants received in the classroom shows the findings are particularly strong, since the participants were exposed to N-A agreement before they were exposed to S-V agreement and yet they acquired the structures in violation of the predicted order. A 90 percent correct acquisition criterion was also used, resulting in a similar finding (see Alhawary 2003). Five (Kay, Viola, John, Jeff, and Mary) of the six participants who acquired S-V agreement before N-A agreement conformed to the same pattern (with Ann reaching criterion for both forms at the same time). In addition, almost all of the participants exhibited more backsliding with N-A agreement than they did with S-V agreement, suggesting the participants had more problems with the former than they did the latter. Thus, the data of the study strongly falsify PT claims with respect to the hypothesized speech-processing hierarchy.

Mansouri's study (2000, 2005) is a third study that investigated PT claims based on a number of syntactic and morphological structures. (See Box 2.7.) The study was based on semi-longitudinal data consisting of four native (Australian) English speakers learning Arabic as an L2, two of them at the beginning level (during their second year of enrollment in Arabic courses) and two at the intermediate level (during their third year of enrollment in Arabic courses).[4] Two data samples were collected from each of the four participants. Elicitation consisted of an oral interview and an oral transformation task (such as story retelling about actors in the dual or plural rather than the singular).[5] Given the limited size of the data samples and the small number of participants, especially given the semi-longitudinal/cross-sectional nature of the study, the findings of the study are somewhat inconclusive.

With respect to the findings of the structures investigated in Nielsen (1997) and Alhawary (1999, 2003), Mansouri claimed that the data are in

Box 2.7 Grammatical markedness and information processing (Mansouri 2000)

Languages: L1 = (Australian) English, L2 = Arabic

Proficiency levels of L2:

MSA	2nd Year	3rd Year
	n = 2 (L2er #1, L2er #2)	n = 2 (L2er #3, L2er #4)

Tasks:
i. Elicited production (oral interview)
ii. Oral transformation

Results: Examples of emergence findings[6]

Structure	Stage #	L2er #1 Time1	L2er #2 Time1	L2er #1 Time2	L2er #2 Time2	L2er #3 Time1	L2er #4 Time1	L2er #4 Time2	L2er #3 Time2
Phrasal Agr	2	+	+	+	+	+	+	+	+
Case	2	-	-	-	-	+/-	+/-	+/-	+
SVO Order	2	+	+	+	+	+	+	+	+
Negation	2	+/-	+/-	+/-	+/-	+	+	+	+
VSO Order	3	+/-	+/-	+/-	+/-	+/-	+/-	+/-	+
Subordination	4	-	-	+/-	+/-	+/-	+/-	+	+

"+" = emergence, "-" = no emergence, "+/-" = "L2er exhibiting signs of emergence"[7]

support of PT in that the N-A agreement had already emerged before the first data set took place and that S-V agreement emerged later (in the second data set) when the learners produced third person plural agreement, even though they had already produced the features first person singular, third person singular masculine, and third person singular feminine (in the first data set). Mansouri dismisses all such features as "default singular number" and not instances involving S-V agreement, since according to Mansouri, the two beginning participants could not yet (in the second data set) produce S-V agreement involving the plural (Mansouri 2000:138).[8] PT does not require that all forms of a given paradigm emerge in order to establish the emergence criterion, only that rule application occurs within morphologically and lexically varied elements to ensure that the elements produced mark actual emergence and are not exemplars of items learned as unanalyzed blocks (see Pienemann 1998; Alhawary 1999, 2003; see also Meisel 1994 for a discussion against defining successful verbal agreement acquisition in terms of completeness of the entire set of the morphological forms available).

However, relying on a more reliable emergence criterion such as that adopted by Nielsen (1997) and Alhawary (1999), since one would not expect L2ers to acquire the *entire* agreement paradigm at an early stage, as Mansouri does, the data in fact show that S-V agreement had also already emerged in the ILs of the two beginning learners (for criticism of this point and others, see also Alhawary 2003). Mansouri reports that the feature "person" agreement "developed predominantly in the two beginning participants when both were producing verbs marked for first, second, and third person" with a high accuracy rate of 87 percent by one of the learners (Mansouri:2000:136, 139). In particular, sentences (5)-(8) (quoted from Mansouri 2000:134-5, 137, 140) illustrate emergence of S-V agreement for the features third person singular masculine and feminine.

(5) *Angela   ta-ʕmalu   muħāsiba*
     Angela   **3.s.f**-work.imperf   accountant
     "Angela works as an accountant."
(6) *ʔab-ī   ya-ʕmal   lākin ʔumm-ī   lā   ya-ʕmal**
     father-my **3.s.m**-work.imperf but   mother-my doesn't **3.s.m**-work
     "My father works but my mother does not."
(7) *Peter ya-drusu   ʔal-luɣa   ʔal-ʕarabiyya*
     Peter **3.s.m**-study.imperf   the-language the-Arabic
     "Peter studies the Arabic language."
(8) *Susan ta-drus   ʔal-luɣa   ʔal-ʕarabiyya*
     Susan **3.s.f**-study.imperf   the-language the-Arabic
     "Susan studies the Arabic language."

Hence, following Nielsen's (1997) and Alhawary's (1999, 2003) emergence criterion, and if both structures had already emerged prior to the first data session, it could not be maintained whether one structure (that is, N-A agreement) emerged before the other (that is, S-V agreement) given the semi-longitudinal/cross-sectional nature of the study. Hence, Mansouri's (2000) findings are neither in support nor against PT with respect to the two structures.

Mansouri (2000) reports on other findings of syntactic and morphological structures. With respect to syntactic structures, Mansouri claims that equational (verbless) word order, analyzed as a stage 1 structure, accordingly emerged early; that SVO word order, analyzed as a stage 2 structure, and VSO order, analyzed as a stage 3 structure, accordingly were acquired later in support of PT syntactic claims;[9] and that "adverb fronting," analyzed as a stage 3 structure, also emerged accordingly, whereas "adverb separation," analyzed as a stage 5 structure, did not emerge yet—following PT predictions.[10]

With respect to morphological forms, Mansouri claims that phrasal agreement, such as definiteness and gender agreement within nominal structure, analyzed as stage 2 structures,[11] was acquired accordingly; that inter-phrasal agreement, such as S-V agreement, analyzed as a stage 3 structure, was acquired accordingly; that clitics, analyzed as a stage 4 structure, did not emerge (as listed in Table 31 in Mansouri 2000:174), although elsewhere it is claimed to have emerged (as listed in Table 28 in Mansouri 2000:163); and that relative pronouns, analyzed as a stage 5 structure, emerged in the learners' Interlanguage in conformity with PT predictions.[12]

Mansouri (2000) does not view any of the findings to be problematic for the validity of the developmental stages hypothesized by PT but rather as manifesting "inter-learner variability" relating to "pace" rather than to order of acquisition stages (Mansouri 2000:161, 163). However, upon examining the data, in addition to the observation made about phrasal (N-A) agreement, analyzed as a stage 2 structure, and inter-phrasal (S-V) agreement, analyzed as a stage 3 structure, as both having already emerged in the learners' Interlanguage systems, one finds other counter-observations from the tables of the findings provided. Thus, one finds that VSO word order, analyzed as a stage 3 structure, emerged in only one of the two intermediate learners although subordination (that is, use of conjunctions such as *and*, *but*, etc.), analyzed as a stage 4 structure, emerged in both intermediate learners. One also finds that negation, analyzed as a stage 2 structure, did not emerge except in the two intermediate learners, even though other stage 2 structures (such as SVO word order) emerged in all the learners, including the beginning learners (Mansouri 2000:161, Table 27).[13] It is also apparent that case, analyzed as a stage 2 structure, emerged in only one of the two intermediate learners, although phrasal agreement, a stage 2 structure, had already emerged in all the L2ers of the study. Thus, considering these observations and the discussion in footnotes 5-8 above, Mansouri's study actually provides either inconclusive evidence or counterevidence to PT claims regarding a number of structures, as illustrated in Box 2.7.

Like the three foregoing studies, Abu Radwan (2002) was conducted from a speech-processing perspective. However, unlike the three studies, which focused on production and investigated Processability Theory, Abu Radwan (2002) focused on comprehension and investigated the Competition Model (Bates and MacWhinney 1987; MacWhinney and Bates 1989) and its application to sentence processing in Arabic. The main assumption investigated is the notion that language processing and language acquisition (both L1 and L2) are conceptualized in terms of the underlying strategies or "competition among various cues for a limited number of channels" in mapping form-function relations (Sasaki 1994). (See Box 2.8.) The study attempted to identify the cues and processing strategies which English L1 learners of Arabic employ in interpreting/comprehending sentences in comparison with cues used by Arabic L1 speakers. The study used three groups, each consisting of nine participants. Two groups of non-native speakers of Arabic consisted of (American) English L1 learners of Arabic: one group enrolled in first semester (first year) Arabic and the other were enrolled in second year Arabic in their academic institution in the US. These were referred to as a beginner and intermediate group, respectively. The third group comprised native Arabic L1 speakers. The participants were presented with a set of 54 sentences, designed following Taman (1993), in which animacy (animate versus inanimate), verbal agreement (singular masculine versus singular feminine), and case markings (nominative versus accusative) were manipulated. Each sentence consisted of a string of three words: two nouns (the subject and the object) and a verb. The participants were requested to interpret each sentence (which they heard being read out loud to them) "as quickly as possible" by identifying the correct subject of each sentence (that is, one of the two nouns occurring with the verb).

Abu Radwan (2002) reported the following favored rankings of cues by all three groups: case → gender → animacy. Abu Radwan further claimed that the findings indicate that both non-native groups exhibit a high sensitivity to cues used by the native speakers of Arabic and do not exhibit transfer of their English L1 processing strategies which would favor word order tendencies.

Box 2.8 Sentence processing strategies (Abu Radwan 2002)

Languages: L1 = (American) English, Arabic; L2 = Arabic

L1 Arabic/Control, n = 9

Proficiency levels of L2:

MSA	1st year (1st semester)	2nd year	Total
	n = 9	n = 9	n = 18

Task: Comprehension: subject/actor identification (54 sentences read out aloud)

Sample stimuli: (cited from Taman 1993:308)[14]

(1) ضربَ الحمارُ الحجرَ. "The donkey hit the rock."

(2) ضربَ الحجرُ الحمارَ. "The rock hit the donkey."

(3) ضربَ الحمارُ الغزالَ. "The donkey hit the gazelle."

(4) ضربَ الحمارَ الحجرُ. "The rock hit the donkey."

(5) ضربَ الحجرَ الحمارُ. "The donkey hit the rock."

(6) ضربَ الحمارَ الغزالُ. "The gazelle hit the donkey."

Results: Sample post hoc Schaffe scores of the three groups (Abu Radwan 2002:203)

Set	Cue	Groups	p
1	C	B and N	.001
		I and N	.000
		B and I	.332
2	C	B and N	.262
		I and N	.026
		B and I	.546
4	G	B and N	.031
		I and N	.207
		B and I	.676
5	C	B and N	.168
		I and N	.000
		B and I	.000

B=beginner; I=intermediate; N=native; C=case; G=gender; p=significance considered at .05.

However, Abu Radwan's conclusions raise at least two questions. First, it is not clear how the non-native, first semester, first year (at Georgetown University) group showed a tendency to case, since they were not exposed to case markings in the book which they used, *Al-kitaab* (Brustad et al. 1995b), until towards the end of the second semester (lessons 16-17). Abu Radwan even claims that in one of the result score sets, the non-native speakers actually tended to "give more weight to case than the native group" (Abu Radwan 2002:202). Second, with respect to the native group, the findings seem to yield a different result than Taman's (1993) study whose test and computation procedure were followed in Abu Radwan (2002). Unlike the findings reported in Abu Radwan (2002), the finding revealed in Taman (1993) yielded the following favored ranking of cues: gender → case → animacy.[15]

However, according to the post hoc statistical (Schaffe) score sets provided, the reported findings seem to indicate mixed evidence. For example, this is evident in the score sets 1-2 and 5 (with respect to case cue): whereas there is a significant difference in the weight assigned to case between the non-native (both beginning and intermediate) groups and native group in set 1, there is no difference between the non-native beginner group and the native group in sets 2 and 5. In addition, the scores provided indicate significance between groups but do not indicate which of the groups actually outscored the others in its use of the case cue. It is likely that this distinction was reversed inadvertently. This seems to be clear in set 4 where there is a statistical difference between the performance of the non-native beginner group and the native group with respect to gender cue. It is therefore likely that the native group outscored the non-native groups in the weight assigned to gender (and case) cue rather than the other way around. Recall also that Taman's (1993) study revealed that in fact gender was the cue on which native speakers tended to assign the most weight. Interpreted accordingly, the data in Abu Radwan (2002) study, with its focus on comprehension, may not necessarily provide evidence against L1 transfer of processing strategies as Abu Radwan claims. What seems to be uncontested, however, is that the non-native intermediate group seems to exhibit gain in weight cues to gender, in particular, as the difference between this group and its native counterpart seems to be diminished in set 4.

2.4   Second Language Acquisition and Universal Grammar

Interest in investigating Arabic L2 acquisition in the last decade or so has not been restricted to the developmental framework and developmental stages. Bolotin (1996a) and, most recently, Alhawary (2002, 2005) investigated issues such as Universal Grammar (UG) access, L1 transfer, and ultimate attainment within the generative framework, in particular, that of Principles and Parameters.

With respect to the notion of UG access, SLA researchers are generally divided into two camps. Proponents of UG access in L2 argue for an indirect access role (through L1) as L2ers are able to reset the parameters of L2 (for example, White 1989, Hulk 1991, Vainikka and Young-Scholten 1994, Schwartz and Sprouse 1996). Opponents of UG availability in L2 argue for limited or no UG access and instead appeal for universal cognitive principles or constraints accessed by L2 learners (for example, Meisel 1983, 1991; Clahsen 1984; Clahsen and Muysken 1986, 1989; Felix 1985; Bley-Vroman 1989; Schachter 1989).

Bolotin (1996a) examined whether L2ers of Arabic exhibit UG access by testing if they could reset the parameter of Arabic relative clause. (See Box 2.9.) The study was based on cross-sectional data of three groups of L2ers who were enrolled in Middlebury's intensive program: 10 beginning, 11 intermediate, and 6 advanced. All participants were (American) English L1 speakers, except for one beginner (whose L1 was Polish) and one from both the intermediate and advanced groups (whose L1 was German). In addition, the study included a control group of six native Arabic speakers (teachers). The data comprised the grammaticality judgment responses of the participants on four types of structures. Two types "represent the Arabic no-movement setting" consisting of simple and complex resumptive pronouns, as in (9)-(10), respectively.

(9)   *hāðā huwa ʔal-radʒulu ʔal-laðī yumsiku ʔal-sullama ʔal-laðī tatasallaqu-hu Fātˤimatu*
         *"This is the man that holds the ladder that Fatima climbs **it**."

(10)   *hāðā huwa ʔal-māʔu ʔal-laðī yamliku ʔaħmadu ʔal-dʒamala ʔal-laðī yašrabu-hu*
         *"This is the water that Ahmad owns the camel that drinks **it**."

Sentence (9) illustrates simple resumptive structure where the resumptive pronoun is related to a constituent located one clause away and sentence (10) illustrates complex resumptive structure where the resumptive pronoun

Box 2.9 Resetting parameters in acquiring Arabic (Bolotin 1996a)

Languages: L1 = (American) English, Arabic; L2 = Arabic

L1 Arabic/Control, n = 6

Proficiency levels of L2:

MSA	Beginners	Intermediate	Advanced	Total
	n = 10	n = 11	n = 6	n = 27

Task: Grammaticality judgment

Results: raw data (mean percent correct)

Structures	Beginners	Intermediate	Advanced	Control
Simple Operators	63	68	81	92
Complex Operators	78	92	97	88
Simple Resumptive	72	73	89	92
Complex Resumptive	27	18	25	61

is related to a constituent located two clauses away. The other two types of structures represent the English movement setting consisting of simple and complex operators, as in (11)-(12), respectively.

(11)   *hāðā huwa ʔal-radʒulu ʔal-laðī yumsiku ʔal-sullama ʔal-laðī tatasallaqu Fātˤimatu
        "This is the man that holds the ladder that Fatima climbs."
(12)   *hāðā huwa ʔal-māʔu ʔal-laðī yamliku ʔaḥmadu ʔal-dʒamala ʔal-laðī yašrabu
        *"This is the water that Ahmad owns the camel that drinks."

Sentence (11) illustrates simple operators where the operator referring back to the clefted element has been moved out of one clause, while sentence (10) illustrates complex operators where the operator has been moved out of two clauses. The consequence of the above structures is that while sentences (9)-(10) are grammatical in Arabic, since no movement is involved, the equivalent English sentences are ungrammatical, as indicated by the asterisks. For sentence (9) to be grammatical in English, the pronoun requires movement. The equivalent English of sentence (12) is also ungrammatical, as it violates the subjacency constraint (which prohibits a constituent from crossing more than one bounding node in a single step) in English, whereas the equivalent English of sentence (11) is grammatical since it does not violate subjacency. However, Bolotin assumes that both (11) and (12) are ungrammatical in Arabic.[16]

The first two types of structures (that is, 9 and 10) were included to check whether the participants would accept such sentences as grammatical in order to test whether they could reset the parameter of Arabic L2 resumptive setting, while the second two types of structures (that is, 11 and 12) were included to test whether they would transfer their English L1 setting. Six sentences of each type were presented to the participants in Arabic, for a total of 24 sentences (in addition to six fillers). Each sentence was accompanied by a picture with the focused element in question colored in for clarification.

The findings revealed a significant difference between the beginning and native group, a significant difference between the intermediate and native group, and no significant difference between the advanced and native group, suggesting that resetting the Arabic parameter to [-movement] is eventually possible, as evident in the advanced group. In addition, even though the beginning and intermediate groups overall underperformed the control group, they performed above chance on simple resumptive structure (with 72-73 percent correct), suggesting that the participants did exhibit the [-movement] parameter from early on. On the other hand, the relatively lower performance of the beginning and intermediate groups on simple operator structure (with 63-68 percent correct) indicates that they also exhibit transfer of their L1 [+movement] setting. Thus, the findings are concluded to be in support of the claim of indirect UG access in L2. Bolotin (1996a) concludes that the study offers findings similar to her previous study (1996b) conducted on Arabic L1 speakers learning English as an L2.

As for the question of L1 transfer in SLA research, a number of specific, competing hypotheses have been advanced. One hypothesis, the Minimal Tree Hypothesis (for example, Vainikka and Young-Scholten 1998), claims that only lexical categories transfer; another, the Weak Transfer Hypothesis (for example, Eubank 1996), claims that both lexical and functional categories transfer but not the feature values associated with functional categories; and a third, the Full Transfer/Full Access Hypothesis (for example, Schwartz and Sprouse 1996), proposes that the entirety of L1 grammar (including lexical categories, functional categories, and feature values associated with functional categories) is available to L2ers from the early stages of L2 acquisition. Accordingly, restructuring (or approximating to the L2 system) takes place upon exposure to input of the target language.

Alhawary (2002) examined the role of L1 transfer in Arabic L2 acquisition in light of the above proposals. Alhawary argues that the findings reached in Alhawary (1999, 2002), based on different acquisition criteria and with strong convergence of results, show that contrary to what a cognitive-interactionist proposal such as PT (above) would assume, L2ers need not wait until they are able to develop category procedures (that is, in order to assign categories such as N, A, V, etc.) and then develop phrasal agreement procedures, then interphrasal agreement, in this order. (See Box 2.6 above.) Moreover, if an alternative proposal assumed that abstract knowledge of inflection (associated with functional categories) needed for acquiring Arabic S-V agreement is already present in English native speakers for transfer to L2 but is absent in nominals (that is, English exhibits S-V agreement but not N-A agreement), this might very well explain the relatively early emergence of S-V agreement in most of the participants' Interlanguage systems before N-A agreement. Thus, of the three hypotheses advanced with respect to L1 transfer, the Full Transfer/Full Access proposal seems to provide the most adequate explanation of the Arabic SLA data. It is argued that the presence of an abstract feature in L1 does seem to transfer to L2 in the sense that speakers of an L1 that exhibits the same abstract feature present in an L2 (such as gender) somehow know to check for the feature (gender) before Spell Out (that is, before the structure is phonologically produced). Hence, Alhawary's findings (2002) offer support to the model from a typological constellation (English L1 speakers who are Arabic L2 learners) not considered earlier in the SLA literature.

A closely related issue to that of L1 transfer in L2 development is the exact status of access to UG in L2 development and in effect the exact status of L2 competence. In essence, this area of investigation aims at explaining the observed difference in ultimate attainment between L1 and L2, an area reminiscent of Krashen's (1977, 1985, 2003) Acquisition-Learning Hypothesis of the Monitor Model. Three main proposals have been posited in this respect. One proposal, the Local Impairment Hypothesis, assumes that functional projections are attainable in L2 but that features associated with functional heads are permanently impaired irrespective of L1 (for example, Beck 1998). Accordingly, no transfer of (abstract) feature strength from L1 takes place. A second proposal, the Failed Functional Features Hypothesis, claims that the Interlanguage system of the L2er, specifically that of the functional feature system, is constrained by what is available in L1 and, therefore, permanently impaired depending on the nature of the L1 system (for example, Hawkins and Chan 1997). It is further maintained that UG is partially unavailable in L2 and that beyond the critical period, the features associated with functional categories (except those already encoded for specific lexical items) become permanently fixed and therefore become inaccessible for modification (or for resetting of parameters). A third proposal, the Missing Surface Inflection Hypothesis, claims that the feature system is temporarily impaired at the morphophonological (surface) level due to complexity in mapping between surface forms and underlying abstract features (for example, Lardiere 2000, De Garavito and White 2002). The nature of impairment according to this proposal depends on the L2 learner's figuring out the mapping complexity and spelling it out properly. The proposal is in line with other UG access proposals such as the Full Transfer/Full Access model (Schwartz and Sprouse 1996).

Alhaway (2005) investigated the predictions made by the three proposals above based on cross-sectional data. (See Box 2.10.) The study was conducted on 53 Arabic L2ers, belonging to two different L1s, (American) English and French. Participants, males and females, of each L1 background were assigned into one of three groups according to their length of exposure to formal instruction in Arabic: first year, second year, and third year. The study investigated the participants' acquisition of morphosyntactic structures involving S-V and N-A agreement as well as N-A word order. Given the participants' L1s and the target structures investigated, the two pairings illustrated in (13)-(14) were aimed at.

(13)   American English participants who were speakers of a [-gender] and
        [-strong] L1, learning a [+gender] and [+strong] L2 (Arabic)
(14)   French participants who were speakers of a [+gender] and
        [+strong] L1, learning a [+gender] and [+ strong] L2 (Arabic)

The data consisted of recorded spontaneous production data from the L1 English and L1 French participants on the target forms discussed above.

Elicitation tasks used included picture description, picture differences, and picture sequencing.

The most significant findings revealed that there was no statistically significant difference in the production of S-V agreement between the French L1 groups, on the one hand, and the English L1 groups on the other, but there was one with respect to N-A agreement. The data further revealed that there was a significant difference between the two sets of groups with respect to N-A agreement involving semantic/natural versus grammatical gender, suggesting that the English L1 participants were more likely to have problems with grammatical gender than natural gender in comparison with their French L1 counterparts. In other words, grammatical gender for the French L1 participants posed no particular problem for them while it did for the English L1 participants, in particular Group 2. A complexity factor in the mapping between underlying abstract features and surface form was ruled out, since the study focused on the regular and straightforward feminine suffix [-a].

Box 2.10   L2 acquisition of Arabic morphosyntactic features (Alhawary 2005)

Languages: L1 = (American) English and French, L2 = Arabic

Proficiency levels of L2:

MSA	1st year	2nd year	3rd year	Total
L1 English	n = 9	n = 9	n = 9	n = 27
L1 French	n = 9	n = 9	n = 8	n = 26

Tasks: Elicited production

Results: Statistical acquisition findings of English L1 versus French L1 participants

Structures	Performance significantly different
S-V Agreement	No
N-A Agreement	Yes
Grammatical Agreement vs. Natural Agreement	Yes

The findings are argued to be in support of a modified temporary (access to UG) impairment view, especially with respect to L2 contexts where the L1 does not exhibit abstract inflectional features similar to those available in the L2. The temporary status is based on the performance of participants in Group 3 (of both L1 backgrounds) where at least one English L1 participant had a 100 percent correct ratio in singular feminine N-A agreement and as many as three had a 100 percent correct ratio in singular feminine S-V agreement (as opposed to 3 and 2 participants, respectively, in the French Group 3). Moreover, at least one of the English L1 participants (Group 3) had 100 percent correct ratios in both forms (so did a French L1 counterpart). This observation suggests that even full attainment in SLA in both groups is possible. Thus, the findings are ultimately significant for comparison between L1 and L2 attainment. Although ultimate attainment in L1 acquisition is often observed and suggested to be different (better) than in L2, there have also been cases, reported anecdotally, where L2ers were able to reach native-like competence. Moreover, studies in Specific Language Impairment have revealed that in fact about 10 percent of children in the United States and Britain exhibit language delay and that not all children eventually catch up on their L1 language competence (Bishop and Leonard 2000:ix). Thus, as more research is conducted, it may be determined that the status of attainment in L1 and L2 may be not so different after all.

2.5 Summary

Arabic SLA research can best be characterized as parsimonious and sporadic. Although it can be argued that Arabic SLA has caught up on most prominent trends of SLA research—including Error Analysis, developmental studies, cognitive, and theoretical accounts—very few studies have been conducted to date. In particular, only two studies (Nielsen 1997; Alhawary 1999, 2003) produced longitudinal data and the remaining few having focused on cross-sectional data. This reality presents a major challenge for researchers working on Arabic SLA, since even some of the most basic data-driven (explanatory in nature) observations available in other languages are not yet documented for Arabic. Aside from limitations to do with some of the studies as discussed above, the data generated in Arabic SLA studies are limited in scope with respect to L1 backgrounds. Apart from Nielsen (1997) and Alhawary (2005), the rest of the data are those gathered from Arabic L2ers who are English L1 speakers.

CHAPTER 3

The Acquisition of Gender Agreement

This chapter discusses acquisition of gender agreement based on both longitudinal and cross-sectional data from native English L1, French L1, and Japanese L1 speakers learning Arabic as an L2. The target structures focused on here include nominal gender agreement, as in (14)-(17) (restated below as (1)-(4)), demonstrative gender agreement, as in (23)-(26) and (29) (restated below as (5)-(9)), and verbal agreement, as in (47)-(48) and (51)-(52) (restated below as (10)-(13)) discussed in Chapter 1.

(1)   *t$^\Omega$ālib*   *qas$^\Omega$īr*
      student.**s.m**   short.**s.m**
      "a short (male) student"

(2)   *t$^\Omega$ālib-a*   *qas$^\Omega$īr-a*
      student-**s.f**   short-**s.f**
      "a short (female) student"

(3)   *Pal-maq$^\Omega$ad*   *Pal-s$^\Omega$ayīr*
      the-desk.**s.m**   the-small.**s.m**
      "the small desk"

(4)   *Pal-t$^\Omega$āwil-a*   *Pal-s$^\Omega$ayīr-a*
      the-table-**s.f**   the-small-**s.f**
      "the small table"

(5)   *hāðā*   *t$^\Omega$ālib(-u-n)*
      this.**s.m**   student.**s.m**-nom-indef
      "This is a (male) student."

(6)   *hāðihi*   *t$^\Omega$ālib-a(t-u-n)*
      this.**s.f**   student-**s.f**-nom-indef
      "This is a (female) student."

(7)   *hāðā*   *t$^\Omega$ālib(-u-n)*   *dʒadīd(-u-n)*
      this.**s.m**   student.**s.m**-nom-indef   new.**s.m**-nom-indef
      "This is a new (male) student."

(8)   *hāðā*   *ʔal-tˤālib(-u)*   *dʒadīd(-u-n)*
       this.s.m   the-student.**s.m**-nom   new.**s.m**-nom-indef
       "This (male) student is new."

(9)   *hāðihi*   *ʔal-sayyār-a(t-u)*   *kabīr-a(t-u-n)*
       This.**s.f**   the-car-**s.f**-nom   big-**s.f**-nom-indef
       "This car is big."

10(a) *ʔal-tˤālib(-u)*   *darasa*
       the-student.**s.m**-nom   study.perf.**3.s.m**
       "The (male) student studied."

10(b) *ʔal-tˤālib(-u)*   *ya-drus(-u)*
       the-student.**s.m**-nom   **3.s.m**-study.imperf-indic
       "The (male) student studies/is studying."

11(a) *ʔal-tˤālib-a(t-u)*   *daras-at*
       the-student-**s.f**-nom   study.perf-**3.s.f**
       "The (female) student studied."

11(b) *ʔal-tˤālib-a(t-u)*   *ta-drus(-u)*
       the-student-**s.f**-nom   **3.s.f**-study.imperf-indic
       "The (female) student studies/is studying."

12(a) *darasa*   *ʔal-tˤālib(-u)*
       study.perf.**3.s.m**   the-student.**s.m**-nom
       "The (male) student studied."

12(b) *ya-drus(-u)*   *ʔal-tˤālib(-u)*
       3.s.m-study.imperf-indic   the-student.**s.m**-nom
       "The (male) student studies/is studying."

13(a) *daras-at*   *ʔal-tˤālib-a(t-u)*
       study.perf-**3.s.f**   the-student-**s.f**-nom
       "The (female) student studied."

13(b) *ta-drus(-u)*   *ʔal-tˤālib-a(t-u)*
       3.s.f-study.imperf-indic   the-student-**s.f**-nom
       "The (female) student studies/is studying."

3.1   Methods (Longitudinal Data)

Eight English L1 speakers and one French L1 speaker were observed longitudinally for a school year. Table 3.1 (below) displays the demographic data of the participants. The participants were selected, because they had no background in Arabic. They were taking their first Arabic language class (a six credit per semester class) at the time as part of their program requirements at their university in the United States. With the exception of one participant, Mark, all the participants attended the same class with the same teacher, but all were using the same textbooks (Brustad et al. 1995a, 1995b).

Table 3.1 Longitudinal participants

Name	Gender	Age	L1	Major	Year at University
Ann	F	21	English	Theology	1st
Beth	F	23	English	History	Graduate 1st
Jeff	M	19	English	Int'l Relations	1st
John	M	19	English	Int'l Economics	1st
Kay	F	18	English	Arabic and History	1st
Mark	M	32	English	Int'l Relations	2nd
Viola	F	18	English	Int'l Economics	1st
Mary*	F	19	English	Arabic	1st
Adam*	M	22	Creole and French	MBNA	4th

* = Early withdrawal in the second half of the school year. All names are pseudonyms.

Data elicitation sessions were held every two weeks for a school year, resulting in ten interviews with each participant except for two: Adam withdrew after the third interview and Mary withdrew after the fourth interview. A number of techniques were used to elicit the agreement contexts of the target structures. Elicitation techniques included picture description, picture differences, picture sequencing, video story retelling, and informal interviews. The elicitation tasks were held constant and were consistently used across all the participants. Elicitation materials were recycled two to three times maximally to control for participants' familiarity. All interviews were audio-recorded. The data were transcribed, transliterated, and coded. Each data sample was triple-checked for accuracy after each step. To preserve the data from contamination due to elicitation errors, the elicitation statements were used consistently across participants and kept general and short and, at times, even said in English. The elicitation materials were piloted before they were used for elicitation. Certain tokens were not coded. These were hesitations and self-corrections except the last attempt in each case. In addition, caution was taken against affecting any gender bias or stereotypes through elicitation materials. The tasks were designed to elicit, for example, tokens such as "Arab woman" and "Arab man," "tall/short woman," and "tall/short man," avoiding stereotypical tokens such as "tall man" and "short woman," etc. Sample elicitation tasks appear in Figures 3.1-3.2 (below).

Figure 3.1

Figure 3.2 From *ExpressWays*, Molinsky and Bliss: 31, 79, 139-141. Copyright Prentice Hall Regents, 1996. Reprinted by permission of Pearson Education, Inc.

3.1.1 *Results of nominal and verbal gender agreement*

The produced data relevant to nominal gender agreement are of the full NP type (that is, with a head lexical noun followed by an attributive lexical adjective). The produced noun phrases range from those occurring as predicates of nominal sentences, to direct/indirect objects, to sentence fragments (that is, just NPs). Focus is on N-A agreement with respect to singular masculine versus singular feminine forms. With respect to verbal agreement (that is, agreement between the subject and the verb), the produced data include tokens with a lexical grammatical subject (with or without a demonstrative pronoun), a pronominal subject, and zero (null) subjects.[1] Like nominal gender agreement, focus of verbal agreement is on third person singular masculine versus third person singular feminine.

3.1.1.1 *Applying an emergence criterion*

To determine whether a form has emerged in the IL systems of the participants, an emergence criterion is adopted. The emergence criterion is defined as:

> "the point in time at which certain skills have, in principle, been attained or at which certain operations can, in principle, be carried out. From a descriptive viewpoint one can say that this is the beginning of an acquisition process." (Pienemann 1998:138)

In other words, the criterion relies on the initial ability to process and apply a rule. Accordingly, this entails that the emergence criterion need not capture a form that is completely target-like (TL). Applying a minimal emergence criterion entails that we rely on one instance of rule application to conclude that emergence of the form has taken place. However, applying a strict one minimal token criterion for emergence may not be reliable with respect to the target structures. Thus, with respect to N-A agreement and the input to which the participants were exposed, to mark an adjective and a noun (in the singular) for the feature feminine, a feminine gender suffix {-*a*} is attached to the end of the form—the default gender marking of the stem being masculine. This means that to mark a form for either gender, the participants had a 50-50 chance to produce the rule correctly (for other problems to do with relying on a strict one minimal token of emergence, see Alhawary 2003:123-124).

On the other hand, a more reliable emergence criterion than that of a strict one minimal token for the Arabic data is one that relies on identifying the first occurrence of the same lexical item in both masculine and feminine contexts in the same data set (for a similar decision and application of the same criterion on Arabic L2 data, see also Nielsen 1997). Accordingly, evidence of rule application (that is, of transferring gender agreement features from the head noun to the attributive adjective) is established for N-A agreement with the first instance of the same attributive adjective being used correctly with both a masculine and a feminine head, as in sentences (14)-(17) (in Chapter 1), restated above as (1)-(4). Similarly, evidence of rule application is established for verbal agreement with the first instance of the same lexical verb occurring in both the third person singular masculine and third person singular feminine, as in sentences (47)-(48) and (51)-(52) (in Chapter 1), restated above as (10)-(13).

Accordingly, the sole contrast of the two target structures of nominal and verbal agreement here is between singular masculine and singular feminine. The advantage of this criterion is that each pair offers two contexts for rule application sufficient to establish emergence with somewhat reasonable certainty, since 1) both elements are varied morphologically (word-finally) and 2) they show suffix manipulation as evidence against learning/memorizing of form as unanalyzed chunk.

Applying the emergence criterion of identical lexical forms in both singular masculine and singular feminine yields the emergence schedules of nominal (N-A) and verbal (S-V) agreement in the participants' IL systems, as listed in Table 3.2 (for raw data as well as a close lexical analysis, see Alhawary 1999:101-146).[2]

As Table 3.2 reveals, a strong pattern of the schedules of nominal (N-A) and verbal (S-V) gender agreement emerges. Verbal agreement emerged in six (Ann, Kay, Viola, John, Jeff, and Mary) of the participants' IL systems before nominal agreement while nominal agreement emerged in only three (Beth, Mark, and Adam) before verbal agreement (for a detailed description of the processing of both structures in the participants' individual IL systems, including an explicit lexical analysis, see Alhawary 1999:108-146). In fact, nominal agreement never emerged in the IL systems of two of the six participants (Jeff and Mary) in whose IL systems verbal agreement emerged first.

Table 3.2 Emergence schedule of N-A and S-V agreement in the participants' IL systems

Participants	Nominal/N-A Agreement		Verbal/S-V Agreement	
	Interview	Week	Interview	Week
Beth	1	8	2	10
Mark	1	8	2	10
Adam	1	8	2	10
Ann	2	10	1	8
Kay	3	14	1	8
Viola	4	16	2	10
John	6	20	2	10
Jeff	0	0	2	10
Mary	0	0	3	14

These findings are particularly strong, because the participants were exposed to nominal (N-A) gender agreement (as early as week 3) before they were exposed to verbal (S-V) agreement (in week 8), as shown in Table 3.3, which lists chronologically the learning objectives of the target structures in the participants' textbooks.

Table 3.3 also lists the dates during which elicitation sessions were held (weeks 8, 10, 14, 16, 18, 20, 22, 24, 26, and 27 in boldface). The elicitation sessions started in the eighth week, because the classroom instruction during the first eight weeks covered mostly phonology and script, cultural notes, and a few discrete meaningful vocabulary items occurring at the phrase level (Unit 5) and a few at the sentence level (Unit 8). Thus, even though the participants of the study were exposed to nominal gender agreement before verbal agreement, the structures emerged differently in most of the participants' IL systems.

Table 3.3 Learning objective schedule of *Alif Baa* and *Al-Kitaab* (Brustad et al. 1995a, 1995b)

Forms		N-A Agreement					S-V (Imperfective) Agreement							
		S.M	S.F	P.M.H	P.F.H	P.Non-H	3.S.M	3.S.F	3.P.M	1.S	1.P	2.S.M	2.S.F	2.P.M
Weeks	Units													
3	5	X	X											
5	7	(/)	(/)											
6	8	X	X											
7	9	(/)	(/)											
	10													
8	1	X	X				X	X		X				
9-10	2	(x)	(x)				(/)	(x)		(x)		(x)		
	3	(/)	(/)			(/)	(x)	(x)						
11-14	4	(x)	(x)	(x)			X	X	X	X	X	X	X	X
	5	X	X	(/)			(x)	(x)	(x)	(x)	(x)		(/)	(/)
	6	(x)	(x)	(/)		(/)	(x)	(x)	(x)	(x)	(x)	(x)	(/)	(/)
15-16	7	(x)	(x)	(x)	(/)	(/)	(x)	(x)	(x)	(x)	(x)	(/)	(/)	(/)
17-18	8	(x)	(x)	(/)		(/)	(x)		(x)	(x)		(/)	(x)	(x)
	9	(x)	(x)			X	X	X	X	X	X	X	X	X
19-20	10	(x)	(x)	(/)		(x)	[x]	[x]	[x]	[x]	[x]	[x]	[x]	[x]
	11	(x)	(x)			(x)	[x]	[x]	[x]	[x]	[x]	[x]	[x]	[x]
21-22	12	(x)	(x)				[x]	[x]	[x]	[x]	[x]	[x]	[x]	[x]
23-24	13	(x)	(x)	(/)		(x)	[x]	[x]	[x]	[x]	[x]	[x]	[x]	[x]
25-26	14	(x)	(x)			(x)	[x]	[x]	[x]	[x]	[x]	[x]	[x]	[x]
27-28	15	(x)	(x)	(/)		(x)	(x)	(x)	(x)	(x)	(/)	(/)	(/)	(x)

X = focused attempt to teach the structure; [x] = indirect focused attempt where main focus is on lexical item/s; (x) = structure is not the focus of instruction but occurs in the lesson and drills more than 4 times; (/) = structure is not the focus of instruction and occurs less than 4 times. Weeks in bold mark the elicitation sessions.

3.1.1.2 *Applying a 90 percent correct acquisition criterion*

Using a 90 percent correct in obligatory contexts measure (with a minimum of three contexts per elicitation session), familiar from the morpheme order studies of the 1970s (see Krashen 1977; Burt and Dulay 1980), leads to similar findings, as shown in Tables 3.4 and 3.5. Accordingly, we find that Beth reached the 90 percent correct criterion in obligatory contexts of N-A agreement in week 10 and exhibited slight backsliding in weeks 20 and 26; she reached criterion for S-V agreement in week 16 and slipped in weeks 20 and 24. Mark reached criterion for N-A agreement in weeks 8, 10, 16, and 24, but slipped below in intervening sessions, most noticeably in week 14; he reached criterion for S-V agreement in weeks 10 and 14 but not again until week 27. Adam reached criteria for neither N-A agreement nor S-V agreement. Ann reached criterion for N-A agreement in week 10 and exhibited backsliding in weeks 20 to 24; she similarly reached criterion for S-V agreement in week 10 and exhibited backsliding in weeks 14 and 16. Kay never reached criterion for N-A agreement but reached criterion for S-V agreement in weeks 10, 16, 24, and 26, backsliding in intervening sessions in weeks 14, 18, 20, 22, and 27. Viola reached criterion for N-A agreement in week 14 and never dropped below it, but she reached criterion for S-V agreement in week 10, backsliding in weeks 18, 20, and 27. John reached criterion for N-A agreement very briefly in week 18 then fell below for the remainder of the year; he reached criterion for S-V agreement earlier, in week 16, and briefly exhibited backsliding in week 20. Jeff seemed to start off fine with N-A agreement, reaching criterion in week 8, but exhibited backsliding until week 26 and then did not reach criterion in week 27; however, for S-V agreement he came very close in week 8 and reached criterion in three sessions, weeks 16, 18, and 24. Mary never reached criterion for N-A agreement (although she came very close in week 16) but reached criterion for S-V agreement in week 16.

As the above analysis reveals, there are two problematic cases when comparing what could be considered *acquired* and *emerged* using these different criteria. These cases are those of Adam and Jeff. Adam reached the *acquisition* criterion for neither N-A agreement nor S-V agreement, but he did reach the *emergence* criterion for both: N-A agreement emerged in his IL in week 8 and S-V agreement emerged in week 10 (Cf. Table 3.2 above). Jeff reached the *acquisition* criterion for N-A agreement in week 8 and for

S-V agreement in week 16, contrary to his *emergence* criterion pattern: he exhibited emergence of S-V agreement in week 10 and exhibited none for N-A agreement. However, neither case disturbs the conclusion of the results (of S-V agreement before N-A agreement) as demonstrated by the general and strong convergence of results using different criteria where the majority of participants seem to acquire S-V agreement before N-A agreement.

Table 3.4 Suppliance ratios of correct rule application of N-A and S-V agreement in the participants' ILs

		W_8	W_{10}	W_{14}	W_{16}	W_{18}	W_{20}	W_{22}	W_{24}	W_{26}	W_{27}
Beth:	N-A	.85	.90	.92	1.0	1.0	.71	1.0	1.0	.75	(1.0)
	S-V	(.0)	.78	.75	1.0	.90	.86	1.0	.66	1.0	1.0
Mark:	N-A	1.0	1.0	.41	.90	.83	.76	.57	1.0	.69	.50
	S-V	.50	.90	1.0	/	.66	.71	.76	.84	.81	.90
Adam:	N-A	.60	.87	.76	-	-	-	-	-	-	-
	S-V	.66	.76	.85	-	-	-	-	-	-	-
Ann:	N-A	.77	1.0	1.0	(1.0)	1.0	.66	.75	.85	1.0	.90
	S-V	.80	1.0	.83	.66	1.0	.91	1.0	1.0	1.0	.95
Kay:	N-A	.66	.50	.57	.57	.50	.80	(.0)	.85	.0	.0
	S-V	.83	1.0	.86	.10	.76	.80	.86	.94	1.0	.89
Viola:	N-A	.83	.87	1.0	1.0	1.0	(1.0)	1.0	(1.0)	1.0	1.0
	S-V	.40	.96	.90	1.0	.66	.88	.92	.10	.92	.71
John:	N-A	/	.70	.62	.66	1.0	.66	.60	(.50)	.60	.75
	S-V	(.0)	.87	.80	1.0	1.0	.73	.94	.93	1.0	1.0
Jeff:	N-A	1.0	.75	.71	.66	.80	.33	(.50)	.40	1.0	.66
	S-V	(1.0)	.85	.50	1.0	1.0	.70	.82	.92	.82	.74
Mary:	N-A	.57	.50	.60	(1.0)	-	-	-	-	-	-
	S-V	.80	.78	.80	1.0	-	-	-	-	-	-

"w" = week; "N-A" = noun-adjective agreement; "S-V" = subject-verb agreement; "/" = zero occurrences; "( )" = less than three tokens; "-" = participant withdrawal.

Table 3.5 Qualitative description of N-A and S-V agreement development in the participants' ILs

		W8	W10	W14	W16	W18	W20	W22	W24	W26	W27
Beth:	N-A	-	+	+	+	+	-	+	+	-	-
	S-V	-	-	-	+	+	-	+	-	+	+
Mark:	N-A	+	+	-	+	-	-	-	+	-	-
	S-V	-	+	+	-	-	-	-	-	-	+
Adam:	N-A	-	-	-							
	S-V	-	-	-							
Ann:	N-A	-	+	+	-	+	-	-	-	+	+
	S-V	-	+	-	-	+	+	+	+	+	+
Kay:	N-A	-	-	-	-	-	-	-	-	-	-
	S-V	-	+	-	-	-	-	-	+	+	-
Viola:	N-A	-	-	+	+	+	-	+	-	+	+
	S-V	-	+	+	+	-	-	+	-	+	
John:	N-A	-	-	-	-	+	-	-	-	-	-
	S-V	-	-	-	+	+	-	+	+	+	+
Jeff:	N-A	+	-	-	-	-	-	-	-	+	-
	S-V	-	-	-	+	+	-	-	+	-	-
Mary:	N-A	-	-	-	-						
	S-V	-	-	-	+						

"+" = acquired; "-" = not acquired; "[blank space] " = participant withdrawal.

Even when aggregating the data of all participants for N-A agreement versus S-V agreement, one can still observe the participants had more problems with nominal gender agreement than they did with verbal agreement, as illustrated in Figure 3.3. The aggregate data of verbal agreement shows the participants' performance started in the mid-50 percent range in the first interview (data session 1: week 8), improved significantly in the second interview to the 80 percent range, maintained the gains throughout and even showed more gains to within the 90 percent range in the last two interviews.

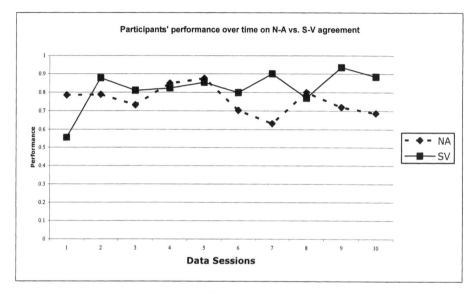

Figure 3.3

On the other hand, the aggregate data of nominal (N-A) agreement shows that the participants exhibited gains to within the 70 percent range (in data session 1: week 8) with higher performance than that of verbal agreement (since input with nominal agreement was presented earlier than input with verbal agreement as explained above), maintained (with somewhat higher) gains until the midpoint of the interviews (data session 5: week 18), and then started to backslide until the end of the observation, ending (in data session: 10, week 27) with even lower gains (in the 70 percent range) than they started (in data session 1: week 8).

3.1.1.3 *Production of gender agreement in non-contexts*

Examining rule application of the target forms in non-contexts is equally significant in order to avoid the pitfalls of the comparative fallacy (see Bley-Vroman 1983). Of the target forms, nominal gender agreement was found to exhibit some particular IL use.[3] In particular, within NP tokens, some participants overproduced the feminine feature {-a} on adjectives following masculine head nouns.[4] These are listed in Table 3.6.

Table 3.6 Oversuppliance of the feminine suffix (in masculine contexts) within NPs

Participants	Week	Total Fem	Oversuppliance/Total Feminine Suffix of a Single Data Sample
Mark	22	1	1/6 (17%)
	24	2	2/4 (50%)
	27	2	2/4 (50%)
Adam	8	4	4/8 (50%)
	10	1	1/6 (17%)
	14	2	2/9 (22%)
Ann	8	1	1/7 (14%)
	24	1	1/3 (33%)
	27	1	1/7 (14%)
Kay	10	1	1/12 (8%)
	16	1	1/3 (33%)
	24	1	1/4 (25%)
Viola	8	1	1/6 (17%)
	10	1	1/7 (14%)
	26	1	1/4 (25%)
John	10	2	2/7 (29%)
	14	2	2/7 (29%)
	16	1	1/1 (100%)
Jeff	10	1	1/6 (17%)
	14	1	1/6 (17%)
Mary	8	2	2/4 (50%)

Recall that, as explained above (see also Chapter 1), the feminine gender feature focused on here is the suffix {-a}. This feature of feminine gender in Arabic (for the items introduced in the input) is quite regular and limited to the suffix {-a}, which is phonologically realized word finally. This is easily verifiable in the content of the textbooks which the participants used in the classroom where all feminine gender adjective forms occur with the suffix {-a} except the word *bint* "girl" with the feminine suffix {-t} (see Brustad et al. 1995a, 1995b). Therefore, in the entire input of the participants, the fully realized phonological marking for the feminine gender feature is always affixed on noun and adjective forms.

In all of the data samples, the participants did produce the feminine gender marking correctly on all of the nouns (within their NP tokens). For example, we do not find any instance where the word *sayyār-a* "car" is produced as *sayyār* in a context such as *sayyār sˤayīr* "a small car" instead of *sayyār-a sˤayīr-a* where the word for "car" in Arabic is thought to be masculine and therefore its adjective "small" is produced in the masculine accordingly. The feminine agreement mismatches in the data samples are almost all of the two following types: *sayyār-a sˤayīr* "a small car" and *ʔimraʔ-a tˤawīl* "a tall woman." In addition, most of the tokens were produced during the second half of the period of the observation rather than at the beginning of the period, which would have indicated the participants had conscious knowledge of the rule from early on.

When we examine all tokens which exhibit overproduction of the feminine gender marking on adjectives following masculine head nouns (that is, all those listed in Table 3.6), we find that most instances of such rule applications in non-contexts are not as significant as they may seem. In fact, the tokens of week 8 (of Ann's IL), week 10 (of Kay's IL), weeks 8-10 (of Viola's IL), week 14 (of Jeff's IL), and one of the two tokens of week 8 (of Mary's IL), are all one NP containing the same lexical element as shown in (14) below:

(14) *xubz   ʔarabiyy-a [ʕarabiyy-a]
       bread-**s.m** Arab-**s.f**
       "Arabic bread"

There are two possible explanations here. One possibility is that the L2ers treated such forms as linguonyms and therefore may have learned them as monomorphemic chunks, since early utterances may include *ʔatakallam ʔal-ʔinklīziyya* "I speak English" *ʔatakallam ʔal-ʕarabiyya* "I speak Arabic" (as it has been suggested by an anonymous reviewer). In fact, even the four tokens produced by Adam in week 8 all contain linguonyms: *shāy turkiyya* "Turkish tea," *xubz ʔ[ʕ]arabiyya* "Arabic bread," *ʔal-xubz ʔal-ʔ[ʕ]arabiyya* "the Arabic bread," and *ʔal-ʔadab ʔal-ʔinklīziyya* "English literature." Another possible explanation is that the participants may have simply produced the feminine suffix at random, since they were introduced to nationality adjectives in feminine and masculine contexts from early on (see Brustad et al. 1995a:133).

Thus, such tokens that exhibit overproduction of the feminine suffix on adjectives following masculine head nouns do not seem to offer much help in exploring the extent to which the participants were aware of applying the feminine gender suffix rule. However, there is some evidence that shows some of the participants were aware of applying the feminine gender suffix rule when we examine productive rule application tokens on adjectives following feminine head nouns. A total of three tokens are found, resulting in novel IL utterances.[5] One token was produced by Beth (in week 18), one by Ann (in week 18), and one by Mark (in week 16): *sayyār-a ʔasˤfar- a* "a yellow car," *sayyār-a ʔal-ʔasˤfar-a* "a yellow car," and *ʔutill-a kabīr-a* "a big hotel," respectively. The first two tokens (produced by Beth and Ann) are non-TL utterances, since color adjectives follow a different gender (pattern) rule (*sayyār-a sˤafrāʔ* "a yellow car"). In the third token (produced by Mark), the masculine head noun for "hotel" *ʔutil* → *ʔutill-a* is treated as feminine and therefore the adjective following it is inflected for the feminine gender feature.

Given the number of the longitudinal participants (a total of 9) as well as the number of data samples gathered (a total of 90), such tokens are not significant and do not indicate the participants were actively applying the feminine gender suffix rule. In fact, most participants scored 100 percent correct on masculine tokens, suggesting that the masculine form (with zero masculine suffix) was often used as a default form (for raw data, see Alhawary 1999:101-105). The main problem observed, therefore, was undersuppliance of the feminine gender suffix {*-a*} on adjectives following feminine head nouns within the NP tokens produced.

3.1.1.4 *Noun-adjective word order*

Although the NP word order of the participants' L1 is adjective-noun, quite the opposite of that of the L2 (that is, noun-adjective), all of the participants seem to have adjusted to Arabic NP word order from early on, as evidenced by the fact that only seven tokens with English word order were found in all of the data samples, as listed in Table 3.7. Thus, Beth produced one token (in week 8), Mark produced two tokens (one in week 14 and another in week 26), Kay produced one token (in week 26), and Jeff produced three tokens (one in week 14 and two in week 16). Examples of the produced (non-target-like) Arabic noun-adjective word order that conform to the word order of the participants' L1 English (adjective-noun) are: *kabīr ?imra?-a "an old woman" (produced by Jeff in week 14), *qasˤīr kitāb "a short book" (produced by Jeff in week 16), *sˤaɣīr sayyār-a "a small car" (produced by Beth in week 8), and *fī ?al-?āxir san-a "in the previous year" (produced by Kay in week 26).

Table 3.7 Participants' noun-adjective word order errors

Participants	Week	Total *A-N	Total *A-N/Total NPs	Ratios
Beth	8	1	1/56	(.02)
Mark	14	1	2/95	(.02)
	26	1		
Kay	26	1	1/74	(.01)
Jeff	14	1	3/63	(.05)
	16	2		

The general observation is that the longitudinal participants were able to adjust to the L2 word order from early on with the exception of the seven tokens discussed above. The very small number of such tokens produced is insignificant compared with the overall production of all NPs during the participants' period of observation.

3.1.2 Results of demonstrative gender agreement

The produced data relevant to gender agreement involving demonstrative pronouns comprise equational sentential agreement between the demonstrative pronoun (as the subject/topic constituent of the sentence) and the predicate/comment (a noun or adjective) constituent, as in sentences (23)-(26) and (29) (in Chapter 1) restated above as (5)-(9). Focus here is on gender (masculine and feminine) in the singular involving the use of hāðā and hāðihi. The participants were presented with pictures such as those in Figure 3.1 and were asked simply to describe what they saw to the

interviewer, referring to each object one at a time and assuming the
interviewer did not know what the participants were describing.

3.1.2.1 *Applying an emergence criterion*

The participants produced a good number of tokens of equational
sentences with the demonstrative as the subject constituent of the sentence,
as in sentences (23)-(26) and (29) (in Chapter 1) and restated above as (5)-
(9). In the majority of tokens produced, the predicate/topic was a noun; a
smaller number of tokens were produced with the predicate/topic as an
adjective, such as *hāðā tˤālib* "This[s.m] is a male student" versus *hāðā
kabīr* "This[s.m] is big." Applying an emergence criterion similar to the one
adopted above, evidence of rule application (that is, of transferring gender
agreement features from the demonstrative pronoun to the predicate/topic) is
established for the first pair of tokens when both demonstrative pronouns are
used correctly with contrasting predicate masculine and feminine predicate,
such as *hāðā tˤālib* "This[s.m] is a male student" versus *hāðihi tˤālib-a*
"This[s.f] is a female student" or *hāðā radʒul* "This[s.m] is a man" versus
hāðihi ʔimraʔ-a "This[s.f] is a woman." Tokens coded include those in
which the participant oversupplied the definite article with the predicate
noun, as in **hāðihi ʔal-tˤālib-a* → *hāðihi tˤālib-a* "This[s.f] is a female
student."[6] The errors produced constituted mainly tokens where the
participants substituted one demonstrative pronoun for the other.

Applying the emergence criterion accordingly yields the emergence
schedules of gender agreement involving demonstratives in equational
sentences in the participants' IL systems listed in Table 3.8. The table also
lists the verbal (S-V) agreement schedule in the participants' IL systems.
Recall that evidence of rule application is established for verbal (S-V)
agreement with the first instance of the same lexical verb occurring in both
the third person singular masculine and third person singular feminine, with
the sole contrast between the two constructions being the features singular
masculine and singular feminine.

As Table 3.8 shows, and according to the emergence criterion, three
acquisition patterns emerge: 1) emergence of verbal agreement and
demonstrative gender agreement at the same time (in the IL systems of Beth,
Adam, Viola, and Jeff in week 10 and in Ann's IL system in week 8), 2)

emergence of demonstrative gender agreement before verbal agreement (in Mark's IL system in weeks 8 and 10 and in Mary's IL system in weeks 10 and 14, respectively), and 3) emergence of verbal agreement before demonstrative gender agreement (in Kay's IL system in weeks 8 and 10 and in John's IL system in weeks 10 and 14, respectively).

Table 3.8 Emergence schedule of demonstrative gender agreement in the participants' ILs

Participants	Demonstrative Gender Agreement		Verbal/S-V Agreement	
	Interview	Week	Interview	Week
Beth	2	10	2	10
Mark	1	8	2	10
Adam	2	10	2	10
Ann	1	8	1	8
Kay	2	10	1	8
Viola	2	10	2	10
John	3	14	2	10
Jeff	2	10	2	10
Mary	2	10	3	14

3.1.2.2 *Applying a 90 percent correct acquisition criterion*

Using a 90 percent correct in obligatory contexts measure (with a minimum of three contexts per elicitation session), shows a totally different pattern, where verbal (S-V) agreement clearly seems to be acquired sooner than gender agreement in demonstrative pronouns with two exceptions, Beth and Mary, as shown in Tables 3.9 and 3.10. Thus, we find that Beth reached 90 percent correct in obligatory contexts of gender agreement in demonstratives in week 14 and exhibited slight backsliding in weeks 18, 20, and 24; she reached criterion for verbal agreement in week 16 and slipped in weeks 20 and 24. Mark never reached criterion for gender agreement in demonstratives; he reached criterion for verbal agreement in weeks 10 and 14 but not again until week 27. Adam reached criterion for neither gender agreement in demonstratives (although he came close in week 8) nor verbal agreement. Ann reached criterion for gender agreement in demonstratives in week 10 and exhibited backsliding in weeks 16 through 20 and again in week 27; she similarly reached criterion for verbal agreement in week 10 and exhibited backsliding in weeks 14 and 16. Kay never reached criterion for gender agreement in demonstratives but reached criterion for verbal agreement in weeks 10, 24, and 26, backsliding in intervening sessions in weeks 14, 16, 18, 20, 22, and 27. Viola reached criterion for gender agreement in demonstratives in week 18, backsliding in weeks 20 and 26,

Table 3.9 Suppliance ratios of correct rule application of demonstrative gender and S-V agreement in the participants' ILs

		W_8	W_{10}	W_{14}	W_{16}	W_{18}	W_{20}	W_{22}	W_{24}	W_{26}	W_{27}
Beth:	DEM	/	.78	1.0	1.0	.86	.82	1.0	.89	1.0	1.0
	S-V	(.0)	.78	.75	1.0	.90	.86	1.0	.66	1.0	1.0
Mark:	DEM	.88	.79	.83	.64	.60	.52	.82	.47	.67	.89
	S-V	.50	.90	1.0	/	.66	.71	.76	.84	.81	.90
Adam:	DEM	(1.0)	.55	.64	-	-	-	-	-	-	-
	S-V	.66	.76	.85	-	-	-	-	-	-	-
Ann:	DEM	.80	.93	.95	.89	.70	.71	1.0	1.0	1.0	.89
	S-V	.80	1.0	.83	.66	1.0	.91	1.0	1.0	1.0	.95
Kay:	DEM	.43	.67	.82	.67	.60	.74	.68	.73	.67	.71
	S-V	.83	1.0	.86	.10	.76	.80	.86	.94	1.0	.89
Viola:	DEM	.54	.68	.86	.78	.91	.69	1.0	1.0	.71	1.0
	S-V	.40	.96	.90	1.0	.66	.88	.92	.10	.92	.71
John:	DEM	.50	.78	.82	.89	.80	.75	1.0	1.0	.92	.75
	S-V	(.0)	.87	.80	1.0	1.0	.73	.94	.93	1.0	1.0
Jeff:	DEM	(1.0)	.72	.69	.67	.43	.42	(.50)	.67	.83	.67
	S-V	(1.0)	.85	.50	1.0	1.0	.70	.82	.92	.82	.74
Mary:	DEM	/	.67	1.0	.92	-	-	-	-	-	-
	S-V	.80	.78	.80	1.0	-	-	-	-	-	-

"w" = week; "DEM" = demonstrative gender agreement; "S-V" = subject-verb agreement; "/" = zero occurrences; "( )" = less than three tokens; "-" = participant withdrawal.

Table 3.10 Qualitative description of demonstrative gender and S-V agreement development in the participants' ILs

		W$_8$	W$_{10}$	W$_{14}$	W$_{16}$	W$_{18}$	W$_{20}$	W$_{22}$	W$_{24}$	W$_{26}$	W$_{27}$
Beth:	DEM	-	-	+	+	-	-	+	-	+	+
	S-V	-	-	-	+	+	-	+	-	+	+
Mark:	DEM	-	-	-	-	-	-	-	-	-	-
	S-V	-	+	+	-	-	-	-	-	-	+
Adam:	DEM	-	-	-							
	S-V	-	-	-							
Ann:	DEM	-	+	+	-	-	-	+	+	+	-
	S-V	-	+	-	-	+	+	+	+	+	+
Kay:	DEM	-	-	-	-	-	-	-	-	-	-
	S-V	-	+	-	-	-	-	-	+	+	-
Viola:	DEM	-	-	-	-	+	-	+	+	-	+
	S-V	-	+	+	+	-	-	+	-	+	-
John:	DEM	-	-	-	-	-	-	+	+	+	-
	S-V	-	-	-	+	+	-	+	+	+	+
Jeff:	DEM	-	-	-	-	-	-	-	-	-	-
	S-V	-	-	-	+	+	-	-	+	-	-
Mary:	DEM	-	-	+	+						
	S-V	-	-	-	+						

"+" = acquired; "-" = not acquired; "[blank space]" = participant withdrawal.

but she reached criterion for verbal agreement in week 10, backsliding in weeks 18, 20, 24, and 27. John reached criterion for gender agreement in demonstratives in weeks 22, 24, and 26 then fell below in the end, week 27; he reached criterion for verbal agreement earlier in week 16 and briefly exhibited backsliding in week 20. Jeff never reached criterion for gender agreement in demonstratives (although he came close in week 8), but he reached criterion for verbal agreement in only three sessions, weeks 16, 18, and 24. Mary reached criterion for gender agreement in demonstratives in weeks 14-16 and for verbal agreement in week 16.

The 90 percent criterion here proves to be a more useful criterion than emergence, as it reveals that most of the participants found demonstrative gender agreement (between the demonstrative pronoun/subject and the predicate within verbless sentences) more problematic than they did verbal agreement (between the subject and the verb). This observation would have been completely missed by relying on one criterion alone such as emergence. The observation that the participants reached the emergence criterion may be due to random hits, as the choice was merely between *hāðihi* and *hāðā*, amounting to a 50 percent chance.

These findings are particularly strong, because the participants were exposed to demonstrative gender agreement (as early as week 6) before they were exposed to verbal (S-V) gender agreement (in week 8), as shown in Table 3.11, which lists chronologically the learning objectives of the target structures in the participants' textbooks. Table 3.11 also lists the dates during which elicitation sessions were held (weeks 8, 10, 14, 16, 18, 20, 22, 24, 26, and 27 in boldface). As previously mentioned, the elicitation sessions started in the eighth week, because the classroom instruction during the first eight weeks covered mostly phonology and script, cultural notes, and a few discrete meaningful vocabulary items occurring at the phrase level (Unit 5) and a few at the sentence level (Unit 8). Thus, even though the participants of the study were exposed to demonstrative gender agreement before they were to verbal (subject-verb) gender agreement, most of them acquired the latter before the former, based on the 90 percent correct acquisition criterion.

Even when aggregating the data of all participants for demonstrative gender agreement versus S-V agreement, one can still observe that the participants had more problems with demonstrative gender agreement than they did with verbal agreement, as illustrated in Figure 3.4. The aggregate data of verbal agreement shows the participants' performance started in the 50 percent range in the first data session, improved significantly in the second data session to the 80 percent range, maintained the gains throughout and even showed more gains to within the 90 percent range in the last two sessions.

Table 3.11 Learning objective schedule of *Alif Baa* and *Al-Kitaab* (Brustad et al. 1995a, 1995b)

Forms		Demonstrative Pronouns					S-V (Imperfective) Agreement							
		S.M	S.F	P.M.H	P.F.H	P.Non-H	3.S.M	3.S.F	3.P.M	1.S	1.P	2.S.M	2.S.F	2.P.M
Weeks	Units													
6	8	X	X											
7	9	(/)	(/)											
	10		(/)											
8	1	(x)	(x)				X	X		X				
9-10	2		(/)			(/)	(/)	(x)		(x)		(x)		
	3	(x)	(x)			(/)	(x)	(x)						
11-14	4	(x)	(x)			(/)	X	X	X	X	X	X	X	X
	5	X	X			(/)	(x)	(x)	(x)	(x)	(x)		(/)	(/)
	6	(/)	(/)			(/)	(x)	(x)	(x)	(x)	(x)	(x)	(/)	(/)
15-16	7	(x)	(x)			(/)	(x)	(x)	(x)	(x)	(x)	(/)	(/)	(/)
17-18	8	(x)	(x)			(/)	(x)		(x)	(x)		(/)	(x)	(x)
	9	(x)	(x)			X	X	X	X	X	X	X	X	X
19-20	10	(/)	(/)			(/)	[x]	[x]	[x]	[x]	[x]	[x]	[x]	[x]
	11	(x)	(/)			(/)	[x]	[x]	[x]	[x]	[x]	[x]	[x]	[x]
21-22	12	(x)	(x)			(/)	[x]	[x]	[x]	[x]	[x]	[x]	[x]	[x]
23-24	13	(x)	(/)			(/)	[x]	[x]	[x]	[x]	[x]	[x]	[x]	[x]
25-26	14	(x)	(x)			(/)	[x]	[x]	[x]	[x]	[x]	[x]	[x]	[x]
27-28	15	(x)	(x)			(/)	(x)	(x)	(x)	(x)	(/)	(/)	(/)	(x)

X = focused attempt to teach the structure; [x] = indirect focused attempt where main focus is on lexical item(s); (x) = structure is not the focus of instruction but occurs in the lesson and drills 4 or more times; (/) = structure is not the focus of instruction and occurs less than 4 times; the figures in bold mark the elicitation sessions.

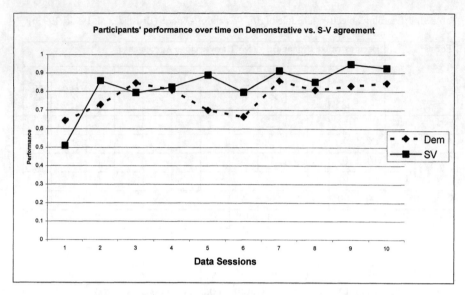

Figure 3.4

On the other hand, the aggregate data of demonstrative gender agreement shows that the participants made gradual gains from the 60 percent to the 80 percent range (in sessions 1-3: weeks 8-14) starting with a higher performance than that of verbal agreement (since input with demonstrative gender agreement was presented earlier than input with verbal agreement as explained above). Their performance backslided in three subsequent sessions (data sessions 4-6: weeks 16-20), regained their earlier performance to the 80 percent range in data session 7 (week 22), and maintained this performance until the end of the observation. In addition to the noticeable U-shaped learning behavior which the participants exhibited for demonstrative gender agreement but did not exhibit for verbal agreement, their performance on verbal agreement was still about 10 percent higher than their performance on demonstrative gender agreement towards the end of the observation. This finding is further corroborated by the similar findings of the gap between the acquisition of nominal gender agreement and verbal agreement above.

3.1.2.3 *Production of demonstrative gender agreement in non-contexts*

To further speculate on the extent to which the participants were aware of applying the demonstrative gender agreement rule as well as to avoid the pitfalls of the comparative fallacy (see Bley-Vroman 1983), the examination of rule application in non-contexts is equally significant. The two following observations are made: random hits where *hāδā* "This[s.m]" is followed by feminine predicate nouns or adjectives (that is, with the feminine suffix {-*a*}) and random hits where *hāδihi* "This[s.f]" is followed by masculine predicate nouns or adjectives (that is, with the masculine zero morpheme suffix {-*0*}). The mismatches of the former were more frequent than the mismatches of the latter, suggesting that the masculine form *hāδā* may have been used as the default form by most participants. Apart from this prevalent pattern of demonstrative pronoun use, only two actual tokens of rule application in non-contexts were found, as illustrated in Table 3.12.

Table 3.12

Participants	Demonstrative S.M Agreement*	Demonstrative S.F Agreement**
Jeff	2 (2/43 = 5%)	0 (0/55 = 0%)

* = rule application of masculine zero suffix {-*0*} on words following *hāδā* in all data sets;
** = rule application of feminine suffix {-*a*} on words following *hāδihi* in all data sets.

The two tokens produced (by Jeff) were *hāδā tˤāyyir* → *hāδihi tˤāʔir-a* "This[s.f] is an airplane[s.f]" and *hāδā tˤawāl* → *hāδihi tˤāwil-a* "This[s.f] is a table[s.f]." Since the participants produced the correct gender (masculine and feminine) on all nouns (following *hāδā* and *hāδihi*), with the exception of two tokens in all the data sets, we can conclude that the main problem which the participants had with demonstrative gender agreement was mainly to do with the correct choice of the demonstrative *hāδā* versus *hāδihi*.

3.2 Methods (Cross-Sectional Data)

Eighty-two Arabic L2 learners belonging to three different L1s, (American) English, French, and Japanese, were invited to participate in the study at their home institutions in the United States, France, and Japan, respectively. The participants were grouped according to their placement by their home institutions (first year, second year, and third year) and according to length of exposure to Arabic as part of their academic programs. Table 3.13 summarizes the details of the participants.

Table 3.13 Cross-sectional participants

Groups English L1	Length of Exposure	Credit Hours Enrolled in	M/F	Age Range	Age Means
Group1 (n=9)	Year 1	6	4/5	18-21	19.22
Group2 (n=9)	Year 2	5	5/4	20-29	22.22
Group3 (n=9)	Year 3	4	6/3	22-34	29.11
French L1					
Group1 (n=9)	Year 1	6.75	5/4	18-32	21.33
Group2 (n=9)	Year 2	6.75	1/8	21-36	26.22
Group3 (n=8)	Year 3	7.5	3/5	23-28	25.75
Japanese L1					
Group1 (n=10)	Year 1	12	8/2	18-20	19
Group2 (n=10)	Year 2	12	5/5	19-21	20
Group3 (n=9)	Year 3	4	1/8	20-23	21.11

M/F = Total Males/Total Females.

The participants were selected, because they had little or no exposure to Arabic prior to joining their academic institutions and were not heritage speakers who would speak Arabic occasionally or often at home. In particular, first year students of all three language groups had zero exposure to Arabic and had made no trips to Arabic-speaking countries. A few participants from the three language groups at other levels had traveled to Arabic-speaking countries but did not stay there for a significant period of time. One student (French L1, Year 3) stayed in Egypt for one year. Her performance in the study, however, was about average among her group. Participants from the three L1 language groups received formal instruction in Arabic with a focus on all grammatical forms from early on. The English L1 groups used mainly Abboud et al. (1983, 1997) and the French L1 groups used mainly Deheuvels (2002, 2003). As for the Japanese L1 groups, some belonged to classes that used Badawi et al. (1983, 1992) and others belonged to classes that used Brustad et al. (1995a, 1995b).

Participants were requested to attend one-on-one interview sessions, one interview per participant (30-45 minutes). Data collection during the interview aimed at eliciting spontaneous/semi-spontaneous production data of the target forms identical to those elicited from the longitudinal participants discussed above (that is, nominal gender agreement, demonstrative gender agreement, and verbal agreement). Elicitation techniques included picture description, picture differences, and picture sequencing (see sample elicitations tasks in Figures 3.1-3.2 above). Since the cross-sectional data consisted of one interview, four additional narrative tasks were used: two in the past tense and two in the present tense divided equally between a female and a male character. Of the two narratives in the past tense, one was about a female character and one was about a male character. The participants were requested to narrate day by day the vacation activities (on a calendar) carried out by each character during his or her vacation (which each character took the previous month for a period of ten days). As a distracter, the participants were asked to figure out and to comment on whether or not the male and female characters were compatible based on what they did on their vacations. The two narratives in the present tense were also about a female and a male character. The participants were requested to describe the daily routines/activities of each of the characters at different times of the day. As a distracter, the participants were asked to figure out where the character was from based on his/her routine activities. The two sets of narratives (past versus present) were not presented sequentially. Rather, the past set was presented towards the middle of the interview and the present towards the end, with tasks of other (unrelated) structures used in the beginning of the first and second halves of the interview, serving as additional distracters. A sample narrative elicitation task appears in Figure 3.5.

The elicitation tasks were held constant and were consistently used across all the participants. All interviews were audio-recorded. The data were transcribed, transliterated, and coded. Each data sample was triple-checked for accuracy after each step. To preserve the data from contamination due to elicitation errors, the elicitation statements were used consistently across participants, kept general and short and at times even said in English or in the L1 of the participants. The elicitation materials were piloted before they were used. Certain tokens were not coded. These

Figure 3.5
A sample (past tense) narrative elicitation task with a male character. The vacation went from the 17th–26th of last month (adapted from *Going Places*, Burton and Maharg: 141, 159. Copyright Addison-Wesley, 1995. Reprinted by permission of Pearson Education, Inc.).

were hesitations and self-corrections except the last attempt. In addition, caution was taken against effecting any gender bias or stereotypes through the elicitation materials (as discussed in Section 3.1). In coding subject-verb agreement tokens, agreement was determined by considering the verbal form and whether it was inflected properly, not by identifying first the subject and then the verb it agreed with. This is significant, since the verb may agree with a discourse referent subject and the participants may be mindlessly producing the wrong subject, especially when the subjects used are the pronouns *hiya* "she" and *huwa* "he," which are close in their pronunciation (see also Poeppel and Wexler 1993, Prévost and White 2000; cf. Meisel 1991).

3.2.1 *Results of verbal (gender) agreement*

Three main results were found with respect to verbal agreement, specifically singular masculine and singular feminine S-V agreement markings, as shown in Table 3.14 and illustrated in Figure 3.6. First, all participants of all three L1 backgrounds had higher correct agreement ratios on singular masculine than on singular feminine, due perhaps to use of the singular masculine as the default form by some of the participants across all groups. Second, the French L1 groups somewhat outperformed their English L1 and Japanese L1 counterparts in producing the appropriate verbal agreement markings for singular feminine and singular masculine in all groups, except for the first year participants (Group 1) on S-V feminine agreement, who slightly underperformed their beginning English and Japanese counterparts (Group 1). Third, the English L1 participants slightly outperformed their Japanese L1 counterparts on feminine S-V agreement with respect to Group 1 and Group 3 and on masculine S-V agreement with respect to Group 3. Fourth, conversely, the Japanese L1 participants slightly outperformed their English L1 counterparts on feminine S-V agreement with respect to Group 2 and on masculine S-V agreement with respect to Group 1 and Group 2.

A series of one-way and two-way MANOVAs as well as follow-up ANOVAs of the MANOVAs were run to detect any statistically significant effect for L1, proficiency, and interaction between proficiency and L1. No effect was found. In other words, neither singular masculine verbal agreement nor singular feminine agreement was found to contribute to the groups' L1 differences.

Table 3.14 Correct ratios: S-V feminine and S-V masculine agreement

Arabic L2 English L1	S-V Feminine Agreement Correct/Total	S-V Masculine Agreement Correct/Total
Group1 (n=9)	135/162 (83%)	168/190 (88%)
Group2 (n=9)	158/236 (67%)	298/347 (86%)
Group3 (n=9)	212/246 (86%)	381/409 (93%)
French L1		
Group1 (n=9)	135/181 (75%)	224/231 (97%)
Group2 (n=9)	204/236 (86%)	293/306 (96%)
Group3 (n=8)	201/217 (93%)	335/342 (98%)
Japanese L1		
Group1 (n=10)	170/210 (81%)	220/236 (93%)
Group2 (n=10)	226/289 (78%)	352/370 (95%)
Group3 (n=9)	184/232 (79%)	288/318 (91%)

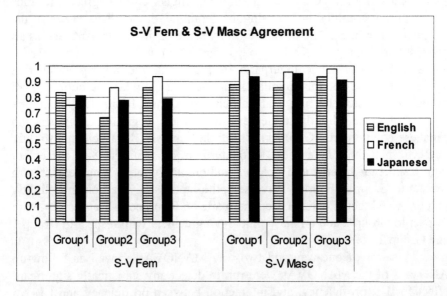

Figure 3.6

3.2.2 Results of nominal (gender) agreement

Unlike the data for verbal agreement, the data for nominal gender agreement—mainly singular feminine (N-A) and singular masculine (N-A) agreement—yield a totally different acquisition pattern. Two main findings are immediately evident in the data listed in Table 3.15 and illustrated in Figure 3.7. First, the participants of all three L1 backgrounds had higher correct agreement ratios on singular masculine than on singular feminine, due perhaps to the use of the singular masculine as the default form by some of the participants across all groups. The second finding is that first year French L1 participants (Group 1) performed better than any of the three English L1 groups (that is, Groups 1-3) as well as better than the first and third year Japanese L1 participants (that is, Groups 1 and 3) on singular feminine. The first year English L1 participants (Group 1) performed slightly better on singular feminine than their Japanese L1 counterparts (Group 1) and the third year English L1 participants (Group 3) outperformed their Japanese L1 counterparts (Group 3). This finding is yielded despite the difference in duration of exposure to input evident in Table 3.13 above (that is, whereas the duration of exposure is somewhat comparable between the English L1 and French L1 participants, the Japanese L1 participants had almost double the amount of instruction time per week). Only the second year Japanese L1 participants (Group 2) outperformed their English L1 counterparts (Group 2) and slightly outperformed their French L1 counterparts (Group 2) on singular feminine.

A series of one-way and two-way MANOVAs as well as follow-up ANOVAs of the MANOVAs reveal the following findings: an effect for L1 between the French and English groups on feminine N-A agreement (Wilks's $\Lambda=.75$, $F(2,46)=7.51$, $p<.002$; $F(1,47)=15.04$, $p<.001$), an effect for L1 between the French L1 and the Japanese L1 groups on feminine N-A agreement (Wilks's $\Lambda=.80$, $F(2,48)=6.3$, $p<.005$; $F(1,49)=11.82$, $p<.002$), and no effect for L1 between the English L1 and Japanese L1 groups. In other words, the French L1 groups found singular feminine N-A agreement significantly less problematic than their English L1 and Japanese L1 counterpart groups. The L1 English and L1 Japanese participants performed comparably on both forms.

Table 3.15 Correct ratios: N-A feminine and N-A masculine agreement

Arabic L2 English L1	N-A Feminine Agreement Correct/Total	N-A Masculine Agreement Correct/Total
Group1 (n=9)	82/135 (61%)	127/149 (85%)
Group2 (n=9)	127/207 (61%)	158/187 (84%)
Group3 (n=9)	145/185 (78%)	179/195 (92%)
French L1		
Group1 (n=9)	116/144 (81%)	112/119 (94%)
Group2 (n=9)	131/165 (79%)	136/160 (85%)
Group3 (n=8)	138/148 (93%)	121/133 (91%)
Japanese L1		
Group1 (n=10)	75/128 (59%)	80/82 (98%)
Group2 (n=10)	154/189 (81%)	133/144 (92%)
Group3 (n=9)	123/177 (69%)	153/170 (90%)

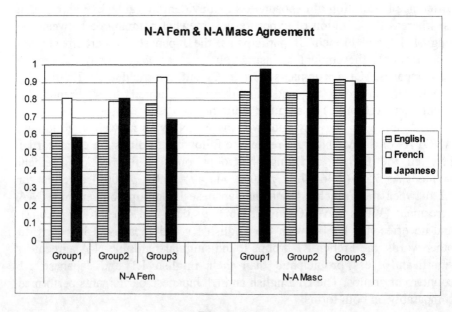

Figure 3.7

3.2.2.1 *Results of natural versus grammatical gender agreement*
    The data of nominal gender (N-A) agreement were further analyzed to determine if there was a difference in the participants' performance on correct natural versus correct grammatical gender agreement markings, since Arabic exhibits both types of gender as discussed in Chapter 1 (Section 1.1.2). The data are summarized in Table 3.16 and illustrated in Figure 3.8. Not unlike the difference in performance between singular feminine N-A and singular masculine N-A agreement, a similar distinction between the production of grammatical and natural gender was found. Here, too, the finding is yielded despite the difference in duration of exposure to input evident in Table 3.13 above (that is, whereas the duration of exposure is somewhat comparable between the English L1 and French L1 participants, the Japanese L1 participants had almost double the amount of instruction time per week). The French L1 groups outperformed their English L1 and Japanese L1 counterparts on correct rule application of N-A agreement involving grammatical gender, except for the Japanese L1 Group 2 which slightly outperformed its French L1 counterpart (Group 2) and more so its English L1 counterpart (Group 2).
    A series of one-way and two-way MANOVAs as well as follow-up ANOVAs of the MANOVAs reveal the following: an effect for L1 between the French L1 and English L1 groups for performance on both natural gender (Wilks's Λ=.75, $F(2,46)$=7.89, $p<.002$; $F(1,47)$=6.7, $p<.014$) and grammatical gender ($F(1,47)$=13.6, $p<.002$) as well as a proficiency effect for grammatical gender (Wilks's Λ=.75, $F(4,92)$=3.64, $p<.009$; $F(2,47)$=7.36, $p<.003$), an effect for L1 between the French L1 and Japanese L1 groups for performance on grammatical gender (Wilks's Λ=.82, $F(2,48)$= 5.19, $p<.01$; $F(1,49)$=8.59, $p<.006$), a near effect for interaction between L1 and proficiency on grammatical gender for the French L1 groups versus the Japanese L1 groups (Wilks's Λ=.81, $F(4,96)$=2.64, p=.038; $F(2,49)$=3.56, p=.036), and neither an L1 nor a proficiency effect was found between the English L1 and Japanese L1 groups. In other words, once again here the French L1 groups outperformed their English L1 and Japanese L1 counterpart groups, especially with respect to nominal grammatical gender involving N-A agreement, whereas no difference was found between the English L1 and Japanese L1 groups despite the significant difference in exposure time between the two (see also Table 3.13 above).

Table 3.16 Correct ratios of natural and grammatical gender

Arabic L2 English L1	Grammatical Gender Correct/Total	Natural Gender Correct/Total
Group1 (n=9)	83/117 (71%)	126/167 (75%)
Group2 (n=9)	102/167 (61%)	183/226 (81%)
Group3 (n=9)	160/188 (85%)	164/192 (85%)
French L1		
Group1 (n=9)	87/100 (87%)	141/163 (87%)
Group2 (n=9)	109/138 (79%)	158/187 (84%)
Group3 (n=8)	114/128 (89%)	145/153 (95%)
Japanese L1		
Group1 (n=10)	65/97 (67%)	90/113 (80%)
Group2 (n=10)	123/148 (83%)	162/185 (88%)
Group3 (n=9)	78/115 (68%)	144/171 (84%)

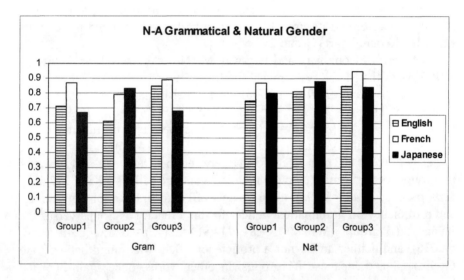

Figure 3.8

3.2.2.2 Rule application of nominal agreement in non-contexts

A small number of productive IL utterances or rule application of singular feminine and singular masculine N-A agreement in non-contexts were found in all the data sets: three produced by the English L1 groups, sixteen by the French L1 groups and four by the Japanese L1 groups (see Table 3.17). These utterances included: 1) feminine nouns correctly produced by the L2 learner but taking a different feminine suffix on the following adjective than the most common feminine suffix {-a}, 2) nouns inflected in Arabic for the feminine gender but produced by the L2 learner inflected for the masculine gender marking followed by an agreeing masculine adjective, and 3) invariant, comparative forms inflected in Arabic for the masculine gender but produced by the L2 learner with the feminine gender marking agreeing with a preceding feminine noun. Examples of nominal gender agreement in contexts, extracted from the participants' data samples, are illustrated in sentences (15)-(17).

(15)	IL:	*sayyār-a*	*ʔaḥmar-a*	
		car-**s.f**	red-**s.f**	
	TL:	*sayyār-a*	*ḥamr-aaʔ*	
		car-**s.f**	red-**s.f**	
		"a red car"		
		(French L1: Group 1; also Japanese L1: Group 3)		
(16)	IL:	*huwa fī*	*ɣurf-in*	*sˤaɣ īr-in*
		he in	room.**s.m**-gen	small.**s.m**-gen
	TL:	*huwa fī*	*ɣurf-at-in*	*sˤaɣ īr-at-in*
		he in	room-**s.f**-gen	small-**s.f**-gen
		"He is in a small room."		
		(French L1: Group 1)		
(17)	IL:	*sayyār-a*	*ʔasˤɣar-a*	
		car-**s.f**	smaller-**s.f**	
	TL:	*sayyār-a*	*ʔasˤɣar*	
		car-**s.f**	smaller	
		"a smaller car"		
		(English L1: Group 3)		

Due to the insignificant number of such tokens with rule applications in non-contexts and the fact that the rest of the nouns were produced with the correct gender inflection (whether masculine or feminine), the learning task that N-A agreement constituted for the participants of the study was to apply the rule on the attributive adjective within the NP by producing the proper gender inflection to agree with the preceding (head) noun.

Table 3.17 Total of N-A agreement tokens in productive contexts

Arabic L2 English L1	N-A Feminine Productive Tokens/Total	N-A Masculine Productive Tokens/Total
Group1 (n=9)	0/284 (.0)	0/284 (.0)
Group2 (n=9)	2/393 (.005)	0/393 (.0)
Group3 (n=9)	1/380 (.003)	0/380 (.0)
French L1		
Group1 (n=9)	8/263 (.03)	1/263 (.004)
Group2 (n=9)	7/325 (.02)	0/325 (.0)
Group3 (n=8)	0/281 (.0)	0/281 (.0)
Japanese L1		
Group1 (n=10)	0/210 (.0)	0/210 (.0)
Group2 (n=10)	2/333 (.006)	0/333 (.0)
Group3 (n=9)	2/286 (.007)	0/286 (.0)

3.2.2.3 *Word order of nominal (noun-adjective) agreement*

The cross-sectional participants produced NPs with almost completely correct noun-adjective word order. The participants produced a significantly small number of NPs with the incorrect adjective-noun word order. Table 3.18 summarizes all the correct and incorrect noun-adjective word placement tokens in all the data sets. Eight NPs exhibiting incorrect adjective-noun placement were produced by the English L1 participants, nineteen by the French L1 participants (nine of which were produced by one participant in Group 2) and only one was produced by a Japanese L1 participant.

Examples of incorrect noun-adjective placement, extracted from the data samples of the participants, are illustrated in sentences (18)-(19). Among these tokens, there are a few that exhibit both incorrect word order placement and gender agreement mismatches; however, the majority of the produced tokens exhibit word order misplacement alone. What is important here to conclude is that the high degree of accuracy ratios of noun-adjective word order placement by all participants within and across groups indicate that the participants did not find it difficult to adjust to Arabic noun-adjective word order, even from early on in their Arabic L2 learning, much like the longitudinal participants discussed above (in Section 3.1.1.4).

Table 3.18 Noun-adjective word order

Arabic L2 English L1	N-A Word Order Total	*A-N Word Order/Total Ratios
Group1 (n=9)	280	4/284 (.014)
Group2 (n=9)	389	4/393 (.010)
Group3 (n=9)	380	0/380 (.0)
French L1		
Group1 (n=9)	259	4/263 (.015)
Group2 (n=9)	311	14/325 (.043)**
Group3 (n=8)	280	1/281 (.004)
Japanese L1		
Group1 (n=10)	210	0/210 (.0)
Group2 (n=10)	333	1/334 (.003)
Group3 (n=9)	286	0/286 (.0)

* = ungrammatical; ** = out of the total 14 tokens, one learner alone exhibited 9 tokens.

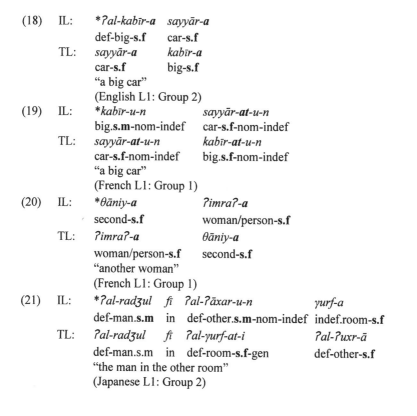

(18) IL: *ʔal-kabīr-*a*   sayyār-*a*
             def-big-**s.f**   car-**s.f**
      TL: sayyār-*a*   kabīr-*a*
             car-**s.f**   big-**s.f**
             "a big car"
             (English L1: Group 2)

(19) IL: *kabīr-u-n   sayyār-*at-u-n*
             big.**s.m**-nom-indef   car-**s.f**-nom-indef
      TL: sayyār-*at-u-n*   kabīr-*at-u-n*
             car-**s.f**-nom-indef   big.**s.f**-nom-indef
             "a big car"
             (French L1: Group 1)

(20) IL: *θāniy-*a*   ʔimraʔ-*a*
             second-**s.f**   woman/person-**s.f**
      TL: ʔimraʔ-*a*   θāniy-*a*
             woman/person-**s.f** second-**s.f**
             "another woman"
             (French L1: Group 1)

(21) IL: *ʔal-radʒul   fi   ʔal-ʔāxar-u-n   ɣurf-a
             def-man.**s.m** in   def-other.**s.m**-nom-indef indef.room-**s.f**
      TL: ʔal-radʒul   fi   ʔal-ɣurf-at-i   ʔal-ʔuxr-ā
             def-man.s.m   in   def-room-**s.f**-gen   def-other-**s.f**
             "the man in the other room"
             (Japanese L1: Group 2)

3.2.3 *Results of nominal versus verbal agreement*

To verify the overall differences among the cross-sectional participants in performance on verbal versus nominal agreement, additional multiple one-way and two-way MANOVA tests as well as follow-up ANOVAs to the MANOVAs were run. These yielded three types of findings accordingly. First, the tests yielded a narrow effect for L1 between the French L1 and English L1 groups for performance on masculine verbal (S-V) agreement (Wilks's $\Lambda=.85$, $F(2,46)=4.05$, $p=.024$; $F(1,47)=7.29$, $p<.011$), an effect for L1 between the French L1 and English L1 groups for performance on feminine nominal (N-A) agreement (Wilks's $\Lambda=.75$, $F(2,46)=7.52$, $p<.002$; $F(1,47)=15.04$, $p<.001$), and a near proficiency effect for feminine nominal (N-A) agreement ($F(2,47)=3.9$, $p=.027$). Accordingly, the results indicate that the French L1 groups outperformed their English L1 counterparts on singular masculine S-V agreement slightly and on singular feminine N-A agreement. Second, the tests yielded an effect for L1 between the French L1 and Japanese L1 groups for performance on singular feminine nominal (N-A) agreement (Wilks's $\Lambda=.80$, $F(2,48)=5.86$. $p<.006$; $F(1,49)=11.82$, $p<.002$) as well as a near effect for interaction between L1 and proficiency for performance on the same form. These results indicate that the French L1 groups outperformed their Japanese L1 counterparts with respect to singular feminine N-A agreement. Third, the tests yielded no effect with respect to the performance of the English L1 groups versus that of the Japanese L1 groups.

Thus, based on these findings, the larger picture that emerges is that there was no difference in the performance of all three L1 groups with respect to feminine verbal (S-V) agreement, the French L1 groups outperformed both the English L1 and Japanese L1 counterparts on feminine nominal (N-A) agreement, and the English L1 and Japanese L1 participants performed comparably on both nominal and verbal agreement.

These findings were obtained despite the presentation of the two forms in the input which the participants received. Tables 3.19-3.21 (and Table 3.3 above) display how often and when verbal agreement and N-A agreement were presented in the textbooks of the English L1, French L1, and Japanese L1 participants. Table 3.19 shows that both structures were introduced in the input (textbook) of the English L1 participants (Group 1) around almost the same time (N-A agreement was formally introduced in Lesson 5 and S-V agreement was formally introduced in Lesson 6) and were both later maintained in the input throughout (until Lesson 15, corresponding to the first year). Table 3.20 shows that although N-A agreement was introduced informally in the textbook of the French L1 participants (Group 1) in Lessons 1-2, and briefly present in Lessons 4-5, it was not until Lesson 6 that it was formally introduced (and was maintained thereafter), whereas verbal agreement was introduced mainly in Lessons 1, 2, and 4 (and was maintained thereafter). As for the Japanese L1 participants, recall that some students belonged to classes that used Badawi et al. (1983, 1992) and others belonged to classes that used Brustad et al. (1995a, 1995b). Tables 3.21A-3.21B show that N-A agreement was informally introduced in Badawi et al. (1983) textbook (for Group 1) in Lesson 2 briefly and later in Unit 7 (and was maintained informally thereafter); it was not formally introduced in the textbook.[7] On the other hand, verbal agreement was informally introduced in the early units focusing on the teaching of phonology and scripts, Units 7-11, in Lessons 1-4, and later formally introduced in Lesson 5 (and was maintained thereafter). Table 3.3 (see above) shows that nominal agreement was formally introduced in Brustad et al. (1995a, 1995b) textbooks in Units 5 and 8 and Lesson 1, was present in the intervening units, and was maintained throughout after Lesson 1; verbal agreement was later introduced (in Lesson 1) and was maintained in the input thereafter.[8]

Based on the analysis of the input which the participants received, the clear observation that we glean here pertains especially to the English L1 and French L1 groups. The English L1 participants were formally exposed to nominal agreement earlier than they were to verbal agreement whereas their French L1 counterparts were formally exposed to verbal agreement before nominal agreement. Thus, in line with the findings of the (English L1) longitudinal participants, the English L1 cross-sectional participants found nominal agreement more problematic than they did verbal agreement while the French L1 participants did not. As for the input of the Japanese L1 participants, it is not possible to make a similarly clear observation due to the mixed nature of the input.

Table 3.19 Learning objective schedule of the first fifteen lessons of *Elementary Modern Standard Arabic* (Abboud et al. 1983)

Lessons	N-A Agreement					S-V Agreement (Perfective and Imperfective)							
	S.M	S.F	P.M.H	P.F.H	P.Non-H	3.S.M	3.S.F	3.P.M	1.S	1.P	2.S.M	2.S.F	2.P.M
1													
2													
3													
4													
5	X	X											
6	(x)	(x)				X	X						
7	(x)	(x)				X	X		X		X	X	
8	(x)	(x)	(x)			X	X	X	(x)		(/)		
9	(/)	(/)	X	X		X	X	X	X	X	X	X	X
10	(x)	(x)		(/)		(x)	(x)	(x)	(x)	(x)	(x)	(x)	(x)
11	(x)	(x)	(/)	(/)	(/)	[x]	[x]	[x]	[x]	[x]	[x]	[x]	[x]
12	(x)	(x)	(x)	(/)	(x)	[x]	[x]	[x]	[x]	[x]	[x]	[x]	[x]
13	(x)	(x)			(/)	[x]	[x]		[x]	(/)	[x]	[x]	
14	(x)	(x)	(x)		(/)	[x]	[x]	[x]	[x]	[x]	[x]	[x]	[x]
15	X	X	(/)	(/)	X	(x)	(x)	(/)	(x)	(x)		(/)	(/)

X = focused attempt to teach the structure; [x] = indirect focused attempt where main focus is on lexical item(s) or mood; (x) = structure is not the focus of instruction but occurs in the lesson and drills 4 or more times; (/) = structure is not the focus of instruction and occurs less than 4 times.

Table 3.20 Learning objective schedule of *Manuel d'Arabe moderne* (Deheuvels 2003)

Lessons	N-A Agreement					S-V Agreement (Perfective and Imperfective)							
	S.M	S.F	P.M.H	P.F.H	P.Non-H	3.S.M	3.S.F	3.P.M	1.S	1.P	2.S.M	2.S.F	2.P.M
1	(x)					X			X		X		
2		(x)				(/)	X		X		(/)	X	
3						(/)	(/)		(x)	X		(x)	X
4	(/)	(/)				X	X	X	X	X	X	X	X
5	(/)					(x)	(x)	(/)	(/)	(x)	(/)	(/)	(/)
6	X	X	X	X		(x)	(/)	(x)	(x)	(x)	(/)		(/)
7	(x)	(x)				(x)	(x)	(x)	(x)	(x)	(/)	(/)	(x)
8	(x)	(x)		(/)	(x)	(x)	(x)	(x)	(x)	(x)	(/)	(/)	(/)
9	(x)	(x)	(/)		(x)	X	X	X	X	X	X	X	X
10	(x)	(x)	(/)	(/)	(x)	(x)	(/)	(x)	(x)	(/)	(x)	(/)	(/)
11	(x)	(x)	(/)		(/)	(x)		(x)	(x)	(/)	(x)		
12	(x)	(x)			(x)	[x]	[x]	[x]	[x]	[x]	[x]	[x]	[x]
13	(x)	(x)			X	[x]	[x]	[x]	[x]	[x]	[x]	[x]	[x]
14	(x)	(x)			(/)	(x)	(x)	(x)	(x)	(x)	(x)		
15	(x)	(x)			(/)	(x)	(x)	(x)	(x)	(x)	(/)	(/)	(/)

X = focused attempt to teach the structure; [x] = indirect focused attempt where main focus is on lexical item(s) or mood; (x) = structure is not the focus of instruction but occurs in the lesson and drills 4 or more times; (/) = structure is not the focus of instruction and occurs less than 4 times.

Table 3.21A Learning objective schedule of *Al-Kitaab Al-Asaasii* (Badawi et al. 1983)

Units and Lessons	N-A Agreement					S-V Agreement (Perfective and Imperfective)												
	S.M	S.F	P.M.H	P.F.H	P.Non-H	3.S.M	3.S.F	3.P.M	1.S	1.P	2.S.M	2.S.F	2.P.M	2.P.F	3.P.F	2.D	3.D.M	3.D.F
1																		
2																		
3																		
4																		
5																		
6																		
7						(x)												
8						(x)												
9						(/)												
10						(/)												
11						(x)												
1											(/)							
2	(/)	(/)				(/)												
3						(x)												
4						(x)			(/)		(/)							
5						X	X		(/)		(/)							
6						X			(/)		(/)	(/)						
7	(x)					X	X	X	X	X	X	X	X	X	X	X	X	X
8	(/)	(x)				X	(x)	X	X		X	X			X			

X = focused attempt to teach the structure; (x) = structure is not the focus of instruction but occurs in the lesson and drills 4 or more times; (/) = structure is not the focus of instruction and occurs less than 4 times.

Table 3.21B Learning objective schedule of *Al-Kitaab Al-Asaasii* (Badawi et al. 1983)

Lessons	N-A Agreement					S-V Agreement (Perfective and Imperfective)												
	S.M	S.F	P.M.H	P.F.H	P.Non-H	3.S.M	3.S.F	3.P.M	1.S	1.P	2.S.M	2.S.F	2.P.M	2.P.F	3.P.F	2.D	3.D.M	3.D.F
9						X	X	X	X	X	(/)	(/)	X	X	X	X	X	
10		(x)				(x)	(x)	(/)	(/)		(/)	(/)	(/)	(/)	(/)	(/)	(/)	(/)
11	(/)	(x)				X	X		X		X							
12		(x)	(/)		(x)	X	X	X	X	X	X		X		X			
13	(x)	(/)			(x)	(x)	(/)		(/)		(x)							
14		(x)				(x)	(x)	(x)	(/)	(/)	(x)	(/)	(/)	(/)	(x)	(/)	(x)	(/)
15						X	(x)	X	(x)		(x)				(/)		X	
16	(x)	(x)				(x)	(x)	(x)	(x)	(x)	(/)	(x)	(/)	(/)	(x)	(/)	(x)	(x)
17	(/)	(/)	(/)			(x)	(x)	(/)	(x)		(x)				(/)		(/)	(x)
18	(x)					(x)	(x)	(x)	X	X	X	X	X	X	(x)	X	(x)	(/)
19	(/)				(x)	(x)	(x)	(x)	(x)		(x)		(x)	(x)	(x)	(x)	(x)	(x)
20	(x)	(x)			(/)	(x)	(x)	(x)	(x)	(/)	(/)			(/)	(/)		(x)	(/)
21	(x)				(x)	(x)	(x)	(/)	(x)	(/)	(x)	(/)	(/)	(/)	(/)	(/)	(/)	(/)
22	(x)	(/)				X	X	X	X	X	X	X	X	X	X	X	X	X
23	(x)	(x)			(/)	(x)	X	(x)	(x)	(x)	(x)	(/)	(/)	(/)	(x)	(/)	(x)	(x)
24	(x)	(x)				(x)			(x)	(/)	(x)							
25	(x)	(x)			(x)	(x)	(x)	(x)	(x)		(x)				(/)			

X = focused attempt to teach the structure; (x) = structure is not the focus of instruction but occurs in the lesson and drills 4 or more times; (/) = structure is not the focus of instruction and occurs less than 4 times.

3.2.4 *Results of demonstrative gender agreement*

As in their performance on nominal and verbal agreement, the cross-sectional participants exhibited a similar acquisition pattern in their performance on demonstrative gender agreement. Based on the ratios listed in Table 3.22 (see also Figure 3.9), similar observations are immediately evident. The participants of all three L1 backgrounds had higher correct agreement ratios on masculine demonstrative agreement than on feminine demonstrative agreement, due perhaps in part to use of the masculine form as the default form by some of the participants across all groups. The French L1 groups had higher correct agreement ratios on demonstrative agreement than their English L1 and Japanese L1 counterparts.

A series of one-way and two-way MANOVA tests as well as follow-up ANOVAs of the MANOVAs were run. An effect was found for L1 between the French L1 and English L1 groups for performance on demonstrative gender agreement (Wilks's Λ=.68, $F(2,33)$=7.6, p<.003) with a near effect for feminine demonstrative agreement on the follow-up ANOVAs ($F(1,34)$=5.3, p=.027) and another near effect on masculine demonstrative agreement on the follow-up ANOVAs ($F(1,34)$=4.4, p=.044). However, no effect for L1 between the French L1 and Japanese L1 groups for performance on feminine or masculine demonstrative agreement was found, but an effect for L1 between the Japanese L1 and English L1 groups on the MANOVA was found (Wilks's Λ=.76, $F(2,32)$=5.1, p<.012) with a near effect for feminine demonstrative agreement on the follow-up ANOVAs ($F(1,33)$=4.6, p=.039). In other words, while the performance of the French L1 groups on demonstrative gender agreement did not differ significantly from that of their Japanese L1 counterparts, the performance of both the French L1 and the Japanese L1 groups differed from that of their English L1 counterparts, especially with respect to feminine demonstrative agreement.

Perhaps equally significant is the observation that the French L1 groups (in particular Group 1 and Group 3) outperformed their English L1 and Japanese L1 counterparts with respect to feminine demonstrative agreement. It is evident in the French L1 Group 1, if examined alone, that it outperformed all of the English L1 and Japanese L1 groups. This finding is yielded despite the difference in duration of exposure to input evident in Table 3.13 above (that is, whereas the duration of exposure is somewhat comparable between the English L1 and French L1 participants, the Japanese L1 participants had almost double the amount of instruction time per week). The Japanese L1 groups had higher correct feminine and masculine agreement ratios than their English L1 counterparts. This is perhaps understandable, since the Japanese L1 participants had almost double the amount of time of instruction of their English L1 counterparts. Indeed, if we factor in the instruction time difference through a two-way MANCOVA test, the significant L1 difference between the two groups of participants disappears.

Table 3.22 Correct ratios of demonstrative gender agreement

Arabic L2 English L1	Feminine Dem. Agreement Correct/Total	Masculine Dem. Agreement Correct/Total
Group1 (n=9)	36/57 (63%)	47/50 (94%)
Group2 (n=9)	17/48 (35%)	23/27 (85%)
Group3 (n=9)	38/79 (48%)	63/66 (95%)
French L1		
Group1 (n=9)	48/54 (89%)	51/51 (100%)
Group2 (n=9)	38/52 (73%)	42/43 (98%)
Group3 (n=8)	32/37 (86%)	15/15 (100%)
Japanese L1		
Group1 (n=10)	70/95 (74%)	42/44 (95%)
Group2 (n=10)	50/58 (86%)	25/26 (96%)
Group3 (n=9)	41/61 (67%)	37/37 (100%)

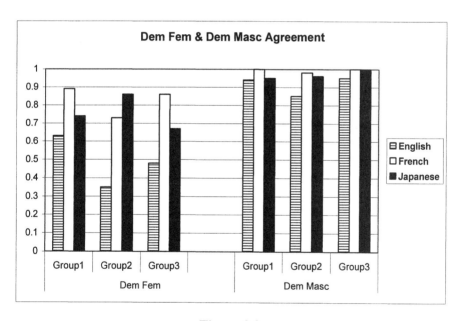

Figure 3.9

These findings are found despite the presentation of demonstrative gender agreement in the input which the participants received. Tables 3.23-25 (and Table 3.11 above) display how often and when demonstrative pronouns (both in predicative and attributive contexts) were presented in the textbooks of the English L1, French L1, and Japanese L1 participants. Table 3.23 shows that the structure was present in the input (textbook) of the English L1 participants (Group 1) from early on. In particular, it was formally introduced in the input as early as Lesson 1, then formally again in Lesson 3 and was maintained in the input throughout (until Lesson 15 corresponding to the first year). Table 3.24 shows that the structure was in fact almost absent from the formal input (textbook) of the French L1 participants (Group 1). Demonstrative pronouns were informally introduced in Lesson 10 and briefly again in Lesson 14. They were formally introduced only in the last lesson (Lesson 15) of the book. Demonstrative pronouns may have been presented formally to the French L1 (Group 1) participants when they occurred in their textbook in Lesson 10. However, the clear observation remains that the form is evidently absent in most of the lessons of the textbook. As for the Japanese L1 participants, recall that some students belonged to classes that used Badawi et al. (1983, 1992) and others belonged to classes that used Brustad et al. (1995a, 1995b). Tables 3.25A-3.25B show that demonstrative pronouns were introduced formally from early on (in the phonology and scripts units) in Units 1-3. Demonstrative agreement was recycled later in Units 6 and 10-11, and was somewhat recycled in the subsequent Lessons 1-25, more intensively so in the latter half of these lessons.

Based on the analysis of the input which the participants received, the clear observation that we can make here pertains especially to the English L1 and French L1 groups. The English L1 participants were exposed to more frequent input on demonstrative gender agreement than their French L1 counterparts. However, despite the fact that the French L1 participants (Group1) received much less focused instruction on demonstrative gender agreement than their English L1 counterparts (Group 1), they exhibited fewer problems with this form. In fact, Group 1 of the French L1 participants even outperformed all three groups of the English L1 participants on both masculine and feminine forms (see Figure 3.9). As for the input of the Japanese L1 participants, it is not possible to make a similarly clear observation due to the mixed nature of the input, although the

French L1 groups somewhat similarly outperformed their Japanese L1 counterparts.

Table 3.23 Learning objective schedule of the first fifteen lessons of *Elementary Modern Standard Arabic* (Abboud et al. 1983)

Lessons	Demonstrative Pronouns				
	S.M	S.F	P.M.H	P.F.H	P.Non-H
1	X	X			
2	(x)	(x)			
3	X	X			
4	(x)	(/)			
5	(x)	(x)			
6	(/)				
7	(x)	(x)			
8	(x)	(x)			
9	(x)	(x)			
10	(x)	(x)			
11	(/)	(/)			
12	(/)	(/)			
13		(/)			
14	(x)	(/)			
15	(x)	(x)			X

X = focused attempt to teach the structure; (x) = structure is not the focus of instruction but occurs in the lesson and drills 4 or more times; (/) = structure is not the focus of instruction and occurs less than 4 times.

Table 3.24 Learning objective schedule of *Manuel d'Arabe moderne* (Deheuvels 2003)

Lessons	Demonstrative Pronouns				
	S.M	S.F	S.M	P.F.H	S.M
1					
2					
3					
4					
5					
6					
7					
8					
9					
10	(/)	(/)			
11					
12					
13					
14	(x)				
15	X	X	X		X

X = focused attempt to teach the structure; (x) = structure is not the focus of instruction but occurs in the lesson and drills 4 or more times; (/) = structure is not the focus of instruction and occurs less than 4 times.

Table 3.25A Learning objective schedule of *Al-Kitaab Al-Asaasii* (Badawi et al. 1983)

Units and Lessons	Demonstrative Pronouns				
	S.M	S.F	S.M	P.F.H	S.M
1	X	X			
2	X	X			
3	X	X			
4					
5					
6	(x)	(x)			
7					
8					
9					
10	(/)	(/)			
11	(x)	(x)			
1	(/)	(x)			
2	X	X			
3					
4	(x)	(x)			
5					
6	(x)	(/)			(/)
7					
8					

X = focused attempt to teach the structure; (x) = structure is not the focus of instruction but occurs in the lesson and drills 4 or more times; (/) = structure is not the focus of instruction and occurs less than 4 times.

Table 3.25B Learning objective schedule of *Al-Kitaab Al-Asaasii* (Badawi et al. 1983)

Lessons	Demonstrative Pronouns				
	S.M	S.F	S.M	P.F.H	S.M
9					
10					
11		(/)			
12					
13	(/)				(/)
14					
15					
16	(/)	(/)	(/)	(/)	
17	X	X	X	X	
18	(/)		(/)	(/)	(/)
19	(/)				
20		(/)			
21	(/)				
22		(/)			
23	(x)	(x)			
24	(/)	(x)			
25	(x)	(x)			(/)

X = focused attempt to teach the structure; (x) = structure is not the focus of instruction but occurs in the lesson and drills 4 or more times; (/) = structure is not the focus of instruction and occurs less than 4 times.

3.2.4.1 *Rule application of demonstrative gender agreement in non-contexts*

Three IL instances of rule application of singular feminine and singular masculine demonstrative gender agreement in non-contexts were found in all the data sets. One was produced by an English L1 participant (Group 3): *ḥāðā ʔal-sˤūr* "This[s.m] picture[s.m]" → *hāðihi ʔal-sˤūr-a* "This[s.f] picture[s.f];" and two identical utterances were produced by a French L1 participant (Group 1): *ḥāði bayt* "This[s.f] is a house[s.f]" →

hāðā bayt "This[s.m] is a house[s.m]." The latter may also be due to treating *bayt* "house" as a feminine word on par with *bint* "girl," since it ends with the consonant /t/. Thus, due to the insignificant number of tokens of rule application in non-contexts, the main observation is that the participants produced nouns occurring after the demonstratives correctly inflected for masculine or feminine. Therefore, the learning task that the use of demonstrative gender agreement constituted for the participants of the study was to correctly choose the demonstrative *hāðā* or *hāðihi* to agree with the noun following it.

3.3   Summary

The preponderance of evidence of both longitudinal and cross-sectional data reveals that the participants have higher rates of correct production of masculine gender than feminine gender agreement within nominal agreement construction, due perhaps in part to use of the masculine as the default form by some of the participants across groups. Another, more significant finding is that the English L1 and Japanese L1 participants (including the longitudinal and cross-sectional participants) significantly undersupplied the productive feminine suffix {-*a*} more so than their French L1 counterparts, even though feminine head nouns produced by the participants were almost all inflected for the correct feminine suffix which is fully phonologically realized in (salient) word final position (resulting in a rhyming effect), and yet participants failed to inflect the adjective similarly for the feminine gender feature. On the other hand, the English L1 and Japanese L1 participants (including the longitudinal and cross-sectional participants) seemed to find verbal agreement less problematic than nominal agreement, as their performance on verbal agreement was found comparable to that of their French L1 counterparts. These findings, especially those pertaining to the English L1 and French L1 participants, are further corroborated when viewed in light of the input which the participants received. The findings were obtained despite the fact that the presentation of both forms should have produced the opposite effect; that is, given that the English L1 participants had a more focused attempt (in their input) to learn nominal gender agreement than their French L1 counterparts. A third significant finding is that the English L1 participants found demonstrative gender agreement more problematic than their French L1 and Japanese L1 counterparts. These and other related questions and issues will be addressed in Chapter 7.

CHAPTER 4

The Acquisition of Tense/Aspect and Verbal Agreement

This chapter discusses acquisition of tense/aspect and verbal agreement based on cross-sectional data from native English L1, Spanish L1, and Japanese L1 speakers learning Arabic as a second/foreign language (L2). The target structures focused on here include tense/aspect (past/perfective and present/imperfective) and verbal (S-V) agreement, as in sentences (47)-(48) and (51)-(52) discussed in Chapter 1 and restated below as (1)-(4).

1 (a) *ʔal-tˤālib(-u)*   *darasa*
       the-student.s.m-nom   study.perf.3.s.m
       "The (male) student studied."

1 (b) *ʔal-tˤālib(-u)*   *ya-drus(-u)*
       the-student.s.m-nom   3.s.m-study.imperf-indic
       "The (male) student studies."

2 (a) *ʔal-tˤālib-a(t-u)*   *daras-at*
       the-student-s.f-nom   study.perf-3.s.f
       "The (female) student studied."

2 (b) *ʔal-tˤālib-a(t-u)*   *ta-drus(-u)*
       the-student-s.f-nom   3.s.f-study.imperf-indic
       "The (female) student studies."

3 (a) *darasa*   *ʔal-tˤālib(-u)*
       study.perf.3.s.m   the-student.s.m-nom
       "The (male) student studied."

3 (b) *ya-drus(-u)*   *ʔal-tˤālib(-u)*
       3.s.m-study.imperf-indic   the-student.s.m-nom
       "The (male) student studies."

4 (a) *daras-at*   *ʔal-tˤālib-a(t-u)*
       study.perf-3.s.f   the-student-s.f-nom
       "The (female) student studied."

4 (b)   *ta-drus(-u)*   *ʔal-tˤālib-a(t-u)*
        3.s.f-study.imperf-indic   the-student-s.f-nom
        "The (female) student studies."

4.1   Methods (Cross-Sectional Data)

Eighty-three Arabic L2 learners belonging to three different native language backgrounds, (American) English, Spanish, and Japanese, were invited to participate in the study in their home institutions in the United States, Spain, and Japan, respectively. The participants were grouped according to their placement by their home institutions (first year, second year, and third year) and according to length of exposure to Arabic as part of their academic programs. Table 4.1 summarizes the details of the participants.

Table 4.1 Participants of the study

Groups English L1	Length of Exposure	Credit Hours Enrolled in	M/F	Age Range	Age Means
Group1 (n=9)	Year 1	6	4/5	18-21	19.22
Group2 (n=9)	Year 2	5	5/4	20-29	22.22
Group3 (n=9)	Year 3	4	6/3	22-34	29.11
Spanish L1					
Group1 (n=9)	Year 1	6	3/6	19-23	20.22
Group2 (n=9)	Year 2	6	2/7	19-26	21.55
Group3 (n=9)	Year 3	6	3/6	20-33	25.33
Japanese L1					
Group1 (n=10)	Year 1	12	8/2	18-20	19
Group2 (n=10)	Year 2	12	5/5	19-21	20
Group3 (n=9)	Year 3	4	1/8	20-23	21.11

M/F= Total Males/Total Females.

The participants were selected, because they had little or no exposure to Arabic prior to joining their academic institutions and were not heritage speakers who would speak Arabic occasionally or often at home. In particular, first year students of all three language groups had zero exposure and had made no trips to Arabic-speaking countries. A few participants from the three language groups at other levels had traveled to Arabic-speaking countries but did not stay there for a significant period of time. Participants from the three L1 language groups received formal instruction in Arabic with a focus on all grammatical forms from early on. The English L1 groups used mainly Abboud et al. (1983, 1997) and the Spanish L1 groups used mainly, though not exclusively, Alkhalifa (1999, 2002). As for the Japanese L1 groups, some belonged to classes that used Badawi et al. (1983, 1992) and some belonged to classes that used Brustad et al. (1995a, 1995b).

Data collection aimed at eliciting spontaneous/semi-spontaneous production data of the target forms from the participants. Elicitation took place in one-on-one interview sessions, one interview per participant (30-45 minutes). Elicitation consisted of four narrative tasks and a random task.

The four narrative tasks consisted of two in the past tense and two in the present tense divided equally between a female and a male character. The two narratives in the past tense were about a female and a male character. The participants were requested to narrate day by day the vacation activities (on a calendar) carried out by each character during his or her vacation (which took place the previous month for a period of ten days). As a distracter, the participants were asked to figure out and to comment on whether or not the male and female characters were compatible based on what they did on their vacations. The two narratives in the present tense were also about a female and a male character. The participants were requested to describe the daily routines/activities of each of the characters at different times of the day. As a distracter, the participants were asked to figure out where the character was from based on his/her routine activities. The two sets of narratives (past versus present) were not presented sequentially. Rather, the past task was presented towards the middle of the interview and the present towards the end, with tasks of other (unrelated) structures used in the beginning of the first and second halves of the interview, serving as additional distracters (see Figure 4.1 for a narrative sample in the past tense with a female character; for a narrative sample in the past tense with a male character, see Figure 3.5, Chapter 3).

The random task was included to control for the present tense narratives tasks due to responses on pilot elicitations. An artifact of the tasks was found when administering the present tense narrative tasks. Some

Figure 4.1

A sample (past tense) narrative task with a female character. The vacation went from the 17th–26th of last month (adapted from *Going Places*, Burton and Maharg: 141, 159. Copyright Addison-Wesley, 1995. Reprinted by permission of Pearson Education, Inc.).

participants misunderstood the present tense narrative task as a narrative in the past (that is, as a story) and accordingly produced past tense verbs. Therefore, the random task was thought necessary to control for the unintended effect of the present tense narrative tasks. The random task elicited production data of present tense as well as verbal agreement through discrete picture description items, each of which showed an individual, male or female, engaged in a common everyday activity. Hence, the random task was included to allow for more immediate and straightforward contexts than the present tense narrative tasks did.

All elicitation tasks were held constant and were consistently used across all the participants. All interviews were audio-recorded. The data were transcribed, transliterated, and coded. Each data sample was triple-checked for accuracy after each step. Certain items were not coded. These included hesitations, repetitions, and self-corrections except for the last attempt. In coding S-V agreement tokens, agreement was determined by considering the verbal form and whether it was inflected properly, not by identifying first the subject and then the verb it agreed with. This is significant, since the verb may agree with a discourse referent subject and the L2 participants may be mindlessly producing the wrong subject, especially when the subjects used are the pronouns *hiya* "she" and *huwa* "he," which are close in their pronunciation (see also Poeppel and Wexler 1993, Prévost and White 2000; cf. Meisel 1991).

4.2 Results

4.2.1 *Tense (narrative tasks)*

Since the four (past and present) narrative tasks elicited utterances within specific time frames of the past and present tense use, production of verbs (past and present) inflected correctly for their context use were coded as tokens of correct rule application and those that were not inflected properly for their context use were coded as tokens of incorrect rule applications.[1] Examples of incorrect rule application of past and present tense are illustrated in sentences (5)-(7), respectively, extracted from the respective participants' data samples.

(5) IL: * *?alxamīs hiya ?a-ðhab   fi   Las Vegas*
            Thursday   she   1.s-go.imperf in   Las Vegas

TL: *ʔalxamīs ðahab-at   ʔilā Las Vegas*
      Thursday go.perf-3.s.f to   Las Vegas
      "On Thursday, she went to Las Vegas ..."
      (Spanish L1: Group 1)

(6) IL: **baʕda raħlata-hu ya-šrab   šāhī* [2]
      after   trip-his   3.s.m-drink tea

TL: *baʕda riħlati-hi šariba   ʔal-šāy*
      after trip-his   drink.perf.3.sm the-tea
      "After his trip/travel, he drank tea ..."
      (English L1: Group 2)

(7) IL: **fī ʔal-sˤabāħ hiya šarib-at   ʔal-šāy* [3]
      in the-morning she drink.perf-3.s.f the-tea

TL: *fī ʔal-sˤabāħ   hiya ta-šrab   ʔal-šāy*
      in the-morning she 3.s.f-drink.imperf the-tea
      "In the morning, she drinks tea ..."
      (Japanese L1: Group 1)

The production data of all participants on past and present tense are summarized in Table 4.2, showing that all participants have higher correct ratios on past tense than present tense. Figure 4.2 illustrates the production trends of the participants via a boxplot. The figure additionally shows that the production of all participants exhibits a greater degree of variability for the present tense than for the past tense as evident in the spread out results of the medial (2nd and 3rd) quartiles. By contrast, the production of the participants for the past tense exhibits less variability as evident in the clustering of their medial (2nd and 3rd) quartiles being higher on their performance ratios, especially the first medial quartile where many participants of most groups scored within 90 percent correct ratios. Looking closely at the data qualitatively, three production patterns seem to emerge: those who exhibited consistently correct rule application of tense, those who exhibited random incorrect use, and those who, perhaps due to the artifact of the tasks, exhibited somewhat consistent wrong rule application of tense.

A series of one-way and two-way MANOVAs as well as follow-up ANOVAs of the MANOVAs were run to detect any statistically significant effect for L1 background, proficiency, and interaction between proficiency and L1 background. However, no effect was found. In other words, neither past nor present tense was found to contribute to group differences.

Table 4.2 Correct rule application of past and present tense

Arabic L2 English L1	Past Tense Correct/Total	Present Tense Correct/Total
Group1 (n=9)	154/170 (91%)	97/144 (67%)
Group2 (n=9)	157/204 (77%)	134/187 (72%)
Group3 (n=9)	150/192 (78%)	111/195 (57%)
Spanish L1		
Group1 (n=9)	81/126 (64%)	37/83 (45%)
Group2 (n=9)	101/135 (75%)	79/132 (60%)
Group3 (n=9)	185/221 (84%)	95/169 (56%)
Japanese L1		
Group1 (n=10)	146/152 (96%)	51/137 (37%)
Group2 (n=10)	211/221 (95%)	111/187 (59%)
Group3 (n=9)	156/190 (82%)	105/174 (60%)

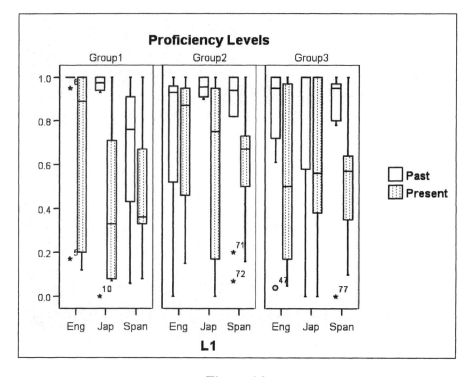

Figure 4.2

4.2.2 *Verbal agreement (narrative tasks)*

The four narrative tasks elicited descriptions of the activities of a female and a male character. Hence, verbal agreement focused on included S-V agreement for third person singular masculine and third person singular feminine. Examples of incorrect rule application of third person singular masculine and third person singular feminine are illustrated in sentences (8)-(10), respectively, extracted from the respective participants' data samples.

(8) IL: * *ʔalxamīs hiya ʔa-ðhab fī*   Las Vegas
           Thursday   she 1.s-go   in   Las Vegas
    TL: *ʔalxamīs   ðahaba-t   ʔilā* Las Vegas
           Thursday   went-3.s.f   to   Las Vegas
           "On Thursday, she went to Las Vegas ..."
           (Spanish L1: Group 1)

(9) IL: * *hiya ya-sˤħū*
           she   3.s.m-wake up
    TL: *hiya ta-sˤħū*
           she   3.s.f-wake up
           "She wakes up."
           (Japanese L1: Group 2)

(10) IL: * *huwa ta-qraʔa ʔal-kitāb*
            he   3.s.f-read   the-book
    TL: *huwa ya-qraʔ   ʔal-kitāb*
            he   3.s.m-read   the-book
            "He reads the book."
            (English L1: Group 1)

While some tokens of incorrect rule application of verbal agreement resulted from affixing the first person singular suffixes {-*ʔa*} (for present tense) and {-*tu*} (for past tense), as in sentence (8) above, the majority of errors resulted from using the third person singular masculine suffix for third person singular feminine and visa versa, as in sentences (9)-(10). The production data of the participants on verbal (S-V) agreement for third person singular masculine and feminine are summarized in Table 4.3 (see also Figure 4.3, illustrating the production trends of all participants across all groups).

A series of one-way and two-way MANOVAs as well as follow-up ANOVAs of the MANOVAs revealed the following findings: an effect for

Table 4.3 Correct rule application of verbal (S-V) agreement

Arabic L2 English L1	Verbal Agreement (Past) Correct/Total	Verbal Agreement (Present) Correct/Total
Group1 (n=9)	150/170 (88%)	128/144 (89%)
Group2 (n=9)	165/204 (81%)	140/187 (75%)
Group3 (n=9)	171/192 (89%)	177/195 (91%)
Spanish L1		
Group1 (n=9)	81/126 (64%)	53/83 (64%)
Group2 (n=9)	88/135 (65%)	98/132 (74%)
Group3 (n=9)	151/221 (68%)	124/169 (73%)
Japanese L1		
Group1 (n=10)	135/152 (89%)	117/137 (85%)
Group2 (n=10)	183/221 (83%)	168/187 (90%)
Group3 (n=9)	169/190 (89%)	147/174 (84%)

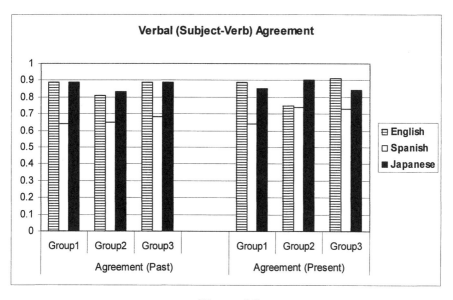

Figure 4.3

L1 between the English L1 and Spanish L1 groups for performance on verbal agreement in the present (Wilks's Λ=.72, $F(4,45)$=4.5, $p<.005$; $F(1,48)$=6.3, $p<.016$) and verbal agreement in the past ($F(1,48)$=17.0, $p<.001$) but no effect for tense; an effect for L1 between the Japanese L1 and Spanish L1 groups for performance on verbal agreement in the present (Wilks's Λ=.64, $F(4,47)$= 6.5, $p<.001$; $F(1,50)$=11.1, $p<.003$) and verbal agreement in the past ($F(1,50)$=18.0, $p<.001$) but no effect for tense; and no L1 effect for English L1 and Japanese L1 was found. In addition, a near proficiency effect for the English groups ($F(2,24)$=2.74, p=.084) with respect to verbal agreement in the present versus agreement in the past was found, while no similar effect was found in their Japanese L1 and Spanish L1 counterparts.

In other words, while there was no significant difference between the performance of the English L1 and Japanese L1 groups, both L1 groups performed significantly better on verbal agreement (both in the present and past tense) than the Spanish L1 groups. All three L1 groups performed comparably on tense (past and present). With respect to the developmental paths of the two forms (tense and verbal agreement) in the IL systems of each of the three native L1 backgrounds, the English L1 participants showed slight improvement on verbal agreement in the present tense with proficiency (that is, with more formal instruction), while no such improvement was found in the performance of the Japanese L1 and Spanish L1 groups. No improvement on tense was exhibited by any of the three native language groups.

4.2.3 *Tense and verbal agreement (random task)*

As discussed above (in Section 4.1), the pilot stage of the elicitation materials revealed that participants may misunderstand the present tense narrative task as a past tense narrative by describing the daily routines of the character as a story in the past tense. Due to this artifact with tasks, it was decided to incorporate an additional random task in which the participants were presented with discrete pictures, each representing an activity being carried out, and which therefore more intuitively captured present tense activities. Thus, the random task was used to provide additional evidence. Table 4.4 summarizes the performance of all participants of all three L1 groups on correct production of present tense as well as verbal (S-V) agreement (see also Figure 4.4, illustrating the distribution of the data by all groups).

Table 4.4 Correct rule application of tense and verbal agreement on the random task

Arabic L2 English L1	Tense (Present) Correct/Total	Verbal Agreement (Present) Correct/Total
Group1 (n=9)	24/42 (57%)	26/42 (62%)
Group2 (n=9)	145/174 (83%)	141/174 (81%)
Group3 (n=9)	252/270 (93%)	237/270 (88%)
Spanish L1		
Group1 (n=9)	28//38 (74%)	24/38 (63%)
Group2 (n=9)	73/88 (83%)	60/88 (68%)
Group3 (n=9)	133/157 (85%)	104/157 (66%)
Japanese L1		
Group1 (n=10)	124/141 (88%)	125/141 (89%)
Group2 (n=10)	212/226 (94%)	207/226 (92%)
Group3 (n=9)	154/168 (92%)	146/168 (87%)

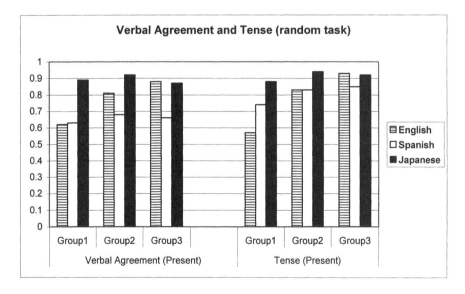

Figure 4.4

The data show that the Japanese L1 groups scored higher correct ratios of rule applications of both (present) tense and S-V agreement (in the present) than their English L1 and Spanish L1 counterparts. The English L1 groups exhibited higher correct ratios than their Spanish L1 counterparts. In addition, while the English L1 participants showed steady gains across groups and with respect to both forms, the Spanish L1 groups did so only with respect to tense. Group 3 of the Spanish L1 participants did not show improvement (over Group 2) with respect to verbal agreement and Group 3 of the Japanese L1 participants did not show gain (beyond that of Group 2) with respect to both forms.

A series of one-way and two-way MANOVAs as well as follow-up ANOVAs of the MANOVAs revealed three findings. First, an effect for L1 between the Japanese L1 and English L1 groups for performance on both verbal agreement (Wilks's Λ=.83, $F(2,49)$=5.04, p<.011; $F(1,50)$=6.8, p<.013) and tense ($F(1,50)$=9.4, p<.005) was found. In addition, an effect for proficiency with respect to the English L1 groups (Wilks's Λ=.51, $F(4,46)$=4.5, p<.005) on their performance of (present) tense ($F(2,24)$=11.1, p<.001) and a near proficiency effect on their performance of verbal agreement ($F(2,24)$=3.99, p=.032) were found. Second, the tests revealed an effect for L1 between the Japanese L1 and Spanish L1 groups for performance on verbal agreement (Wilks's Λ=.72, $F(2,49)$=9.7, p<.001; $F(1,50)$=19.1, p<.001) and a near effect for their performance on tense $F(1,50)$=3.9, p=.054). Third, a near effect for L1 between the English L1 groups and their Spanish L1 counterparts on their performance of verbal agreement (Wilks's Λ=.88, $F(2,47)$= 3.3, p=.044; $F(1,48)$=5.4, p<.025) was found. In other words, the Japanese L1 groups outperformed their English L1 and Spanish L1 counterparts on their performance of both verbal agreement and tense, whereas the English L1 groups slightly outperformed their Spanish L1 counterparts on their performance of verbal (S-V) agreement.

Finally, the participants' performance on present tense in the random task exhibited less variability than their performance in the past narrative task, as illustrated in Figure 4.5, as well as less variability than their performance on present tense in the present (non-random) narrative task (cf. Figure 4.3). Thus, for example, apart from Group 1 of the English L1 participants, the performance of all participants on present tense in the random task is generally less variable than their performance on past tense.

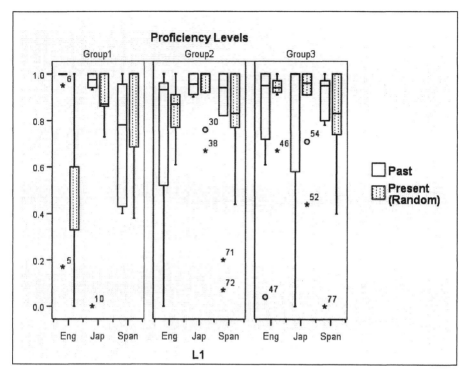

Figure 4.5

4.3   Summary

Based on the acquisition data for tense (past and present) and verbal (S-V) agreement presented in this chapter, the findings show that both the Japanese L1 and English L1 groups performed significantly better on verbal agreement (both in the present and past tense) than the Spanish L1 groups, all three L1 groups having performed comparably on tense (past and present). When we consider the data generated via the random task, which was used due to artifact of the present narrative task thereby excluding the near effect of verbal agreement (in the present) showing slight improvement over time, the data show that the Japanese L1 groups outperformed their English L1 and Spanish L1 counterparts in their performance of both verbal agreement and tense, whereas the English L1 groups slightly outperformed their Spanish L1 counterparts in their performance of verbal (S-V) agreement. Thus, the finding that the data seem to converge on, given all tasks, is that the performance of the participants from the three L1 language backgrounds was significantly different from each other on verbal agreement and to a lesser extent on (present) tense. In addition, if we exclude (or interpret more cautiously) the near effect for improvement on verbal agreement over time, the findings show that, of all participants, only the English L1 groups seemed to exhibit two developmental paths for the two target forms, showing more improvement on (present) tense than on verbal agreement (that is, with the acquisition of verbal agreement slightly lagging behind that of tense). The issue of why the Spanish L1 participants surprisingly underperformed their Japanese L1 and English L1 counterparts on verbal agreement given the typological constellations (of the L1s and L2) of the participants and given the difference in duration of exposure to input evident in Table 4.1 above (that is, whereas the Japanese L1 participants had almost double the amount of instruction time of their English L1 and Spanish L1 counterparts, the latter had somewhat comparable duration of exposure) will be addressed in Chapter 7. In addition, Chapter 5 discusses additional data which reveal a correlation in the use of null subjects and verbal agreement in the production output of the Spanish L1 groups.

The Acquisition of Null Subjects

This chapter discusses acquisition of null subjects based on cross-sectional data from native English L1, Spanish L1, and Japanese L1 speakers learning Arabic as an L2. The target structure of null subjects is of the non-embedded construction type, as illustrated in sentences (44)-(45) discussed in Chapter 1 and restated below as (1)-(2), where use of an overt pronominal or NP/lexical subject in the matrix (main) clause is optional.

    (1)   *daras-ū*
            study.perf-3.p.m
            "They studied."
    (2)   *ya-drus-ū-na*
            3-study.imperf-p.m-indic
            "They study."

5.1   Methods (Cross-Sectional Data)

Eighty-three Arabic L2 learners belonging to three different L1s, (American) English, Spanish, and Japanese, were invited to participate in the study at their home institutions in the United States, Spain, and Japan, respectively.[1] The participants were grouped according to their placement by their home institutions (first year, second year, and third year) and according to length of exposure to Arabic as part of their academic programs. Table 5.1 summarizes the details of the participants.

What is significant about the participants is that they had little or no exposure to Arabic prior to joining their academic institutions and were not heritage speakers who would speak Arabic occasionally or often at home. In particular, first year students of all three language groups had zero exposure and had made no trips to Arabic-speaking countries. A few participants from the three language groups at other levels had traveled to Arabic-speaking countries briefly but did not stay there for a significant period of time. Participants from the three L1 language groups received formal instruction in Arabic with a focus on all grammatical forms from early on. The English L1 groups used mainly Abboud et al. (1983, 1997) and the Spanish L1 groups used mainly, though not exclusively, Alkhalifa (1999, 2002). As for the Japanese L1 groups, some belonged to classes that used Badawi et al. (1983, 1992) and others belonged to classes that used Brustad et al. (1995a, 1995b).

Table 5.1 Participants of the study

Groups English L1	Length of Exposure	Credit Hours Enrolled in	M/F	Age Range	Age Means
Group1 (n=9)	Year 1	6	4/5	18-21	19.22
Group2 (n=9)	Year 2	5	5/4	20-29	22.22
Group3 (n=9)	Year 3	4	6/3	22-34	29.11
Spanish L1					
Group1 (n=9)	Year 1	6	3/6	19-23	20.22
Group2 (n=9)	Year 2	6	2/7	19-26	21.55
Group3 (n=9)	Year 3	6	3/6	20-33	25.33
Japanese L1					
Group1 (n=10)	Year 1	12	8/2	18-20	19
Group2 (n=10)	Year 2	12	5/5	19-21	20
Group3 (n=9)	Year 3	4	1/8	20-23	21.11

M/F= Total Males/Total Females.

In addition, six native speakers of Arabic were invited to participate in the study as a control group. The demographic information for the control participants is displayed in Table 5.2. The native speakers were from different Arab countries (including Egypt, Jordan, Palestine, Syria, and Tunisia) with a mean age of 32. They were all graduate students pursuing different graduate programs at a university in the United States.

Table 5.2 Control participants

Controls Arabic L1	Country of Origin	Graduate Major	Gender	Ages
1	Egypt	Geology	M	32
2	Jordan	Industrial Engineering	M	33
3	Palestine	Education	M	37
4	Palestine	Mathematics	M	33
5	Syria	Biochemistry	M	32
6	Tunisia	Computer Engineering	M	25

Data collection aimed at eliciting spontaneous/semi-spontaneous production data of the target forms from the English L1, Spanish L1, Japanese L1, and control participants. Elicitation took place in one-on-one interview sessions, one interview per participant (30-45 minutes). Elicitation consisted of four narrative tasks: two in the past tense and two in the present tense divided equally between a female and a male character. The two narratives in the past tense were about a female and a male character. The participants were requested to narrate day by day the vacation activities (on a calendar) carried out by each character during his or her vacation (which took place the previous month for a period of ten days). As a distracter, the participants were asked to figure out and to comment on whether or not the two characters were compatible based on what they did on their vacations. The two narratives in the present tense were also about a female and a male character. The participants were requested to describe the daily routines/activities of each of the characters at different times of the day. As a distracter, the participants were asked to figure out where the character was from based on his/her routine activities. The two sets of narratives (past versus present) were not presented sequentially. Rather, the past set was presented towards the middle of the interview and the present towards the end, with tasks of other (unrelated) structures used in the beginning of the first and second halves of the interview as additional distracters (for sample narrative tasks, see Figure 4.1, Chapter 4, and Figure 3.5, Chapter 3).

All elicitation tasks were held constant and were consistently used across all the participants. All interviews were audio-recorded. The data were transcribed, transliterated, and coded. Each data sample was triple-checked for accuracy after each step. The elicitation materials were piloted before they were used for elicitation. Certain items were not coded. These included hesitations, repetitions, and self-corrections except for the last attempt. In addition, a small number of null verb contexts were produced where a pronominal or lexical subject was produced followed by a pause or verbal noun (instead of a verb). These tokens were too few and were not included in the analysis. In coding subject-verb agreement tokens, agreement was determined by considering the verbal form first and whether it was inflected properly, not by identifying first the subject and then the verb it agreed with. This is crucial, since the verb may agree with a discourse referent subject and the L2 participants may be mindlessly producing the wrong subject, especially when the subjects used are the pronouns *hiya* "she" and *huwa* "he," which are close in their pronunciation (see also Poeppel and Wexler 1993, Prévost and White 2000; cf. Meisel 1991).

5.2 Results

5.2.1 *Null subjects production*

The focus of null subject production was on third person singular masculine and feminine. Given the description of the four narrative tasks above, one would expect each of the six native (control) speakers to produce between 0-4 contexts with overt subjects (NPs or pronouns), with one token for each task, introducing the first event. Once the first event in each narrative is anchored with an explicit pronominal or NP subject, producing a pronominal or NP subject for each subsequent event of a narrative becomes redundant.[2] This is also true for two of the L1s of the participants, Spanish and Japanese, which allow null subjects. The third L1 (that is, English) does not allow null subjects. The control participants produced tokens within the predicted range. All of the six native Arabic speakers produced 11 contexts with overt subjects (four pronominal and seven lexical) and all except one occurred as a description of the first event of a narrative. Apart from one token, all contexts occurred with the overt subjects in a pre-verbal position. Only one control participant produced 100 percent zero overt subject contexts. In addition, the control group occasionally produced (obligatory) overt pronominal subjects in lower or embedded clause with verbs such as *yabdū* "it seems," *kaʔanna* "looks like," and *yumkin* "it is possible" and the complementizer *ʔanna*, as illustrated in (3)-(4).

(3)   *ya-bdū   ʔanna-**hā** ta-sˤ ʰū   bākiran*
      3.s.m-seem that-she   3.s.f-wakes up early
      "It seems that she wakes up early."

(4)   *kaʔanna-**hu**   kāna   ya-ʔkulu kaθīran*
      looks.like-he   be.perf.3.s.m   3.s.m-eat a lot
      "It looks like he was eating a lot."

The control participants produced a total of 24 such tokens in the middle of the narratives.

As for the English L1, Japanese L1, and Spanish L1 participants, they mainly produced null subject and overt (pronominal and lexical) subject contexts in matrix clauses, as in sentences (5)-(7).

(5)   *ʔal-sabt ðahab-at   ʔilā ʔal-bayt*
      Saturday go.perf-3.s.f to   the-house
      "On Saturday, she went home."
      (English L1, Group 1: past narrative)

(6)   *fī ʔal-sabt hiya radʒaʕ-at   [ʔilā] bayti-hā*
      on Saturday she return.perf-3.s.f [to] house-her
      "On Saturday, she returned to her house."
      (Japanese L1, Group 1: past narrative)

(7) IL: **ʔal-bint ya-ðhabu ʔal-kulliya*
         the-girl   3.s.m-go   the-college

    TL: *ʔal-bint ta-ðhabu ʔilā ʔal-kulliya*
         the-girl 3.s.f-go to   the-college
         "The girl goes to college."
         (Spanish L1, Group 1: present narrative)

Of all the participants, only two Spanish participants (in Group 3) produced a total of four contexts of overt pronominal subjects with the complementizer *liʔanna* in embedded clause. All four tokens were correctly used with the obligatorily expressed pronominal subject on a par with those produced by the control group. Production data of the cross-sectional participants also included null subjects and overt lexical and pronominal subjects in conjoined contexts. Tokens of both contexts were collapsed together. All overt subject contexts were produced with the subjects in a pre-verbal position. The vast majority of overt subjects produced were pronominal subjects; the rest were lexical subjects.

Table 5.3 displays the distribution of the production data of all participants in null and overt contexts, including those of the control group (see also Figure 5.1). The data show that generally the English L1 participants noticeably produced the most subjectless clauses compared with their Spanish L1 and Japanese L1 counterparts. The Japanese L1 participants produced more subjectless clauses than their Spanish L1 counterparts. Most noticeably, the English L1 Group 1 produced a total of 280 tokens of null subjects, almost twice the number of their Japanese L1 counterparts in Group 1 (who produced a total of 163 tokens) and more than five times the number of their Spanish L1 counterparts in Group 1 (who produced a total of 55 tokens). As for Group 2, whereas the Japanese L1 group caught up with their English L1 counterparts in dropping more subjects, doing so in 321 contexts (versus 353 by the English L1 Group 2), the Spanish L1 Group 2 dropped subjects in fewer than half as many contexts, with a total of 156. The difference in dropping subjects among the three L1 groups shrank in Group 3, where the English L1, Spanish L1, and Japanese L1 dropped subjects in 303, 232, and 236 contexts, respectively.

Table 5.3 Distribution of null subjects in the participants' IL systems

Participants	Null/Total Subjects	Ratios %	Lexical/Pronominal Subjects
(Arabic L1) Controls (n=6)	264/275	96	7/4
Arabic L2 (English L1)			
Group 1 (n=9)	280/314	89	9/25
Group 1 (n=9)	353/388	91	11/24
Group 1 (n=9)	303/385	79	18/64
Arabic L2 (Spanish L1)			
Group 1 (n=9)	55/200	28	18/127
Group 2 (n=9)	156/256	61	10/90
Group 3 (n=9)	232/371	63	9/130
Arabic L2 (Japanese L1)			
Group1 (n=10)	163/293	56	3/127
Group2 (n=10)	321/409	78	6/82
Group3 (n=9)	236/365	65	8/121

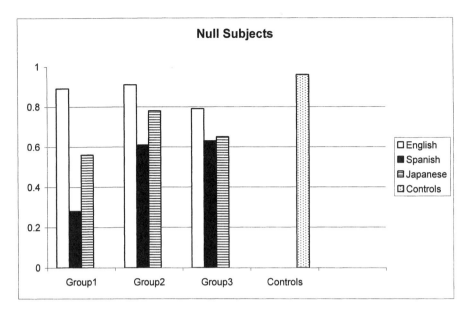

Figure 5.1

Table 5.3 also lists the number of contexts where an overt subject is produced. The data reveal that contexts with pronominal subjects represented the largest number of contexts with overt subjects; contexts with lexical subjects were far fewer. The data also show that the control group by far outperformed all three L1 groups, dropping subjects in 264 out of 275 contexts (that is, producing overt lexical or pronominal subjects in 11 contexts only).

Two-way MANOVAs and follow-up ANOVAs of the MANOVAs (as well as post hoc pair-wise comparisons of the ANOVAs) mainly revealed a significant effect for L1 on null subject production between the control, English L1, and Japanese L1 groups on one hand, and the Spanish groups on the other (Wilks's Λ=.598, $F(6,156)$=7.6, p<.001; $F(3,79)$=8.4, p<.001). In other words, the Arabic L1, English L1, and Japanese L1 participants dropped significantly more subjects than their Spanish L1 counterparts.

5.2.2 *Null subjects and verbal agreement production*

The data become more revealing of the participants' use of null subjects, particularly those of the Spanish L1 participants, when production of verbal agreement in null and overt subject contexts is examined. Table 5.4 displays the distribution of correct rule application of verbal agreement in null and overt subject contexts (see also Figure 5.2). As discussed above, the English L1 groups overall produced far more subjectless sentences than sentences with overt (lexical and pronominal) subjects. Their production also exhibited high ratios of correct verbal agreement in both null subject contexts (88 percent, 80 percent, and 91 percent) and overt subject contexts (91 percent, 68 percent, and 89 percent), as shown in Table 5.4. Similarly, the Japanese L1 groups overall produced far more subjectless sentences than sentences with overt subjects. Not unlike their English L1 counterparts, the Japanese L1 groups exhibited high ratios of correct verbal agreement in both null subject contexts (89 percent, 84 percent, and 83 percent) and overt subject contexts (85 percent, 93 percent, and 86 percent). However, the production of the Spanish L1 groups exhibited a contrasting pattern to that of their English L1 and Japanese L1 counterparts. The beginning Spanish L1 group (Group 1) not only produced far fewer sentences with null subjects (55) than sentences with overt subjects (145) but also exhibited a lower ratio of verbal agreement in null subject contexts (42 percent) than that of overt subject contexts (70 percent). Unlike Group 1, the intermediate group (Group 2) produced a higher number of null subject contexts (156) than overt subject contexts (100) with somewhat equal ratios of correct verbal agreement in both contexts (71 percent and 68 percent, respectively). The advanced group (Group 3) produced far more tokens of both null subjects and overt subjects than Groups 1 and 2 did (232 and 139, respectively), coming close to the number of tokens of dropped subjects by the English L1 and Spanish L1 counterparts of Group 3. Unlike Spanish L1 Group 1 but like Group 2, Spanish L1 Group 3 exhibited somewhat equal ratios of correct subject-verb agreement in null subject and overt subject contexts (69 percent and 77 percent, respectively).

As indicated above, two-way MANOVA and follow-up ANOVAs of the MANOVA tests (as well as post hoc pair-wise comparisons of the ANOVAs) revealed a significant effect for L1 on null subject production between the control, English L1, and Japanese L1 participants on one hand,

Table 5.4 Distribution of verbal (S-V) agreement in the participants' IL systems

Participants	Correct Agreement: Null Subjects	Ratios %	Correct Agreement: Overt Subjects	Ratios %
(Arabic L1)				
Controls (n=6)	264/264	100	11/11	100
Arabic L2 (English L1)				
Group 1 (n=9)	246/280	88	31/34	91
Group 1 (n=9)	283/353	80	24/35	68
Group 1 (n=9)	276/303	91	73/82	89
Arabic L2 (Spanish L1)				
Group 1 (n=9)	23/55	42	102/145	70
Group 2 (n=9)	111/156	71	68/100	68
Group 3 (n=9)	160/232	69	107/139	77
Arabic L2 (Japanese L1)				
Group1 (n=10)	145/163	89	111/130	85
Group2 (n=10)	271/321	84	82/88	93
Group3 (n=9)	196/236	83	104/121	86

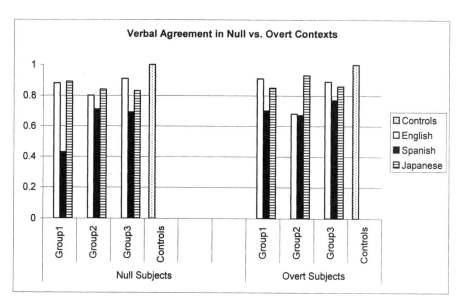

Figure 5.2

and the Spanish L1 participants on the other. Here, too, the same tests revealed a significant difference between the control group, English L1, and Japanese L1 groups on one hand, and the Spanish L1 participants on the other, with respect to correct verbal agreement in null subject contexts (Wilks's Λ=.598, $F(6,156)$=7.6, p<.001; $F(3,79)$=8.4, p<.001).[3]

5.3 Summary

The data reveal that the English L1 and Japanese L1 groups dropped significantly more subjects than the Spanish L1 groups. The data also show that the English L1 and Japanese L1 groups significantly produced more correct verbal (S-V) agreement tokens in null subject contexts than their Spanish L1 counterparts. Thus, the data reveal a close correlation between the production of subjectless clauses and verbal agreement. While the English L1 and Japanese L1 groups produced a good number of subjectless clauses and from the beginning stage of L2 development (that is, Group 1), the Spanish L1 group produced fewer sentences with null subjects and with much lower ratios of correct verbal agreement. However, with more exposure to Arabic L2 input during later L2 development, the Spanish L1 Groups (2-3) exhibited an increase in both correct verbal agreement ratios and null subject production. The unexpected finding as to why the Spanish L1 participants underperformed their English L1 and Japanese L1 counterparts on null subject production given the typological constellations of the L1s and L2 (where Arabic, Japanese, and Spanish are all null subject languages and English is not) will be addressed in Chapter 7.

CHAPTER 6

The Acquisition of Negation, Mood, and Case

This chapter discusses acquisition of negation as well as the morphological inflections of case and mood based on longitudinal data from native English L1 speakers learning Arabic as an L2. The negation constructions focused on here include the use of *lā*, *mā*, *lam*, and *lan*, as in sentences (55)-(58) and (61)-(64) discussed in Chapter 1 and restated below as (1)-(8).

(1) *lā   ya-drus(-u)*[1]   *ʔal-tˤālib(-u)*[2]
    not 3.s.m-study.imperf-indic   the-student.s.m-nom
    "The (male) student does not study."

(2) *ʔal-tˤullāb(-u)*   *lā   ya-drus-ū-na*
    the-student.p.m-nom not 3-study.imperf-p.m-indic
    "The (male) students do not study."

(3) *mā darasa*   *ʔal-tˤālib(-u)*
    not study.perf.3.s.m the-student.s.m-nom
    "The (male) student did not study."

(4) *ʔal-tˤullāb(-u)*   *mā daras-ū*
    the-student.p.m-nom not study.perf-3.p.m
    "The (male) students did not study."

(5) *lam ya-drus-0*   *ʔal-tˤālib(-u)*
    not 3.s.m-study.imperf-juss   the-student.s.m-nom
    "The (male) student did not study."

(6) *ʔal-tˤullāb(-u)*   *lam   ya-drus-ū-0*
    the-student.p.m-nom not   3-study.imperf-p.m-juss
    "The (male) students did not study."

(7) *lan ya-drus(-a)*   *ʔal-tˤālib(-u)*
    not 3.s.m-study.imperf-subjunc   the-student.s.m-nom
    "The (male) student will not study."

(8)   *Pal-tˤullāb(-u)*   *lan*   *ya-drus-ū-0*
       the-student.p.m-nom   not   3-study.imperf-p.m-subjunc
       "The (male) students will not study."

The morphological inflections of mood that are focused on include the indicative (on the default imperfect stem and imperfect stem following the negation particle *lā*), the jussive (following the negation particle *lam*), and the subjunctive (following the negation particle *lan*), as in sentences (1)-(8) above. The focus on mood also includes the subjunctive following the complementizer *Pan*, as in sentences (9)-(10) below.

(9)   *yu-rīd-(u)*   *Pal-tˤālib(-u)*   *Pan ya-drus(-a)*
       3.s.m-want-indic   the-student.s.m-nom   to   3.s.m-study-subjunc
       "The (male) student wants to study."

(10)   *Pal-tˤullāb(-u)*   *yu-rīd-ū-(na)*   *Pan ya-drus-ū-0*
       the-student.p.m-nom   3-want-p.m-indic   to   3-study-p.m-subjunc
       "The (male) students want to study."

As for case, the focus is on the accusative case of subjects and predicates occurring with the past copular verb *kana* and the verbless sentential negator *laysa*, as in sentences (32)-(37) and (38)-(43) discussed in Chapter 1 and restated below as sentences (11)-(22).

(11)   *kāna*   *Pal-tˤālib(-u)*   *mubakkir(-a-n)*
       be.perf.3.s.m   the-student.s.m-nom   early.s.m-acc-indef
       "The (male) student was early."

(12)   *kāna*   *Pal-tˤullāb(-u)*   *mubakkir-īna*
       be.perf.3.s.m   the-student.p.m-nom   early-p.m-acc
       "The (male) students were early."

(13)   *Pal-tˤullāb(-u)*   *kān-ū*   *mubakkir-īna*
       the-student.p.m-nom   be.perf-3.p.m   early-p.m-acc
       "The (male) students were early."

(14)   *kān-at*   *Pal-tˤālib-a(t-u)*   *mubakkir-a(t-a-n)*
       be.perf-3.s.f   the-student-s.f-nom   early-s.f-acc-indef
       "The (female) student was early."

(15)   *kān-at*   *Pal-tˤālib-āt(-u)*   *mubakkir-āt(-i-n)*
       be.perf-3.s.f   the-student-p.f-nom   early-p.f-acc-indef
       "The (female) students were early."

(16) *ʔal-tˤālib-āt(-u)*   *kun-na*   *mubakkir-āt(-i-n)*
      the-student-p.f-nom   be.perf-3.p.f   early-p.f-acc-indef
      "The (female) students were early."

(17) *laysa*   *ʔal-tˤālib(-u)*   *mubakkir(-a-n)*
      not.3.s.m   the-student.s.m-nom   early.s.m-acc-indef
      "The (male) student is not early."

(18) *laysa*   *ʔal-tˤullāb(-u)*   *mubakkir-īna*
      not.3.s.m   the-student.p.m-nom   early-p.m.acc
      "The (male) students are not early."

(19) *ʔal-tˤullāb(-u)*   *lays-ū*   *mubakkir-īna*
      the-student.p.m-nom   not-3.p.m   early-p.m.acc
      "The (male) students are not early."

(20) *lays-at*   *ʔal-tˤālib-a(t-u)*   *mubakkir-a(t-a-n)*
      not-3.s.f   the-student-s.f-nom   early-s.f-acc-indef
      "The (female) student is not early."

(21) *lays-at*   *ʔal-tˤālib-āt(-u)*   *mubakkir-āt(-i-n)*
      not-3.s.f   the-student-p.f-nom   early-p.f-acc-indef
      "The (female) students are not early."

(22) *ʔal-tˤālib-āt(-u)*   *las-na*   *mubakkir-āt(-i-n)*
      the-student-p.f-nom   not-3.p.f   early-p.f-acc-indef
      "The (female) students are not early."

6.1 Methods (Longitudinal Data)

6.1.1 *Participants*

Eight (American) English L1 speakers and one French L1 speaker were observed longitudinally for a school year. The demographic data of the participants are discussed in Chapter 3 and restated here in Table 6.1. As discussed in Chapter 3, the participants were selected, because they had a zero background in Arabic. They were taking an Arabic language (a six credit per semester course) at the time as part of their program requirements at their university in the United States. With the exception of one participant, Mark, all the participants attended the same class with the same teacher, but all were using the same textbook (Brustad et al. 1995a, 1995b).

Table 6.1 Longitudinal participants

Name	Gender	Age	L1	Major	Year
Ann	F	21	English	Theology	1st
Beth	F	23	English	History	Graduate 1st
Jeff	M	19	English	Int'l Relations	1st
John	M	19	English	Int'l Economics	1st
Kay	F	18	English	Arabic and History	1st
Mark	M	32	English	Int'l Relations	2nd
Viola	F	18	English	Int'l Economics	1st
Mary*	F	19	English	Arabic	1st
Adam*	M	22	Creole and French	MBNA	4th

* = Early withdrawal in the second half of the school year. All names are pseudonyms.

6.1.2 *Formal classroom input*

Table 6.2 lists the structures presented in the participants' classroom textbooks (Brustad et al. 1995a, 1995b). The table also lists in bold the dates during which data elicitation interviews were held (weeks 8, 10, 14, 16, 18, 20, 22, 24, 26, and 27). The data elicitation sessions started in the 8th week, because the classroom instruction during the first eight weeks covered mostly phonology and script, cultural notes, and a few discrete meaningful vocabulary items occurring at the phrase level (Unit 5) and a few sentences (Unit 8).

In addition to the formal classroom input, a four-lesson design was prepared to expose the participants to additional input of the target structures via the computer, beginning in week 19. This input was added to reinforce exposure to the target forms together with their associated case and mood endings; the latter were not emphasized in the textbooks of the participants (Brustad et al. 1995b). Six of the nine participants were randomly selected to receive instruction on two out of four target structures. Three participants (Mark, Viola, and Mary) were selected to receive instruction on negation constructions with *lā*, *mā*, *lam*, and *lan* and the past tense copular verb *kāna*. The three others (Kay, Beth, and Jeff) received instruction on *?an* construction and negation construction with *laysa*. One participant, Mary, withdrew from the study after the first (computer) session. The other participants (Ann, Adam, and John) did not receive additional input and were observed based on their exposure to classroom input alone.[3] Table 6.3

displays various details about the additional input which six of the participants received during computer sessions, including the number of times the sessions were held and the time frame with respect to elicitation interviews.

Table 6.2 Schedule of the learning objectives in Brustad et al. (1995a, 1995b)

Study Weeks	Units and Lessons	Elicitation Interviews	Negation						
			Imperfect	Perfective	Perfective	Future			
			lā	mā	lam	lan	laysa	kāna	?an
3	5								
5	7								
6	8								
7	9								
	10		(/)	(/)					
8	1	**1**							
9-10	2	**2**							
	3								
11-14	4	**3**	X					(x)	
	5		(x)					(/)	
	6		(x)						
15-16	7	**4**	(/)					X*	
17-18	8	**5**	(x)	X					(x)
	9		(x)			(/)*			(x)
19-20	10	**6**	(x)	(/)					X
	11		(x)	(/)				(/)	(x)
21-22	12	**7**	(x)	(x)	(/)	X	(/)	(x)	(x)
23-24	13	**8**	(x)	X	X	(/)	(/)	(x)	(x)
25-26	14	**9**	(x)		(/)		(/)	(/)	(x)
27-28	15	**10**	(x)	(/)	(x)	(/)	(x)	(x)	(x)

Numbers in bold = elicitation interviews; X = focused attempt to teach the structure; (x) = structure is not the focus of instruction but occurs in the lesson and drills more than 4 times; (/) = structure is not the focus of instruction and occurs less than 4 times; * = case is associated with *laysa* and *kāna* but not targeted in the textbook.

Table 6.3 Content and schedule of additional input during computer sessions

Mark, Viola, and Mary*	Kay, Beth, and Jeff	Study Weeks	Computer Sessions	Elicitation Interviews
lā, mā, lam, lan, kāna	ʔan, laysa	19	1-2	6
		20	3-4	
		21	5-6	7
		22	7-8	
		23	9-10	8
		24	11-12	
		25	13-14	9
		26	15-16	
		27		10

* = Participant withdrew from the study after first (computer) session.

Thus, each of the six (out of the nine) participants attended sixteen sessions, eight for each structure, once a week for two months. The sessions were held individually in a medium size conference room in the participants' university library. The duration of the sessions was timed by the computer. On average, the participants spent less time on negation constructions with *lā, mā, lam, lan*, and *ʔan* construction (10-15 minutes) than on the past tense copular *kāna* and copular negation structures (20-30 minutes).

The additional input consisted of four lessons and each lesson consisted of three components. Each lesson started with a dialogue with three buttons for the user's access to audio recordings, vocabulary glosses, and a *help* menu that provided explanations of instruction statements in English (since these were provided in Arabic) and other components of the lessons. The participants were told they could listen and read or read and listen to the dialogue as many times as they wished. The second component let users record themselves as they listened to and read from a list of discrete words with and without the relevant case and mood endings. The third component presented ten multiple choice questions, one question at a time. The order of the questions was automatically randomized after each session. Some of the questions were contextualized (that is, they consisted of a two-turn short dialogue by two speakers) so that both the rule and the function of the target forms were emphasized.

When attempting to answer each question, the participants had the option of consulting a button that gave clues about the answer and a grammar button that allowed access to an explanation of the rule relevant to the question. The participants were encouraged to use these two buttons before they attempted an answer. Then, the participants were required to choose from the multiple answers. Depending on the rule and question, the screen clue contained the glossing of key words and other relevant information such as number, gender, and case or mood. The user could not figure out the answer by using the clue button without consulting the rule accessible by clicking on the grammar button. For this reason, the participants were given as many as four trial errors before the next question popped up.[4]

6.1.3 *Data collection and coding*

Data elicitation sessions were held every two weeks for a school year, resulting in ten interviews with each participant except for two: Adam withdrew after the third interview and Mary withdrew after the fourth interview. A number of techniques were used to elicit agreement contexts of the target structures. Elicitation techniques included picture description, picture differences, picture sequencing, video story retelling, and informal interviews. The elicitation tasks were held constant and were consistently used across all the participants. Elicitation materials were recycled two to three times maximally to control for participants' familiarity. All interviews were audio-recorded. The data were transcribed, transliterated, and coded. Each data sample was triple-checked for accuracy after each step. To preserve the data from contamination due to elicitation errors, the elicitation statements were used consistently across participants, kept general and short, and, at times, even said in English. The elicitation materials were piloted before they were used for elicitation. Certain tokens were not coded. These were hesitations and self-corrections except the last attempt in each case.

6.2   Results

6.2.1 *Emergence criterion*

To assess the participants' gains following their exposure to formal classroom and computer-assisted language sessions input, emergence is relied on here as a measure for L2 development (adopted earlier by other researchers, for example, Cazden et al. 1975, Bahns 1981, Meisel et al. 1981). Following Pienemann (1998), emergence is defined as follows:

> "Emergence can be understood as the point in time at which certain skills have, in principle, been attained or at which certain operations can, in principle, be carried out. From a descriptive viewpoint one can say that this is the beginning of an acquisition process." (Pienemann 1998:138)

In other words, the notion of emergence does not rely on full mastery of form but rather on the initial ability to process and apply a rule. Accordingly, this entails that the emergence criterion need not capture a form that is completely target-like. The advantage of this approach, as Pienemann suggests, is "to allow the researcher to trace every step in the development of the relationship between grammatical forms and their functions from the first emergence of the most modest (non-standard) systematicity to the full use of the target language systems" (Pienemann 1998:149). This has the additional advantage of avoiding the pitfalls of the "comparative fallacy" (Bley-Vroman 1983) which would otherwise result in a misleading assessment of the systematicity of the learner's Interlanguage system (that is, by comparing the learner's production directly to the target language rather than analyzing it as part of the Interlanguage system as a system by itself).

Emergence is operationalized here in terms of two minimal tokens of rule application provided the two tokens occur within morphologically and lexically varied elements. This condition is to ensure that the elements produced mark actual emergence and are not exemplars of items learned as unanalyzed chunks. Thus, to establish emergence of the present tense negation construction with *lā*, two tokens with two different lexical verbs need to be produced, as in (23)-(24) below where *taktub* and *ʔa-ʕrif* are two different lexical verbs occurring with *lā* in the same data set.

(23) *hiya lā ta-ktub*
      she not 3.s.f-write
      "She is not writing."
      (Jeff: Interview 3)

(24) *lā ʔa-ʕrif*
      not 1.s-know
      "I do not know ..."
      (Jeff: Interview 3)

Additionally, in applying the emergence criterion and confirming acquisition claims, the continuity assumption, following Brown (1973) and Pienemann (1998), is adopted. The rationale of this assumption is based on the notion that the Interlanguage development of a form takes on a "steady" trend: "If a structure has been acquired it will be a constant part of the Interlanguage system at later levels of development" (Pienemann 1998:147; see also 122-62).

6.2.2 Negation construction with lā and the indicative mood

The present tense negation construction with *lā* was present in the classroom input as early as week 7 in the expression *lā ʔaʕrif* "I don't know" just before present tense was formally introduced in week 8 (see Table 6.2 above). Table 6.4 lists the suppliance ratio of the negation particle *lā* by the participants (see also Table 6.5).

The figures in bold indicate that evidence of emergence was reached by the participants according to the emergence criterion discussed in the preceding section (that is, two minimal tokens occurring with different lexical elements; in this case, two different lexical verbs are required to co-occur with the negation particle in order to conclude that emergence took place). The figures represent the ratios of rule application (in this case suppliance of *lā*) and suppliance of the proper negation particle. As displayed in Tables 6.4-6.5, emergence took place from early on and in all of the participants' Interlanguage systems, except one (Adam). Emergence also seems to exhibit a steady pattern throughout the period of the observation.

As for emergence of the morphological inflection for the indicative mood affixed to the end of the verb following *lā*, no production of the morphological inflection for the indicative mood was found in the participants' production data, including those of the participants (displayed in Tables 6.4-6.5 in bold in the two top rows) who received the additional computer input, except for one participant, Mary, who produced one token in the singular (that is, with an {-u} suffix).[5]

Table 6.4 Suppliance ratios of the present tense negation particle *lā*

Weeks	8	10	14	16	18	20	22	24	26	27
Mark	/	**(1.0)**	/	**(1.0)**	**(1.0)**	**(1.0)**	**(1.0)**	.60	(1.0)	/
Viola	**1.0**	**(1.0)**	**(1.0)**	**(1.0)**	**1.0**	**(1.0)**	**(1.0)**	**(1.0)**	**(1.0)**	**(1.0)**
Kay	**(.75)**	.62	**1.0**	**(1.0)**	**(1.0)**	**1.0**	**1.0**	**(1.0)**	(.0)	**(1.0)**
Beth	**(1.0)**	**1.0**	**1.0**	**(1.0)**	**(1.0)**	**(1.0)**	**(1.0)**	**(1.0)**	**(1.0)**	**(1.0)**
Jeff	/	**(1.0)**	**(1.0)**	**(1.0)**	**1.0**	**1.0**	**1.0**	**(1.0)**	**(1.0)**	/
Ann	**1.0**	**1.0**	/	**(1.0)**	**(1.0)**	**1.0**	**(1.0)**	**(1.0)**	/	**(1.0)**
John	.0	/	.75	/	**(1.0)**	**(1.0)**	**(1.0)**	**(1.0)**	/	/
Mary	(.0)	(.0)	**(1.0)**	**(1.0)**						
Adam	.25	/	.33							

"( )" = less than 4 tokens; "/" = zero occurrence; figures in bold = reaching emergence criterion; names in bold = participants who received additional computer input; blank spaces = absence from elicitation interview.

Table 6.5 Emergence of the present tense negation particle *lā*

Weeks	8	10	14	16	18	20	22	24	26	27
Mark	-	+	-	-	+	+	+	+	-	-
Viola	+	-	+	+	+	+	+	+	+	+
Kay	+	+	+	-	+	+	+	+	-	-
Beth	+	+	+	+	+	+	+	+	+	-
Jeff	-	-	+	+	+	+	+	+	+	-
Ann	+	+	-	-	+	+	+	+	-	+
John	-	-	+	-	+	+	+	+	-	-
Mary	-	-	-	+						
Adam	-	-	-							

"-" = non-emergence; "+" = emergence; names in bold = participants who received additional computer input; blank spaces = absence from elicitation interview.

6.2.3 *Negation constructions with mā and lam and the jussive mood*

The past tense negation construction with *mā* was introduced before negation with *lam*. Recall *mā* is supplied with the perfective form of the verb while *lam* is supplied with the imperfective. The negation construction with *mā* occurred once in the input in week 7 in the expression *mā fahimt* "I did not understand" and was later directly introduced in week 17; *lam* was introduced later in weeks 21-22. Expectedly, this excludes Mary, since she withdrew after week 14. Table 6.6 lists suppliance ratios of *lam* and *mā* in obligatory contexts that required past tense negation. As Table 6.6 shows, the form emerged in only four of the participants' Interlanguage systems (Mark, Viola, Kay, and Ann), with Mark being the first participant to produce the form, and Mark and Viola were the only ones to reach criterion more than once. Furthermore, among all the participants, Mark was the only one to produce the negation particle *lam*; the rest produced only *mā* (see also Table 6.7). Production errors of the negation particles constituted mainly use of the present tense negation particle *lā* instead of *mā* or *lam*.

Table 6.6 Suppliance ratios of the past negation particles *mā* and *lam*

Weeks		8	10	14	16	18	20	22	24	26	27
Mark	*mā*	/	/	/	/	/	(.0)	/	/	**(1.0)**	/
	lam	/	/	/	/	/	/	**(1.0)**	(1.0)	/	/
Viola	*mā*	/	/	/	/	(.0)	(.33)	(.0)	(.50)	**(1.0)**	**(1.0)**
Kay	*mā*	/	/	/	/	/	(.0)	(.33)	(.0)	(.0)	**(.66)**
Beth	*mā*	/	/	/	/	(.0)	(.50)	.75	(.0)	(.0)	/
Jeff	*mā*	/	/	(.0)	(.0)	/	(.0)	(.0)	(.0)	.25	(.0)
Ann	*mā*	/	/	/	(.0)	/	(.0)	(.0)	**(1.0)**	(.0)	(1.0)
John	*mā*	/	/	/	/	/	(.0)	(.0)	(1.0)	(.50)	/
Mary	*mā*	/	/	/	(.0)						
Adam	*mā*	/	/	/							

"( )" = less than 4 tokens; "/" = zero occurrence; figures in bold = reaching emergence criterion; names in bold = participants who received additional computer input; blank spaces = absence from elicitation interview.

As for emergence of the morphological inflection for the jussive mood affixed to the end of the verb following *lam*, there is no indication that the participants, except for Mark, attempted to produce the jussive mood and caution should be used in interpreting the data.[6] Even in Mark's case, Mark being the only one who reached criterion for suppliance of the negation particle *lam* (see Table 6.7), it cannot be concluded that the jussive mood emerged in Mark's Interlanguage system, since he dropped the final ending of the indicative elsewhere (that is, in non-jussive contexts).

Table 6.7 Emergence of past tense negation constructions with *mā* and *lam*

Weeks		8	10	14	16	18	20	22	24	26	27
Mark	*mā*	-	-	-	-	-	-	-	-	+	-
	lam	-	-	-	-	-	-	+	-	-	-
Viola	*mā*	-	-	-	-	-	-	-	-	+	+
	lam	-	-	-	-	-	-	-	-	-	-
Kay	*mā*	-	-	-	-	-	-	-	-	-	+
	lam	-	-	-	-	-	-	-	-	-	-
Beth	*mā*	-	-	-	-	-	-	-	-	-	-
	lam	-	-	-	-	-	-	-	-	-	-
Jeff	*mā*	-	-	-	-	-	-	-	-	-	-
	lam	-	-	-	-	-	-	-	-	-	-
Ann	*mā*	-	-	-	-	-	-	-	+	-	+
	lam	-	-	-	-	-	-	-	-	-	-
John	*mā*	-	-	-	-	-	-	-	-	-	-
	lam	-	-	-	-	-	-	-	-	-	-
Mary	*mā*	-	-	-	-						
	lam	-	-	-							
Adam	*mā*	-	-	-							
	lam	-	-	-							

"-" = non-emergence; "+" = emergence; names in bold = participants who received additional computer input; blank spaces = absence from elicitation interview.

6.2.4 *Negation construction with lan and the subjunctive mood*

The future tense negation construction with *lan* was first introduced in weeks 21-22. Table 6.8 displays the production data of the participants and their suppliance of the future tense negation particle *lan* (see also Table 6.9). Table 6.8 shows that, with the exception of Mary and Adam (who both withdrew long before the form was introduced in the input), suppliance of the future negation particle *lan* emerged in all the Interlanguage systems of the participants within the last four weeks of the study. Production errors of suppliance of the correct negation particle constituted mainly use of the present tense negation particle *lā* or the past negation particle *lam* instead of *lan*.

Table 6.8 Suppliance ratios of the future tense negation particle *lan*

Weeks	8	10	14	16	18	20	22	24	26	27
Mark	/	/	/	/	/	(.0)	(.33)	**(.66)**	**.66**	**1.0**
Viola	/	/	/	/	/	(.0)	(.0)	(.0)	**.75**	**.80**
Kay	/	/	/	/	/	/	(.0)	(.33)	**.80**	**1.0**
Beth	/	/	/	/	/	(.0)	(.0)	(.0)	**1.0**	**.83**
Jeff	/	/	/	/	/	(.0)	(.0)	(.0)	**.83**	(.0)
Ann	/	/	/	/	/	(.0)	/	(.0)	(.0)	**1.0**
John	/	/	/	/	/	(.0)	(.0)	(.0)	**1.0**	**.66**
Mary	/	/	/	/						
Adam	/	/	/							

"( )" = less than 4 tokens; "/" = zero occurrence; figures in bold = reaching emergence criterion; names in bold = participants who received additional computer input; blank spaces = absence from elicitation interview.

Table 6.9 Emergence of future negation construction with *lan*

Weeks	8	10	14	16	18	20	22	24	26	27
Mark	-	-	-	-	-	-	-	+	+	+
Viola	-	-	-	-	-	-	-	-	+	+
Kay	-	-	-	-	-	-	-	-	+	+
Beth	-	-	-	-	-	-	-	-	+	+
Jeff	-	-	-	-	-	-	-	-	+	-
Ann	-	-	-	-	-	-	-	-	-	+
John	-	-	-	-	-	-	-	-	+	+
Mary	-	-	-	-						
Adam	-	-	-							

"-" = non-emergence; "+" = emergence; names in bold = participants who received additional computer input; blank spaces = absence from elicitation interview.

As for emergence of the morphological inflection for the subjunctive mood affixed to the end of the verb following *lan*, which has mainly two different realizations (the final vowel {-*a*} for the singular (first person, third person masculine and feminine and second person masculine) and the final consonant /n/ deletion {-*uu-0*} for the plural (third person masculine and second person masculine) and second person singular feminine), it emerged in only one participant, Mark, who was one of the participants who received additional input on the target form.[7] Table 6.10 displays the production of the subjunctive by the participants in both singular and plural verbal agreement contexts (see also Table 6.11). Tables 6.10-6.11 show that, apart from Mark, none of the participants supplied the subjunctive ending on the singular. Jeff produced it only once, not enough to qualify as an instance of emergence. Given the small number of tokens in which the subjunctive was supplied on the plural verb (hence the figures within brackets) and the fact that the participants did on occasion drop the final plural consonant ending elsewhere (for example, in the indicative) and no one other than Mark produced the subjunctive in the singular, it cannot be concluded that the subjunctive emerged in the participants' Interlanguage systems (including Viola's) other than Mark's—who happened to be one of the three participants who received additional input via computer sessions. In other words, only in Mark's case did emergence of the subjunctive in the singular and the plural take place if caution is to be followed and the data are to be interpreted conservatively.

Table 6.10 Suppliance ratios of the subjunctive mood on the verb following *lan*

Weeks		8	10	14	16	18	20	22	24	26	27
Mark	S	/	/	/	/	/	/	(1.0)	(1.0)	(.50)	**(.66)**
	P	/	/	/	/	/	/	/	/	**(1.0)**	(.0)
Viola	S	/	/	/	/	/	/	/	/	(.0)	(.0)
	P	/	/	/	/	/	/	/	/	(1.0)	(.50)
Kay	S	/	/	/	/	/	/	/	/	(.0)	/
	P	/	/	/	/	/	/	/	/	(1.0)	/
Beth	S	/	/	/	/	/	/	/	/	(.0)	(.0)
	P	/	/	/	/	/	/	/	/	(.0)	(.75)
Jeff	S	/	/	/	/	/	/	/	/	(0.50)	/
	P	/	/	/	/	/	/	/	/	(1.0)	/
Ann	S	/	/	/	/	/	/	/	/	/	(.0)
	P	/	/	/	/	/	/	/	/	/	(1.0)
John	S	/	/	/	/	/	/	/	/	(.0)	(.0)
	P	/	/	/	/	/	/	/	/	(.33)	(.0)
Mary	S	/	/	/	/						
	P	/	/	/	/						
Adam	S	/	/	/							
	P	/	/	/							

"( )" = less than 4 tokens; "/" = zero occurrence; figures in bold = reaching emergence criterion; names in bold = participants who received additional computer input; blank spaces = absence from elicitation interview.

Table 6.11 Emergence of the subjunctive mood on the verb following *lan*

Weeks		8	10	14	16	18	20	22	24	26	27
Mark	S	-	-	-	-	-	-	-	-	-	+
	P	-	-	-	-	-	-	-	-	+	-
Viola	S	-	-	-	-	-	-	-	-	-	-
	P	-	-	-	-	-	-	-	-	-	-
Kay	S	-	-	-	-	-	-	-	-	-	-
	P	-	-	-	-	-	-	-	-	-	-
Beth	S	-	-	-	-	-	-	-	-	-	-
	P	-	-	-	-	-	-	-	-	-	-
Jeff	S	-	-	-	-	-	-	-	-	-	-
	P	-	-	-	-	-	-	-	-	-	-
Ann	S	-	-	-	-	-	-	-	-	-	-
	P	-	-	-	-	-	-	-	-	-	-
John	S	-	-	-	-	-	-	-	-	-	-
	P	-	-	-	-	-	-	-	-	-	-
Mary	S	-	-	-	-						
	P	-	-	-	-						
Adam	S	-	-	-							
	P	-	-	-							

"-" = non-emergence; "+" =emergence; names in bold = participants who received additional computer input; blank spaces = absence from elicitation interview.

6.2.5 *Ɂan construction and the subjunctive mood*

The particle *Ɂan* was introduced in the additional computer sessions in week 19 after being casually introduced in the textbook/classroom input 1-2 weeks earlier (see Tables 6.2 and 6.3). Table 6.12 lists the ratios of *Ɂan* suppliance by the participants. The form emerged in all of the Interlanguage systems of the participants except for two participants, Mary and Adam, who withdrew from the study after the third and fourth elicitation interviews, respectively. Additionally, Tables 6.12 and 6.13 show that suppliance of the particle *Ɂan* emerged in Mark's Interlanguage system the earliest. It was mentioned above in the course of discussing the future negation particle *lan* that it emerged in Mark's Interlanguage system earlier than in the rest of the participants'. Recall, Mark was in a different class. In fact, it turned out that the class which he was in was slightly ahead of the other class. This explains perhaps his non-steady suppliance of the form following its emergence in his Interlanguage system in week 16.

Table 6.12 Suppliance ratios of *ʔan*

Weeks	8	10	14	16	18	20	22	24	26	27
Kay	/	/	/	(.0)	**.80**	**1.0**	**1.0**	**1.0**	**1.0**	**1.0**
Beth	/	(1.0)	/	(1.0)	**1.0**	**1.0**	**1.0**	**.91**	**1.0**	**1.0**
Jeff	/	/	/	/	(.50)	.0	**.80**	**1.0**	**1.0**	**1.0**
Mark	/	/	(1.0)	**(1.0)**	(.0)	.28	.0	.33	(.0)	.0
Viola	/	.0	/	.33	.83	1.0	1.0	1.0	.87	1.0
Ann	/	/	/	(.0)	(.50)	.72	1.0	1.0	1.0	1.0
John	/	/	/	(.0)	.0	**.80**	.33	.77	.75	.77
Mary	/	/	/	(.0)						
Adam	/	/	/							

"( )" = less than 4 tokens; "/" = zero occurrence; figures in bold = reaching emergence criterion; names in bold = participants who received additional computer input; blank spaces = absence from elicitation interview.

Table 6.13 Emergence of the particle *ʔan*

Weeks	8	10	14	16	18	20	22	24	26	27
Kay	-	-	-	-	+	+	+	+	+	+
Beth	-	-	-	-	+	+	+	+	+	+
Jeff	-	-	-	-	-	-	+	+	+	+
Mark	-	-	-	+	-	+	-	+	-	-
Viola	-	-	-	-	-	+	+	+	+	+
Ann	-	-	-	-	-	-	+	+	+	+
John	-	-	-	-	-	+	+	+	+	+
Mary	-	-	-	-						
Adam	-	-	-							

"-" = non-emergence; "+" = emergence; names in bold = participants who received additional computer input; blank spaces = absence from elicitation interview.

The production errors of all the participants with respect to the suppliance of the *ʔan* particle constituted particle omission. The participants may not have been aware of certain verbs, such as *yurīd* "he wants" and *yuḥib* "he likes," subcategorizing for a finite complement clause with *ʔan*.

As for suppliance of the morphological inflection for the subjunctive mood on the verb following *ʔan*, although all the participants (with the exception of the two who withdrew from the study earlier) acquired use of the particle *ʔan*, a few participants reached criterion for the subjunctive mood marking somewhat briefly. Table 6.14 displays the ratios of subjunctive mood suppliance in obligatory contexts in all the weeks in which the interview sessions were held (see also Table 6.15). In particular, three participants each reached criterion once for the singular subjunctive mood ending on the verb following *ʔan*: Kay, Mark, and Ann. Two participants, Jeff and Viola, each reached criterion (twice) for the singular subjunctive mood ending. The other participants (Beth, John, Mary, and Adam) never reached criterion. In addition, only one participant, Viola, reached criterion for the plural subjunctive mood ending.

Table 6.14 Suppliance ratios of the subjunctive mood on the verb following *ʔan*

Weeks		8	10	14	16	18	20	22	24	26	27
Kay	S	/	/	/	/	.0	.11	**.28**	.0	(.33)	.14
	P	/	/	/	/	/	(.0)	(.0)	(1.0)	/	(.0)
Beth	S	/	(.0)	/	(.0)	(.0)	.0	.14	.10	(.0)	.09
	P	/	/	/	/	(.0)	(.50)	(.0)	(.0)	(.0)	(1.0)
Jeff	S	/	/	/	/	/	/	**.33**	**.55**	.0	.12
	P	/	/	/	/	(.0)	/	(.0)	(1.0)	(1.0)	/
Mark	S	/	/	/	(1.0)	/	**(1.0)**	/	/	/	/
	P	/	/	/	(1.0)	/	/	/	(.0)	/	/
Viola	S	/	/	/	(.50)	/	.36	.33	.0	.0	.0
	P	/	/	/	/	(.0)	(.50)	(1.0)	(1.0)	(.0)	**(1.0)**
Ann	S	/	/	/	/	(.0)	**.25**	.08	.12	.25	.10
	P	/	/	/	/	/	/	/	/	/	(1.0)
John	S	/	/	/	/	/	.0	(.0)	.0	(.0)	.12
	P	/	/	/	/	/	/	/	/	(.0)	(.0)
Mary	S	/	/	/	/						
	P	/	/	/	/						
Adam	S	/	/	/							
	P	/	/	/							

"( )" = less than 4 tokens; "/" = zero occurrence; figures in bold = reaching emergence criterion; names in bold = participants who received additional computer input; blank spaces = absence from elicitation interview.

Table 6.15 Emergence of the subjunctive mood ending on the verb following *ʔan*

Weeks		8	10	14	16	18	20	22	24	26	27
Kay	S	-	-	-	-	-	-	+	-	-	-
	P	-	-	-	-	-	-	-	-	-	-
Beth	S	-	-	-	-	-	-	-	-	-	-
	P	-	-	-	-	-	-	-	-	-	-
Jeff	S	-	-	-	-	-	-	+	+	-	-
	P	-	-	-	-	-	-	-	-	-	-
Mark	S	-	-	-	-	-	+	-	-	-	-
	P	-	-	-	-	-	-	-	-	-	-
Viola	S	-	-	-	-	-	+	+	-	-	-
	P	-	-	-	-	-	-	-	-	-	+
Ann	S	-	-	-	-	-	+	-	-	-	-
	P	-	-	-	-	-	-	-	-	-	-
John	S	-	-	-	-	-	-	-	-	-	-
	P	-	-	-	-	-	-	-	-	-	-
Mary	S	-	-	-	-						
	P	-	-	-	-						
Adam	S	-	-	-							
	P	-	-	-							

"-" = non-emergence; "+" = emergence; names in bold = participants who received additional computer input; blank spaces = absence from elicitation interview.

6.2.6 *Case within kāna and laysa constructions*

The accusative case (affixed on the predicative adjective/noun of *kāna* and *laysa*) was not presented directly in the classroom input, although it was occasionally present (especially in the case of *kāna*) since *kāna* and *laysa* were first introduced in weeks 11-14 and 15-16 and weeks 17-18 and 21-22, respectively (see Table 6.2 above). However, input of the computer sessions of both forms aimed at focusing directly on the use and function of *kāna* (and verbal agreement) as well as on the accusative case of the predicate of *kāna* and *laysa* during weeks 19-27; that is, from week 19 until the end of the period of the observation (see Table 6.3 above).[8] The results show that in all of the data sets gathered there was only one occurrence of rule application of suppliance of the accusative case on the predicate of *kāna*. The single token of the accusative case on the predicate of *kāna* was produced by Kay in week 9, cited below as (25).

(25) IL: *ʔal-tˤaqs   *kān-ū   mušmis-**an**
          the-weather.s.m   be.perf-3.p.m sunny.s.m-**acc**
      TL: ʔal-tˤaqs   kāna   mušmis-**an**
          the-weather.s.m   be.perf.3.s.m sunny.s.m-**acc**
      "The weather was sunny."

This single instance does not, of course, qualify for emergence. In fact, this instance is a reproduction of one of the sentences that occurred in the computer treatment lessons. Additionally, the copular *kāna* is not accurately inflected for number as indicated by the ungrammaticality of the sentence.

One possible explanation for the non-emergence of the accusative case (affixed on the predicative adjective/noun of *kāna* and *laysa*) is that agreement has not *fully* emerged with respect to number and gender between *kāna/laysa* and the predicative adjective/noun—a prerequisite for accusative case suppliance. These morphological agreement inflections are hierarchical in nature, since inserting the proper case suffix presupposes figuring out the proper gender and number marking. Tables 6.16-6.17 reveal the low ratios of gender and number agreement in both cases between *kāna/laysa* and the predicate element, especially in the plural feminine and masculine (of most participants) and to a lesser extent the singular feminine. The high ratios of singular masculine agreement suggest that the participants probably used the singular masculine as the default form. The figures to the left of the slash are the total number of correct agreement tokens, while those to the right are the total number of all contexts. (Note Mary's and Adam's data are omitted due to the low number of tokens, since the two participants discontinued participating after week 14.)

Table 6.16 Gender and number agreement ratios between the subject and predicate of *kāna*

	S.M	%	S.F	%	P.M	%	P.F	%
Mark	28/28	100	0/3	(0)	3/17	18	0/4	0
Viola	27/28	96	3/4	75	2/15	13	0/3	(0)
Kay	31/32	97	7/8	87	4/15	27	0/4	0
Beth	29/31	93	6/6	100	0/14	0	0/4	0
Jeff	27/28	96	1/4	25	0/14	0	0/5	0
Ann	23/26	88	4/5	80	7/11	64	0/4	0
John	28/28	100	2/4	50	0/13	0	0/5	0

Total of rule application/Total of all contexts; names in bold = participants who received additional computer input.

Table 6.17 Gender and number agreement ratios between the subject and predicate of *laysa*

	S.M	%	S.F	%	P.M	%	P.F	%
Kay	11/13	84	4/19	21	3/7	43	/	
Beth	17/17	100	5/5	100	5/11	45	0/2	(0)
Jeff	21/23	91	11/17	65	1/4	25	0/1	(0)
Mark	21/21	100	2/4	50	1/9	11	/	
Viola	15/16	94	6/6	100	4/11	36	/	
Ann	12/12	100	7/8	87	4/7	57	/	
John	8/10	80	3/5	60	3/12	25	/	

Total of rule application/Total of all contexts; names in bold = participants who received additional computer input.

As Tables 6.16-6.17 show, agreement mismatches are the highest in the plural feminine and plural masculine. Production of feminine plural is even absent in most cases, especially in Table 6.17. Examples (26)-(28) below show the types of gender and number mismatches made.

(26)   IL: *?al-bināy-a   lays-at   kabīr
           the-building-**s.f**   not-**3.s.f**   big.**s.m**
       TL: ?al-bināy-a(t-u)   lays-at   kabīr-at-an
           the-building-**s.f**-nom   not-**3.sf**   big-**s.f-acc**
           "The building is not big."
           (Kay: Interview 10)

(27)   IL: *?al-ban-āt kān-at   saʕīd-a
           the-girl-**p.f** be.perf-**3.s.f** happy-**s.f**
       TL: ?al-ban-āt(-u)   kun-na   saʕīd-āt-in
           the-girl-**p.f**-nom   be.perf-**3.p.f** happy-**p.f-acc**
           "The girls were happy."
           (Mark: Interview 10)

(28)   IL: *hum   lays-at   zaʕlān-ūn wa lays-at   saʕīd-a
           they.**p.m**   not-**3.s.f** sad-**p.m**   and not-**3.s.f** happy-**3.s.f**
       TL: hum   lays-ū   zaʕlān-īn wa lays-ū   saʕīd-īn
           they.**p.m**   not-**3.p.m** sad-**p.m.acc** and not-**3.p.m** happy-**3.p.m.acc**
           "They are not sad and not happy."
           (Jeff: Interview 10)

As illustrated in the above examples, case (especially the accusative) endings differ across different agreement patterns. Thus before producing the case endings {-*an*} for singular masculine/feminine, {-*in*} for plural feminine, and {-*īn*} for masculine (sound) plural, the proper gender and number agreement between *kāna*/*laysa* and the predicate element needs to be produced. One might expect that one form or another of case ending is overgeneralized across all agreement patterns, but this does not take place even in the Interlanguage systems of the participants who received the additional computer sessions input. Upon close examination of the data, we find that until the last interview (Interview 10, week 27), the participants were still struggling with gender and number agreement, as the examples above suggest. Hence this is perhaps why there is a total absence of accusative ending suppliance on the predicate of *kāna*/*laysa* except for the single instance cited above.

6.3   Summary

The data reveal the following findings with respect to negation constructions with *lā*, *mā*, *lam*, and *lan*: 1) emergence of *lā* took place from early on and in all except one of the participants, exhibiting a somewhat steady pattern throughout the period of the observation; 2) emergence of *mā* occurred in only four of the participants' Interlanguage systems, only two reaching criterion more than once; 3) emergence of *lam* could not be confirmed in the participants, since only one participant produced the negation particle *lam* only once; and 4) emergence of *lan* occurred in all the participants within the last four weeks of the study. As for emergence of the morphological inflection of mood on the verbs following the negation particles, there is no indication that the participants exhibited use of the indicative mood inflection affixed to the end of the verb following *lā* or the jussive inflection affixed to the verb following *lam*, but there is evidence that the subjunctive mood inflection on the verb following *lan* emerged in only one participant. As for the *ʔan* construction, it emerged in the Interlanguage systems of the participants (except for two who withdrew at an early stage), but only a few participants reached criterion briefly for the subjunctive mood on the verb following *ʔan*. Finally, the accusative case inflection (affixed on the predicative adjective/noun of *kāna* and *laysa*) did not emerge in the Interlanguage systems of the participants; only one occurrence of suppliance of the accusative case inflection on the predicate of *kāna* was found. Finally, a general observation is that the participants who received additional input on the target forms (via the computer sessions) did consistently better than the other participants.

CHAPTER 7

Theoretical Implications

This chapter relates the findings reported on in the foregoing chapters (3-6) to the most recent second language acquisition (SLA) models and hypotheses as well as to central issues to do with language learnability and processability, L1 transfer, Universal Grammar (UG) access, and ultimate attainment. The chapter discusses in specific ways how the findings contribute to cross-linguistic evidence on these issues.

7.1 L2 Learnability and Processability

One of the most recent well-formulated attempts at explaining learnability/teachability and processability of second language grammatical development is Processability Theory (PT), formulated by Pienemann (1998). Although the PT model is claimed to account for syntactic phenomena as well as morphological and morphosyntactic features, due to the scope of the data here, focus is on the latter (for a complete account of PT, see Pienemann 1998; Pienemann and Håkansson 1999).

The PT model relies on the main assumption that speech production is by nature constrained in that working memory is a "limited capacity" processor of information. Therefore, additional "memory buffers" are posited in which "processing procedures" deposit grammatical information for temporary storage (Pienemann1998:60). The processing procedures, following Levelt (1989) and Kempen and Hoenkamp (1987), are further posited to operate hierarchically in an implicational order. From an L2 perspective, these procedures are considered to be language-specific; hence the L2er would have to create such language-specific prerequisites necessary for L2 grammatical development.

In concrete L2 terms, the model claims that the L2er cannot initially process L2 grammatical structures, since the L2er is not immediately able to code conceptual information (the initial stage of speech production) into L2 syntactic structure for two reasons: first, the lexicon is not fully annotated; second, even if the lexical annotation were transferred into L2, the syntactic procedures "have not specialized to hold the specific L2 syntactic information" in the proposed memory buffers (Pienemann 1998:76). The extent of this specialization is claimed to be the principle or "core" mechanism of L2 processability (Pienemann and Håkansson 1999:384).

The assumption of specialization or of holding grammatical information in temporary memory buffers is explained in terms of the specific morpheme types held. Three such morphemes are identified: lexical morphemes, phrasal (that is, "phrasal" as in phrase structure à la Lexical Functional Grammar, or LFG) morphemes, and inter-phrasal morphemes.[1] These are assumed to be processable by the L2er along five distinct stages in an implicational set sequence as follows:

Stage 1   Absence of any language-specific procedures where words are entered into the lexicon and conceptual structures are simply mapped into individual words and fixed phrases

Stage 2   Development of "category procedures" where grammatical categories (that is, S,V, N, etc.) are assigned and "lexical morphemes" (for example, the {-ed} tense marker in English) are produced; these morphemes can be activated and realized in the same location once grammatical categories are assigned

Stage 3   Development of "phrasal procedures" where development from word level to phrase level becomes possible and "phrasal morphemes" are produced (that is, lexical morphemes, such as tense, number, gender, and case markers when unified between a head of a phrase and its modifier/s)

Stage 4   Development of "S-procedures" where "Inter-phrasal morphemes," involving exchange of information across phrases, are developed (for example, S-V agreement features); here, functional destinations are determined and sentences assembled

Stage 5   Development of "S'-procedures" where subordinate/embedded clauses are developed (Pienemann 1998:83-85)

The hierarchical stages of processing procedures is illustrated in Table 7.1. The implicational nature of the above hierarchy "derives from the assumption that the processing resources developed at one stage are necessary prerequisites for the following stage" (Pienemann 1998:87). Hence, the claim that "stages cannot be skipped [even] through formal instruction" (Pienemann 1998:250). Skipping a stage is hypothesized to cause the hierarchy to be "cut off in the learner grammar at the point of the missing processing procedure and that the rest of the hierarchy will be

replaced by a direct mapping of conceptual structures onto surface form"
(Pienemann and Håkansson 1999:391; also Pienemann 1998:250).

Table 7.1 PT hierarchy of implicational sequence of speech processing procedures

| Procedures | Developmental Stages | | | | |
	T1	T2	T3	T4	T5
S'-procedure	-	-	-	-	+
S-procedures/Inter-phrasal procedures	-	-	-	+	+
Phrasal procedures	-	-	+	+	+
Category procedures	-	+	+	+	+
Word or lemma access	+	+	+	+	+

"T" = time/stage, "+" = emergence, "-" = non-emergence.

In addition to the PT mechanism claim, two main claims with respect
to learnability/teachability of grammatical structures are introduced, as
stated in (1)-(2).

1. Stages cannot be skipped [even] through formal instruction.
2. Instruction will be beneficial if it focuses on structures from the next stage
   (Pienemann 1998:250).[2]

Pienemann (1998) further qualifies claim (2) as "optimistic" and that "there
is no reason to assume that learners will acquire a structure just because they
can process it; [a] functional need would have to be present for the structure
to emerge" (1998:250).[3]

Given the nature of the longitudinal data reported on in chapters 3 and
6, being formal and classroom-based, both the processability and
teachability/learnability claims of PT can be examined. Recall, the data
reported on in chapters 3 and 6 include nominal (N-A) agreement, verbal
(S-V) agreement, negation and mood markings on the verb following
negation particles, ʔan construction and mood marking on the verb
following ʔan, and case within laysa and kāna (in particular the accusative
case on the predicate of laysa and kāna) constructions. Table 7.2 lists the
structures that are most relevant and obvious in terms of their findings for
examining PT claims according to their hypothesized stages of emergence à
la PT.

Table 7.2

Processing Prerequisites	Arabic L2 Structures	Stage
Inter-phrasal procedures	-Verbal (S-V) agreement	4
	-Subjunctive mood on the verb following ʔan	4
	-Case on the predicate of kāna/laysa	4
Phrasal procedures	-Nominal (N-A) agreement	3

To illustrate the points of comparison between stage 3 and stage 4 structures listed in Table 7.2 and the types of agreement procedures involved, figures 7.1-7.3 offer examples with simplified constituent structures (c-structures) of the four forms à la LFG.[4] Figure 7.1 illustrates

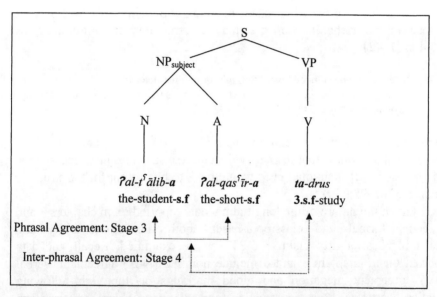

Figure 7.1 Simplified c-structure of "The short (female) student studies/is studying," illustrating phrasal and inter-phrasal agreement.

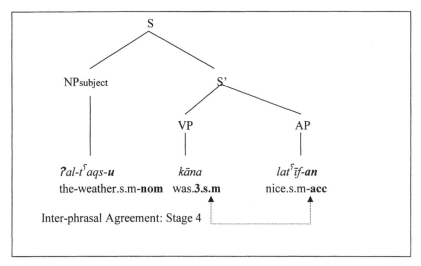

Figure 7.2 Simplified c-structure of "The weather was nice,"
illustrating inter-phrasal agreement.

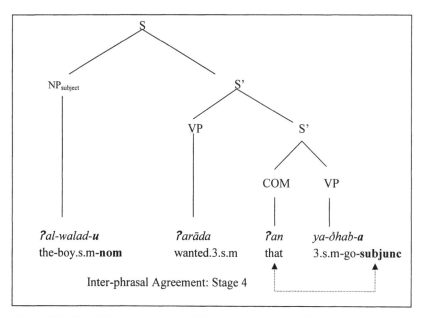

Figure 7.3 Simplified c-structure of "The boy wanted to go,"
illustrating inter-phrasal agreement.

two types of agreement: nominal agreement at the phrasal level (claimed by PT to be processable at stage 3) between the head noun agreeing with the attributive adjective in gender and number (that is, singular feminine) and verbal agreement at the inter-phrasal level (claimed by PT to be processable at stage 4) between the subject NP and the verb agreeing in person, gender, and number (that is, third person singular feminine). Figure 7.2 illustrates the exchange of grammatical information for the accusative case (between the copular verb and the predicate constituent of the sentence) at the inter-phrasal level (claimed to be processable at stage 4). Figure 7.3 illustrates the exchange of grammatical information for the subjunctive mood on the verb between *ʔan* and the verb and the structural position of *ʔan* as a complementizer of the finite complement clause (subcategorized for by the verb *ʔarāda*) at the inter-phrasal level (claimed to be processable at stage 4).

With respect to nominal (N-A) and verbal (S-V) agreement, illustrated in Figure 7.1, and based on the emergence criterion, the findings reported on in Chapter 3 (Table 3.2) show that six out of the nine participants were able to process N-A agreement after S-V agreement. If PT predictions were correct, one would expect all participants to instead be able to process N-A agreement before S-V agreement—the former is hypothesized to emerge at stage 3 and the latter at stage 4. Using a 90 percent correct acquisition criterion, the data nonetheless reveal similar, converging evidence where the majority of the participants acquired S-V agreement before N-A agreement (see Tables 3.4-3.5, Chapter 3). The findings are particularly strong, since N-A agreement was present in the formal input of the participants before S-V agreement (Table 3.3, Chapter 3); yet, the participants found N-A agreement more problematic than S-V agreement. Hence, the findings clearly show that the hypothesized notion of speech processing prerequisites constraining stages of acquisition, particularly claim (1) above that stages cannot be skipped through formal instruction, is untenable.[5]

Another finding that is problematic for PT claims can be found in the data reported on in Chapter 6, in particular the data (from the same participants reported on in Chapter 3) to do with production of the subjunctive mood on the verb following *ʔan* (claimed to be processable at stage 4) and of the accusative case on the predicate of *kāna/laysa* (claimed to be processable at stage 4). Recall that the data reveal that while the latter structure emerged in none of the participants, the former emerged in six of the Interlanguage systems of the participants, at least once in four participants, and twice in two (see Tables 6.14-6.15, Chapter 6).[6] Thus, the problem posed for PT is how is it that the participants acquired S-V agreement but did not acquire the accusative case marking on the predicate of *kāna/laysa*. According to PT, the participants were ready to process other forms processable at the same stage as that of S-V agreement (stage 4), yet the participants did not, even though additional instruction was provided that nevertheless proved to be non-beneficial.[7] Perhaps it can be reasonably explained from the PT perspective that, following the PT claim (2) above, there was no apparent functional need for the participants to process the form. However, this argument would not explain the finding that some of the participants were able to acquire the subjunctive mood marking on the verb following *ʔan* (stage 4), yet none acquired the accusative case on the predicate of *kāna/laysa* (stage 4). It is not clear how one can argue for a functional need behind producing the subjunctive mood marking on the verb following *ʔan*, which is affixed for none other than structural accuracy considerations.[8] Thus, the findings of the data reported on in Chapters 3 and 6 pose problems for both of PT's claims that: 1) stages cannot be skipped [even] through formal instruction and 2) instruction will be beneficial if it focuses on structures from the next stage.[9] In fact, other language factors such as L1 transfer may be at play, as discussed in the next section.[10]

7.2   L1 Transfer and UG Access

A better account for the findings may be provided by L1 transfer, a factor not acknowledged by PT. Three accounts of L1 transfer within Principles and Parameters (Generative framework) have been proposed in the past two decades. Vainikka and Young-Scholten (1994, 1996, 1998) propose the "Minimal Tree Hypothesis" which posits that L2ers already have access to lexical categories and that functional projections develop upon exposure to L2 input in successive stages: a VP stage, an under-specified functional projection (FP) stage, an AGR stage, and a CP stage, in this order.[11] Eubank (1993/1994, 1996) proposes the "Valueless Feature Hypothesis," or what others (Schwartz and Sprouse 1996) refer to as the "Weak Transfer Hypothesis." Eubank proposes that both lexical and functional categories and the linear orientation of the L1 grammar transfer in L2 acquisition but that the feature values (strength) associated with functional categories do not. Schwartz and Sprouse (1994, 1996) and

Schwartz (1998) propose a stronger version of L1 transfer, "The Full Transfer/Full Access Hypothesis," disagreeing with both proposals by suggesting that the entirety of L1 grammar, including lexical categories, functional categories, and feature values associated with functional categories (excluding the phonetic matrices of lexical/morphological items), is available to L2ers from the early stages of L2 acquisition; restructuring (or approximation of the L2 system) takes place upon exposure to input of the target language and that obscurity in input leads to fossilization.[12]

The data reported on here, in particular on N-A and S-V agreement, suggest that of the three hypotheses, the Full Transfer/Full Access proposal seems to provide the most adequate explanation. Thus unlike PT and the other transfer accounts, the implication of the Full Transfer/Full Access Hypothesis is that L2ers need not wait until they are able to develop category procedures and then develop agreement procedures as, for example, PT assumes. Further, L2ers have access to abstract knowledge of inflection (associated with functional categories) and feature checking mechanism (for example, Chomsky 1995) available in L1 and therefore the L2ers somehow *know* to check for a certain feature (if present in L1) in L2 (see also Lardiere 1998, 2000, who argues that due to L1 transfer, the L2ers know to look for functional categories present in L1).

Thus, with respect to N-A agreement, we would predict, based on the Full Transfer/Full Access account, that L2ers who are speakers of an L1 that does not exhibit the feature gender would find nominal agreement in Arabic more problematic than L2ers who are speakers of an L1 that exhibits the feature gender. Recall, eight of the nine longitudinal participants were English L1 speakers, while one was a French L1 speaker, resulting in the following typological constellation (3)-(4):

(3) Eight American English participants who are speakers of a [-gender] and
     [-strong] L1, learning a [+gender] and [+strong] L2
(4) One French participant who is a speaker of a [+gender] and
     [+strong] L1, learning a [+gender] and [+ strong][13] L2

The findings show that six of the eight English L1 speakers acquired S-V agreement earlier than they did N-A agreement, finding the latter form more problematic, whereas the data of the French L1 speaker (Adam) did not show that he necessarily found N-A agreement more problematic than S-V agreement; he acquired neither form prior to his early withdrawal after the third data set.[14] Similarly, the data of the demonstrative-predicate gender agreement (of the same longitudinal participants, see Chapter 3) show that the majority of participants found demonstrative-predicate agreement more problematic than S-V agreement.

This is further supported by the cross-sectional data of nominal and verbal agreement reported on in Chapter 3. Recall, the cross-sectional data were gathered from English L1, French L1, and Japanese L1 participants. With respect to nominal agreement, both the English L1 and Japanese L1 participants belonged to typological constellation (3) and the French L1 to (4) listed above. The data reveal that the French L1 participants performed significantly better than both their English L1 and Japanese L1 counterparts. In particular, the first year French L1 participants (Group 1) performed better than any of the three English L1 groups (that is, Groups 1-3) as well as better than the first and third year Japanese L1 groups (that is, Groups 1 and 3) on singular feminine (see Table 3.15, Chapter 3). The first year English L1 participants (Group 1) performed only slightly better on singular feminine than their Japanese L1 counterparts (Group 1) and the third English L1 participants (Group 3) outperformed their Japanese L1 counterparts (Group 3). This finding is yielded despite the difference in duration of exposure to input evident in Table 3.13, Chapter 3 (that is, whereas the duration of exposure is somewhat comparable between the English L1 and French L1 participants, the Japanese L1 participants had almost double the amount of instruction time per week).

In addition, performance of the same cross-sectional participants on correct natural versus grammatical gender agreement markings provide similarly consistent findings. Not unlike the difference in performance between singular feminine N-A agreement and singular masculine N-A agreement, a similar statistically significant distinction between the production of grammatical and natural gender was found. The French L1 groups outperformed their English L1 and Japanese L1 counterpart groups, especially with respect to nominal grammatical gender involving N-A agreement (see Table 3.16, Chapter 3). Here, too, the finding is yielded despite the difference in duration of exposure to input evident in Table 3.13, Chapter 3 (that is, whereas the duration of exposure is somewhat comparable between the English L1 and French L1 participants, the Japanese L1 participants had almost double the amount of instruction time per week). The French L1 groups outperformed their English L1 and Japanese L1 counterparts on correct rule application of N-A agreement involving grammatical gender, except for the Japanese L1 Group 2 which slightly outperformed its French L1 counterpart (Group 2) and more so its English L1 counterpart (Group 2).

The conclusion drawn here is that the English L1 and Japanese L1 participants seemed to have more problems with singular feminine agreement than their French L1 counterparts, since they made more significant errors in singular feminine (by undergenerating the feminine agreement suffix) than they did in singular masculine. Absence or presence of the φ-feature gender seems to have a role in L2 grammatical development. Thus, the Full Transfer/Full Access Hypothesis as discussed above can provide a better account of the N-A agreement data than PT, which allows for no role for L1 transfer.

Furthermore, performance of the same cross-sectional participants on demonstrative-predicate and verbal agreement provides further support of the L1 transfer account adopted here. Most significantly, the French L1 groups (Groups 1 and 3) outperformed their English L1 and Japanese L1 counterparts with respect to feminine demonstrative agreement. The beginning French L1 group (that is, Group 1) alone outperformed any of the English L1 or Japanese L1 groups. This finding is yielded despite two observations to do with the type and duration of input which the participants received, in particular Group 1. First, the French L1 participants received a far less focused input for the demonstrative agreement structure (see Table 3.24, Chapter 3; cf. Tables 3.23-3.25, Chapter 3) than their English L1 and Japanese L1 counterparts. Second, although the duration of exposure to input is somewhat comparable between the English L1 and French L1 participants, the Japanese L1 participants had almost double the amount of instruction time per week (see Table 3.13, Chapter 3). Yet, the French L1 participants outperformed both. The Japanese L1 groups had higher correct ratios than their English L1 counterparts, but this is perhaps understandable considering the significantly higher amount of instruction time the Japanese L1 groups received.[15] Thus, it is clear that the French L1 participants (most evidently in Group 1) demonstrate L1 transfer. They seem ready to check demonstrative-predicate agreement for the feature gender more readily than, in particular, their English L1 counterparts.

As for S-V agreement, we would expect (according to the L1 transfer account advanced above) L2ers who are speakers of an L1 that does not exhibit the feature gender in verbal agreement to find verbal agreement in Arabic more problematic than L2ers who are speakers of an L1 that exhibits the feature gender. We would also expect no difference in performance among speakers of L1s that do not exhibit the feature gender. We would expect this effect in the data, since none of the L1s (English, French, and Japanese) of the cross-sectional participants exhibits the gender feature in verbal agreement.[16] In fact, this is borne out by the data. Recall that no statistically significant difference in performance on S-V agreement was found in the three L1 groups (Section 3.2.1, Chapter 3). In other words, neither singular masculine verbal agreement nor singular feminine verbal agreement was found to contribute to L1 group difference.

However, a residual, seemingly problematic aspect of the data (as mentioned in the concluding paragraph of the previous section) remains. Although the three L1s of the participants do not exhibit the ϕ-feature gender in verbal agreement, there is a somewhat qualitative difference between the three languages with respect to verbal agreement. While Japanese exhibits zero verbal agreement, both French and English exhibit S-V agreement features albeit the latter (being restricted to {-s} for third person singular and {-0} elsewhere) has a verbal agreement paradigm that is more impoverished than the former. As discussed above and although the findings reveal no statistically significant difference in the performance of the three L1 groups, some slight differences were found (see Table 3.14, Chapter 3). Recall, the French L1 groups somewhat outperformed their English L1 and Japanese L1 counterparts in producing the appropriate verbal agreement markings for singular feminine and singular masculine in almost all groups; the English L1 participants slightly outperformed their Japanese L1 counterparts in their performance on feminine S-V agreement with respect to Group 1 and Group 3 and in their performance on masculine S-V agreement with respect to Group 3. However, since no statistically significant effect was found, the issue remains with respect to presence or absence of the feature verbal agreement altogether and the lack of significant difference in the performance of the French L1 and English L1 on the one hand and that of the Japanese L1 on the other. This issue will be returned to in Section 7.4 (below) discussing the Split-INFL hypothesis.

7.3   Ultimate Attainment and Near Nativeness

Related to the role of L1 transfer is the exact status of access to UG in L2 grammatical development and the exact status of L2 competence or ultimate attainment. In other words, this area of investigation aims at explaining the observed difference in attainment between L1 and L2, an area reminiscent of Krashen's (1977, 1985) acquisition-learning hypothesis of his Monitor model. Due to the widely observed difference in ultimate attainment between L1 and L2, the term "near nativeness" has gained more currency recently (see also Sorace 2003). Three main theoretical proposals, speculating on the nature of ultimate attainment in L2, have been advanced. The Local Impairment Hypothesis assumes that functional projections are attainable in L2 but that features associated with functional heads are permanently impaired (or 'inert') irrespective of L1 (Beck 1997, 1998; Eubank et al. 1997; Eubank and Beck 1998). Accordingly, no transfer of (abstract) feature strength from L1 takes place. The Failed Functional Features Hypothesis claims that the Interlanguage system of the L2er, specifically that of the functional feature system, is constrained by what is available in L1 and, therefore, permanently impaired depending on the nature of the L1 system (Hawkins and Chan 1997; Hawkins 1998, 2001). It is further maintained that UG is partially unavailable in L2 and that beyond the critical period, the features associated with functional categories (except those already encoded for specific lexical items) become permanently fixed and therefore become inaccessible for modification (or for resetting of parameters). The Missing Surface Inflection Hypothesis claims that the feature system is temporarily impaired at the morphophonological (surface) level due to complexity in mapping between surface forms and underlying abstract features and that the presence or absence of a feature in L1 is irrelevant (Lardiere 1998, 2000; Prévost and White 2000; De Garavito and White 2002). The nature of impairment according to this proposal depends on the L2 learner figuring out the mapping complexity and spelling it out properly. This proposal is in line with other UG access proposals such as the Full Transfer/Full Access model (Schwartz and Sprouse 1994, 1996).

Given the varied typological constellations of the participants, the Arabic L2 production data reported on here can be used to confirm or disconfirm the specific claims made by these hypotheses. According to the Local Impairment Hypothesis, agreement features are assumed to be permanently impaired in L2 regardless of the status of L1. Although "syntactic" S-V agreement is excluded as a locus of potential impairment, N-A agreement is not (Beck 1998). This allows us to test the Local Impairment Hypothesis' claim on N-A agreement based on the cross-sectional data reported on in Chapter 3. In order for the prediction of the Local Impairment Hypothesis to be confirmed, the performance of the participants would have to exhibit greater variability in agreement inflection on nouns and adjectives in the Interlanguage systems of all three L1 participants: English L1, French L1, and Japanese L1. This prediction is not borne out by the findings, especially those of the French L1 participants. Recall, N-A agreement in the Interlanguage systems of the French L1 participants shows highly consistent correct rule application (Tables 3.15-3.16, Chapter 3, especially Group 3).

As for the Failed Functional Features Hypothesis, the findings confirm one prediction but disconfirm another. On one hand, the data confirm the prediction that L2ers whose L1 systems exhibit functional feature specifications similar to those of the L2 will approximate quite closely to the L2 system as exposure to L2 increases. This is evident in the performance of the French L2ers who outperformed their English L1 and Japanese L1 counterparts in almost all groups, although this prediction does not seem to follow from an a priori explanation, since the assumption is that functional features associated with functional categories which determine parametric differences between languages become inaccessible to modification beyond the critical period. In other words, although Hawkins (2001) acknowledges that it is possible that certain values associated with functional categories can be acquired in L2 (but others cannot), this does not follow from an a priori explanation as to why this is so and no explanation is provided. On the other hand, the findings disconfirm the prediction of the Failed Functional Features Hypothesis that L2ers, faced with a different feature specification in L2, will not achieve a performance level similar to that of native speakers. There is nothing to suggest that impairment is permanent in this case, since the English L1 participants in particular continued to show improvement with increased exposure to both N-A and S-V agreement. In fact, some of them even attained 100 percent correct rule application, as evident in Figure 7.4 illustrating the performance of Group 3 of both the English L1 and French L1 participants for both singular feminine N-A agreement and singular feminine S-V agreement. As Figure 7.4 shows, at least one English L1 participant had a 100 percent correct ratio in singular feminine N-A agreement and as many as three had a 100 percent correct ratio in singular feminine S-V agreement (as opposed to three and two participants, respectively, in the French group). Moreover, Participant 1 had 100 percent correct ratios in both forms; so did the French L1

Participant 1. This observation suggests that even full attainment in L2 is possible (see also Alhaway 2005).

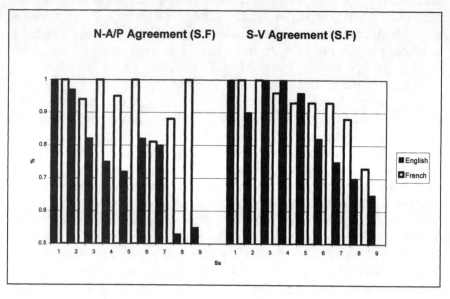

Figure 7.4

Further support for the conclusion reached here, contrary to the predictions made by the Local Impairment and Failed Functional Features hypotheses, is provided in the findings of noun-adjective word placement within Arabic DPs of the same cross-sectional participants (see Table 3.18, Chapter 3). The participants of all three L1s (English, French, and Japanese) were able to acquire the strong inflection feature that licenses N raising; hence the almost 100 percent correct ratios for noun-adjective word order placement across and within all groups.[17] This finding is problematic for the Local Impairment Hypothesis, which would otherwise predict greater variability (or optionality) in noun-adjective word order in all groups. The finding is similarly problematic for the Failed Functional Features Hypothesis, since the English L1 and Japanese L1 participants were able to reset feature strength to [+strong] for their Arabic L2 although neither L1 shares the same feature specification with that of Arabic (for similar treatment and crosslinguistic evidence for resetting the nominal feature strength and word order in L2, see also White 2003:133-135).

Thus, contrary to the predictions made by the Local Impairment and Failed Functional Features hypotheses, the findings seem to show no serious impairment in the ability of the L2ers to acquire functional categories and functional features, including the ability to reset feature strength. Further, in principle, there is no reason to assume that the L2ers are not capable of achieving full grammatical attainment/competence in L2.

As for the Missing Surface Inflection Hypothesis, the findings are only partially in support of the predictions. According to the Missing Surface Inflection Hypothesis: 1) temporary impairment is due to a problem of mapping underlying abstract features onto surface forms resulting from complexity of form-function relationship and communication demands and 2) absence or presence of feature inflection, in this case gender, from L1 is irrelevant. The mapping problem indeed may be a contributing factor in L2 development when it comes to forms that exhibit a complex form-function relationship such as accusative case realization on the predicate of *kāna* and *laysa*. Thus, according to the notion of mapping complexity that De Garavito and White (2002) rely on, following Lardiere (2000) and Beard (1995), and upon triggering the computational feature checking mechanism, two sets of algorithms must proceed for the production of the proper case ending on the predicate of *kāna* and *laysa*. The first is an algorithm of mapping syntax to morphology, as in (5); the second is an algorithm of mapping morphological category of the accusative case to phonological form (PF) based on classes of nouns/adjectives, number and gender, as in (6).[18]

(5)   Iff predicate of *kāna* and *laysa*, then Accusative
(6)   Iff accusative
        a.   singular, suffix {-an}
        b.   sound plural masculine, suffix {-īn}
        c.   sound plural feminine, suffix {-in}

In order to produce case properly, the Arabic L2er needs to figure out these two types of mapping. Recall from Chapter 6, the participants did not even produce the singular form of the accusative case (on singular nouns and adjectives) in the entire data sets of the longitudinal participants, except only once by one of the participants (Kay).

However, relying on the mapping complexity as a factor alone does not provide a satisfactory explanation of the findings for N-A agreement. The findings suggest that the absence or presence of a feature in L1, contrary to the Missing Surface Inflection Hypothesis, does contribute to group difference (Chapter 3). In the case of the Arabic target forms and in the absence of any complexity of mapping gender agreement feature onto surface forms, the L1 [-gender] English and L1 [-gender] Japanese participants still had a problem producing gender agreement (mainly singular feminine in noun-adjective agreement) while the L1 [+Gender] French participants did not. This is quite likely, in light of the distinction between gender agreement in the Arabic target forms and that in the Spanish target forms of De Garavito and White's (2002) study. In fact, De Garavito and White (2002) acknowledge that the generalization of the endings {-0} and {-a} as masculine and feminine gender markers, respectively, is misleading in Spanish and insufficient to account for many other obscure cases. For example, there are some feminine nouns that end with {-o}, numerous and common masculine nouns that end with {-a}, and many (invariant) adjectives that lack overt gender agreement. Following Harris (1991), De Garavito and White consider these endings as word markers rather than gender markers; hence justifying, and perhaps correctly so, their attributing the problems of their participants with respect to nominal gender agreement to the mapping problem. Such observations indeed suggest that the input relating to gender agreement in Spanish DPs which the participants of De Garavito and White's study received is in fact obscure. Under the Full Transfer/Full Access model (Schwartz and Sprouse 1994, 1996), in the event input is obscure, problems of gender agreement are predicted to occur.

However, by contrast, the longitudinal as well as the cross-sectional participants (the English L1, the French L1, and the Japanese L1), as discussed in Chapter 3, received a clearer, more transparent input where the gender agreement is to a large extent regular (in Modern Standard Arabic). In the vast majority of cases, N-A agreement for singular feminine is achieved by attaching the suffix {-a} in word final (salient) position on both nouns and adjectives, resulting in a rhyming effect that can serve as a phonological clue to the Arabic L2er. For singular masculine, agreement is realized as zero {-0}, the stem form being the default masculine form (see also Sections 1.1.2 and 1.2.1, Chapter 1). As stated above, a statistically significant difference in performance on rule application of singular feminine gender agreement was found between the French L1 participants on one hand and the English L1 and Japanese L1 participants on the other. Accordingly, under the Full Transfer/Full Access model (Schwartz and Sprouse 1994, 1996), with the additional assumption that if abstract features associated with functional categories (not the surface, phonetic matrices of lexical/morphological items) transfer to L2 in the sense that the L2er knows to check for the feature if available in L1, then surface problems of gender agreement may result. Hence, the distinct difference in the performance of the French L1 participants on one hand and the English L1 and Japanese L1 participants on the other; the latter encountered significantly more problems with nominal gender agreement than the former.

Thus, the findings here are essentially in support of the Missing Surface Inflection Hypothesis with respect to the source of impairment as long as the hypothesis reflects the essential view of the Full Transfer/Full Access model with respect to the nature of the input. In the case of obscure input or forms involving a complex mapping between abstract underlying features and surface forms, then a mapping problem can be suspected as a contributing factor for problems with surface forms. However, in the case of transparent input, it would be unwarranted to assume that problems with surface forms are due to a (mapping) problem that does not exist. Absence or presence of a feature in L1 does seem to be relevant, at least in light of the findings presented here. As for the nature of the impairment (that is, the temporary notion), the findings seem to be in support of this assumption. According to the findings, close approximation and attainment of L2 is possible; hence the continued improvement of all English L1, Japanese L1, and French L1 participants with increased proficiency.

7.4   The Split-INFL Hypothesis: More on L1 Transfer

In modifying and refining the Minimalist Program (as the current version of Generative grammatical theory), Chomsky (1995, 1998, 1999, 2001) abandoned earlier proposals of the Split-INFL Hypothesis (Pollock 1989) and Agr-based theory of clause structure (Chomsky 1991, 1993) and adopted instead a single INFL projection "Tense Phrase" (TP) within which Agreement, Case, and the Extended Projection Principle feature of "Tense" (T) are checked. This is illustrated in (7)-(8) where (8) now replaces (7).

(7)   [AgrsP NP$_i$ Agrs [TP [VP t$_i$ V ...]]]

(8)   [TP NP$_i$ T [vP t$_i$ v [VP ...]]]

Findings reported in the L1 acquisition literature, for example, on German, French, and English, seem to suggest that tense develops before agreement properties (for a detailed review of such studies, see Griffin 2003; Alhawary 2007a). Accordingly, TP and "Agreement Phrase" (AGRP) seem to be independent projections. Chomsky's current reformulation would, therefore, inaccurately predict that tense and agreement properties are developed simultaneously (see also Griffin 2003).

L2 acquisition findings are less clear with respect to emergence of tense and agreement. Most such findings were presented in the morpheme order studies of the 1970s. Although such studies suffer from a number of methodological limitations, as pointed out in the literature, the findings seem to suggest that emergence of tense (regular and irregular past) and the third singular {-s} S-V agreement suffix seem to cluster together at a later stage, with respect to other morphemes. The exact ordering of emergence of tense and agreement in those studies is mixed, including: 1) emergence of both tense and agreement at the same time (for example, Krashen 1977), 2) emergence of tense before agreement (for example, Anderson 1978; Bailey et al. 1974), and 3) emergence of either regular past tense then agreement followed by irregular past tense or irregular past tense then agreement followed by regular past tense (for example, Larsen-Freeman 1975; see also Zobl and Liceras 1994). A more recent study on L2 German, based on one participant (José) from the ZISA project (Meisel et al. 1981), reveals that S-V agreement and tense emerged at around the same stage (Eubank 1992). Most other L2 acquisition studies examine emergence of tense and aspect and do not include any comparative findings with respect to emergence of tense and S-V agreement.

Recall, the data reported on in chapter 4 offer findings on this exact phenomenon: emergence of tense and agreement. The data were gathered from Arabic L2ers who are English L1, Spanish L1, and Japanese L1 speakers with the typological constellations illustrated in (9)-(11).

(9) Spanish participants who are speakers of a [+ Tense], [+AGR], and [+strong][19] L1, learning a [+Tense], [+AGR], and [+strong] L2

(10) English participants who are speakers of a [+ Tense], [+AGR], and [-strong] L1, learning a [+Tense], [+AGR], and [+strong] L2

(11) Japanese participants who are speakers of a [+Tense], [-AGR], and [-strong] L1, learning a [+Tense], [+AGR], and [+ strong] L2

With these three types of typological constellation, it is also possible to control for L1 transfer.

As discussed in Chapter 4, although the findings reveal L1 effects among the three L1 groups, no significant proficiency effect with respect to performance on both forms between each of the Spanish L1 and Japanese L1 groups was found. As for the English L1 groups, a near effect for verbal agreement in the present tense (with no such effect for verbal agreement in the past tense) was found based on the narrative tasks. However, given the artifact to do with the narrative tasks, it was decided that the (present) random tasks would be a better predictor of participants' performance. The random task revealed no proficiency effect between the Spanish and Japanese L1 groups, suggesting that both forms had the same developmental paths in the Interlanguage systems of these participants. However, the random task revealed a significant proficiency effect for (present) tense and a near significant effect for verbal agreement, suggesting performance on verbal agreement was lagging slightly behind that of tense. Two types of conclusions can be drawn here. A literal interpretation of the data suggests that the findings provide mixed evidence: whereas the Spanish L1 and Japanese L1 data provide evidence that the Split-INFL view may be untenable, the English L1 data are in support of the Split-INFL proposal, suggesting that the two target forms had two developmental routes in the Interlanguage systems of the English L1 participants alone (as suggested in Alhawary 2007b). A more cautious interpretation of the data may suggest that the difference in performance between verbal agreement and tense is minimal and does not justify the conclusion that the two forms were developing along two separate paths; therefore, the entire data of the three L1 backgrounds seem to suggest that both feature properties of AGR and Tense develop within a single functional projection/node.

Given the nature of the target verb stem and agreement and tense features, one may tend to lean on the latter conclusion. Perhaps a contributing factor to the findings is due in part to the nature of the target forms examined and the participants' hypothesizing that both features of verbal agreement and tense are conflated together within the verbal agreement morphological features without paying attention to the nature of the verb stem at the root-vocalic melody level in the past versus the present. This may be the only remaining, subtle clue to tease apart from agreement and tense features, as illustrated in the distinction between *darasa* "he studied" and *ya-drusu* "he studies" (see also Figure 1.1, Chapter 1). The participants do not seem to be aware of the distinction based on their production data.[20] More Arabic SLA research needs to be conducted to explore this factor either experimentally or observationally similar to Badry's (2005) study on Arabic L1.

To conclude this section, a final discussion of L1 transfer is in order. The findings discussed above may be surprising, since all three L1s of the participants exhibit tense but only two of them (English and Spanish) additionally exhibit verbal agreement. In particular, it may be surprising that the Spanish L1 participants underperformed their Japanese L1 and English L1 counterparts on verbal agreement given the typological constellations of the participants: Spanish exhibits verbal agreement and tense while Japanese exhibits only tense and no verbal agreement. However, there are many reasons for confounding L1 transfer effects. First, as discussed above, the nature of the target forms may have led the participants to hypothesize that both features of verbal agreement and tense are conflated together without paying attention to the nature of the verb stem at the root-vocalic melody. On this account, and since Japanese also exhibits the feature tense, the Japanese L1 participants knew to check for the feature tense in Arabic whenever they needed to produce a verb, generating high ratios of correct tense and concomitantly verbal agreement features. Second, there is a significant difference in the duration of exposure to input (Table 4.1, Chapter 4), with the Japanese L1 groups having almost double the instructional time of their English L1 and Spanish L1 counterparts. This may well have contributed to the Japanese L1 groups outperforming their English L1 and Spanish L1 counterparts; hence the statistically significant effects found for L1. However, this still leaves unanswered the question of why the English L1 participants outperformed their Spanish L1 counterparts even though both L1s exhibit tense and verbal agreement features and both groups had comparable exposure time. Upon examining the formal input (the textbooks of the participants of all three L1 backgrounds), we find a qualitative difference with respect to the input of verbal agreement. Thus, although the textbooks used by the Spanish L1 (Al-Khalifa 1999, 2002), Japanese L1 (Brustad et al. 1995, 1995b; Badawi el al. 1983, 1992), and the English L1 (Abboud et al. 1983, 1997) participants all focus on form from early on, of the three only the English and Japanese textbooks recycle verbal agreement rigorously throughout, whereas the textbook used by the Spanish L1 participants hardly recycles verbal agreement. This may very well explain the difference in performance by the three L1 groups. In fact, the observation that the Spanish L1 participants underperformed on verbal agreement is further supported by their use of null subjects, dropping significantly fewer subjects than their English L1 and Japanese L1 counterparts, resulting in an obvious correlation between their low scores on verbal agreement and low scores on subject dropping (see Chapter 5). This will be further discussed in the next section. Finally, perhaps L1 transfer with respect to tense and verbal agreement can be better explained in future studies with different typological constellations that include L1s that exhibit rich morphological agreement inflections (including gender) and L1s that lack both tense and verbal agreement.

7.5   Null Subjects and Setting of Parameters: More on UG Access and L1 Transfer

The null subject phenomenon has received perhaps the most extensive investigations in second (and first) language acquisition. In particular, the main questions that have preoccupied second language researchers (within the Principles and Parameters framework) include setting the null subject parameter, access to UG, and L1 transfer. Research conducted on these issues produced mixed results that can be summarized as follows (for a detailed review, see Sauter 2002; Alhawary 2007a):

• Studies provided mixed evidence with respect to the association between development of verbal inflection and null subjects.
• Studies produced mixed evidence that L2ers can reset the parameter in L2.
• Studies generally show evidence that adult speakers of null subject and non-null subject languages learning a null subject language produce subjectless clauses from early on. Conversely, speakers of null subject and non-null subject languages learning a non-null subject language do supply overt subjects from early on.
• Studies generally seem to provide evidence in support of L1 transfer. This comes from at least three main directions. First, speakers of null subject languages learning null subject languages produce null subject clauses and seem to adjust to the L2 system from early on. Second, speakers of null subject languages learning non-null subject languages (for example, English and German) still produce some subjectless clauses even though they seem to adjust to the system of L2 from early on. Third, speakers of non-null subject languages learning non-null subject languages noticeably reject more subjectless clauses (on grammaticality judgment tasks) than speakers of null subject languages learning non-null subject languages.

Although many such studies relied on data from participants of many different L1s (including both null subject and non-null subject languages), an additional observation of the research literature is that the research mainly focused on three languages as L2s: English [-null], German [-null], and Spanish [+ null]. The data reported on in Chapter 5 contribute to the debate by investigating a fourth language (Arabic) as an L2.[21] Furthermore, the data are gathered from speakers of three different L1s, resulting in the typological constellation (12)-(14).

(12) Spanish participants who are speakers of a [+null] and [+strong] L1, learning a [+null] and [+ strong] L2

(13) Japanese participants who are speakers of a [+null] and [-strong] L1, learning a [+null] and [+ strong] L2

(14) English participants who are speakers of a [-null] and [-strong] L1, learning a [+null] and [+strong] L2

The data reported in Chapter 5 have significant implications for the three main issues of the null subject phenomenon. Recall, the data show that the English L1 and Japanese L1 groups dropped significantly more subjects than their Spanish L1 counterparts. However, the data also reveal that the English L1 and Japanese L1 groups significantly produced more correct verbal (S-V) agreement tokens in null subject contexts than their Spanish L1 counterparts.[22] Thus, the data reveal a close correlation between the production of subjectless clauses and verbal agreement. While the English L1 and Japanese L1 groups produced a good number of subjectless clauses, and from the beginning stage of L2 development (through Group 1), the Spanish L1 group produced far fewer sentences with null subjects and with much lower ratios of correct subject agreement. However, with more exposure to Arabic L2 input during later L2 development, the Spanish L1 groups (2-3) exhibited an increase in both correct verbal agreement ratios and null subject production.

Thus, the data offer strong evidence for a contingent relationship between the development of null subjects and the development of verbal agreement morphology. This is primarily manifest in the Spanish L1 data and evident in the close correlation found between their use of null subjects and that of verbal agreement. This contributes to the general body of cross-linguistic evidence found in the field.

The data also provide evidence that all three L1 participants seem to have managed to set the parameter value to [+null] and to have managed to adjust to the grammar of null subjects in Arabic from early on, although the participants do not seem to have made the adjustment equally readily across groups. The Spanish L1 participants, who are speakers of a null subject language, did not seem to adjust to the Arabic L2 system as readily as their Japanese L1 counterparts, who are similarly speakers of a null subject language, nor did they seem to adjust as well as the English L1 participants, who are speakers of a non-null subject language. This is mostly evident in (the Spanish L1) Group 1 who dropped the subjects in 55 out of the 200 null subject contexts (see Table 5.3, Chapter 5). Yet, the number of tokens where the subjects were dropped shows that the Spanish L1 participants adjusted to the Arabic L2 system, albeit rather conservatively. However, this finding is in line with cross-linguistic evidence where speakers of null subject (and non-null subject) languages do produce overt subjects from early on.

Finally, the data can be argued to concomitantly provide evidence for L1 transfer based on the performance of the Japanese L1 and Spanish L1 participants, both of whose L1s are null subject languages. Two observations to do with the English L1 and Spanish L1 data may seem to be problematic for an L1 transfer argument. First, the Spanish L1 participants seemed to exhibit L1 transfer rather conservatively, since they were speakers of a null subject language learning a null subject language. Second, the English L1 participants, who were speakers of a non-null subject language learning a null subject language, mostly produced subjectless clauses. However, these observations are not necessarily problematic for an L1 transfer role.

First, with respect to the English L1 observation, it is evident from the data that the English L1 participants were able from early on to figure out from the input that Arabic allows null subjects. Indeed, null subject use is prevalent in the input (Abboud et al. 1983, 1997). The participants also seem to have established an association between verbal agreement and null subjects as evident in the correlation between their high scores on both null subjects and verbal agreement from an early stage of their Arabic L2 acquisition. Accordingly, all they had to do was pay attention to verbal inflection and simply drop the subject. Two additional factors may make this task easy for them. First, Arabic exhibits a functional projection similar to their own language, albeit verb raising in Arabic occurs overtly rather than covertly (as in English) at Logical Form (LF): feature strength in Arabic is

[+strong]. Second, subjects occur in a perceptually salient position within word order (see also Slobin 1973; Corder 1978).[23] Additionally, the English L1 participants did indeed produce many contexts with overt subjects.

As for the Spanish L1 participants, we can speculate, at least, on two likely scenarios to help explain the conservative production of null subjects, particularly those at the beginner level (Group 1). One possibility is that the Spanish L1 participants may have used (pronominal) subjects as a processing strategy to gain time to retrieve the verb form with the proper agreement inflections (see Liceras et al. 1997 for a similar explanation); hence their conservative dropping of subjects. However, a more plausible scenario is that it may be the case that the Spanish L1 participants figured out the null subject feature of Arabic and preferred not to drop the subjects, since they did not master Arabic verbal agreement, as evident in the low ratios of verbal agreement (see Chapters 5-6), and therefore wanted to ensure the recoverability of the content of subjects simply by not dropping them.

Thus, although a strong argument cannot be made for an L1 transfer role in the cases of the English L1 and Spanish L1 data on null subjects, the findings are not necessarily contradictory to L1 transfer. The explanation provided here remains sketchy, since null subjects investigated in this study included only third person singular masculine and feminine, both of which are not marked differently in Spanish. Future research should include other forms in the verbal agreement paradigm and should also examine the use of overt pronominal subjects in embedded clauses. Additionally, since a period of three years of formal instruction, such as that of Group 3, is not sufficient to attain a near-native status, future research should include participants at higher advanced levels to examine the near-native status of the null subject parameter in such L2ers (see Sorace 2003).

7.6   Summary and Areas of Future Research

The data reported on in the foregoing chapters are significantly relevant to a number of models, proposals, and central issues in recent and current second language acquisition research. The data (reported on in Chapters 3 and 6) show that the Processability Theory (Pienemann 1998) proposal of speech process prerequisites constraining L2 grammatical development along a set implicational sequence is untenable and does not provide an adequate account of the data based on many target structures and different L1 speakers. Rather, the role of L1 transfer, not acknowledged within Processability Theory, seems to have a significant role. In particular, the Full Transfer/Full Access Hypothesis (Schwartz and Sprouse 1994, 1996; Schwartz 1998) seems to provide the most satisfactory L1 account for the data. The proposal holds that the entirety of L1 grammar, including lexical categories, functional categories, and feature values associated with functional categories (excluding the phonetic matrices of lexical/ morphological items), is available to L2ers from the early stages of L2 acquisition; restructuring (or approximation of the L2 system) takes place upon exposure to input of the target language and that obscurity in input leads to fossilization. Since full indirect (through L1) access to UG is posited, no permanent impairment is assumed in L1 competence. The data indeed provide further evidence that since some cases are found where participants were able to achieve 100 percent ratios of rule application on grammatical forms, there is no reason to assume that L1 grammatical development is permanently impaired. Accordingly, the data show that the Missing Surface Form Hypothesis (for example, De Garavito and White 2002), which is essentially derived from the Full Transfer/Full Access Hypothesis, is similarly sound in its assumption of the nature of ultimate attainment. However, while the mapping complexity between underlying abstract forms and surface structures does play a role, presence or absence of a feature in L1 can also play a role contrary to what is assumed, especially when no case of a mapping problem or complexity can be made. In addition, the data (reported on in Chapter 4) seem to indicate that Chomsky's collapsing AGR and T features into one projection TP may be warranted against a Split-INFL proposal, at least in L2, and based on the data, since the overwhelming results seem to indicate that acquisition of verbal agreement and tense are developmentally related and seem to proceed along the same developmental route. Finally, the data (reported on in Chapter 5) contribute to the cross-linguistic body of evidence on the null subject phenomenon: that there seems to be a close correlation between development of null subjects and development of verbal agreement inflection, that L2ers can reset the null subjects parameter in L2, that L2ers who are speakers of null subject and non-null subject languages learning a null subject language produce subjectless clauses from early on, and that although a strong case for L1 transfer cannot be made, the findings do not necessarily contradict the role of L1 transfer.

CHAPTER 8

Pedagogical and Applied Implications

This chapter aims at explaining implications and suggesting practical applications of the findings in a number of subfields of Arabic applied linguistics, including Arabic curriculum design, Arabic foreign language teaching pedagogy, teacher preparation, and Arabic proficiency testing. Such areas can be informed by Arabic SLA data through knowledge of acquisition tendencies, especially time and pattern of emergence of the structures investigated, and other factors that may contribute to L2 acquisition. The chapter will first discuss what information the data reported on here can generally offer in the way of Arabic acquisition tendencies and emergence patterns and then identify who can benefit from such data.

8.1 Acquisition Tendencies of the Target Structures

As a general rule, an observational conclusion about the emergence and acquisition of a form should be made only when and after it has been introduced and maintained steadily in the input beyond its occasional introduction once or twice. Thus, for example, a conclusion of late or non-emergence of a form should not be drawn if the form has been introduced late in the input or introduced only once or twice. For such a conclusion about emergence and acquisition to be warranted, the form should be introduced from early on in the period of the observation and maintain reasonable presence in the input. The observations made about the target forms here are based on this rationale. With respect to longitudinal data, the form must additionally exhibit emergence at many times (that is, in different data sets), following Brown's (1973) Continuity Principle.[1]

8.1.1 *Gender of nouns*

From observation of the present data, nouns inflected for both masculine and feminine gender are prevalent in the input and from early on. Based on the findings with respect to gender in nouns, we can speculate that

English L1 (longitudinal and cross-sectional), French L1 , and Japanese L1 learners of Arabic are likely to produce the gender feature {-a} on almost all nouns correctly (as reported in Chapter 3), suggesting that they are able to acquire the masculine-feminine gender distinction on nouns throughout and from early on. The (cross-sectional) participants produced a small number of tokens in all the data sets where nouns were inflected for the wrong gender (see section 3.2.2.2, Chapter 3). It is possible that the participants of the present study may have learned and produced nouns initially based on instance learning of the stem noun and inflection together as a monomorphemic chunk as is usually the case at the initial stage of L2 acquisition. However, the conclusion remains that all such learners are likely to acquire nouns inflected with the proper gender ending from early on.

8.1.2 *Gender of adjectives*
Provided that adjectives (inflected for the masculine and feminine gender, especially those following head nouns within NPs) are available and maintained in the input from early on, French L1 speakers are likely to acquire the form early on and exhibit mostly correct use. As for English L1 and Japanese L1 speakers, they are likely to make significant errors in their production of adjectives even until a later stage (third year) of learning and even though the form is available and prevalent in the input. The other observation is that they are likely to produce adjectives correctly inflected for the proper gender with naturally gendered nouns sooner than they will produce correctly inflected adjectives following nouns inflected for grammatical gender.

8.1.3 *Gender of demonstrative pronouns*
Not unlike the observation of gender on adjectives, French L1 learners of Arabic are likely to demonstrate significant correct use of demonstrative pronouns, whereas English L1 learners of Arabic are likely to make noticeable errors in their production of demonstrative pronouns even until a later stage of learning (well into the third year) even though the form is available and prevalent in the input. Japanese L1 speakers are likely to exhibit the same pattern as English L1 speakers but the former may make noticeably fewer errors with probably double the instruction time and input (as data of the Japanese L1 participants here seem to demonstrate). The additional observation with respect to the French L1 participants is that even

though demonstrative gender agreement was scarcely present in the input, they outperformed their English L1 and Japanese L1 counterparts, likely due to other factors such as L1 transfer (as discussed in Chapter 7).

8.1.4 *Verbal agreement*

Provided that verbal (S-V) agreement is present and maintained in the input throughout, English, French, and Japanese L2ers of Arabic are likely to improve their performance with length of exposure and may exhibit more feminine than masculine agreement errors in their production of S-V agreement beyond the early stage of exposure. Furthermore, learners with the same L1s may not exhibit differences in performance among themselves. However, if the form is not maintained throughout in the input, such learners are likely to exhibit significant errors (as is the case with the Spanish L1 participants here).

8.1.5 *Tense (past and present)*

Performance of English, Spanish, and Japanese L2ers of Arabic on tense is likely to exhibit the same pattern as that of verbal agreement. Such learners are likely to improve their performance with length of exposure without exhibiting significant differences in errors between the past and the present tense. Ability to narrate within past and present tense frames is expected to improve equally among all these learners with more time and exposure to the target language.

8.1.6 *Negation*

Four negation constructions were observed (in the longitudinal participants reported on in Chapter 6) resulting in different acquisition tendencies. Negation of the present tense with *lā* is likely to be readily acquired by English L1 speakers when it is presented in the input and upon introducing the present tense. Recall, it was introduced and maintained in the input consistently.

Negation of the past tense with *mā* by the English L1 speakers emerged occasionally and at the end of the first year of observation. It emerged in both participants who received additional input and in only one who received classroom input alone. It was presented in classroom input after the past tense but was not maintained in the input consistently thereafter; the past tense was presented towards the middle of the year of the observation. Therefore, no observational generalization can be made about *mā* here.

Negation with *lam*, as another optional rule of the past tense, emerged in only one L2er who received additional input one month after negation with *mā* was introduced. The former was presented briefly in the classroom input. As in the case of *mā*, no generalization can be made about *lam* due to limitations of the formal input and its later introduction in the input.

Negation of the future tense with *lan* is likely to be readily acquired by English L1 speakers, as it emerged in all the participants in the last two weeks of the observation. Recall, it was introduced in the input towards the end of the observation and was only presented occasionally after the future tense was introduced.

Based on the above observations, the developmental stages of negation that are yielded here are: *lā* → *mā* → *lan* → *lam*, somewhat resembling Al-Buanain's (1986) conclusion based on her cross-sectional data: *lā* → *lam* → *lan*. Of course, this conclusion is mostly constrained by the teaching schedule of these negation particles in the instructional materials, with only *lam* violating the order. However, this finding indicates that the negation construction with *lam* may be more problematic (for the English L1 speakers) than the other negation constructions, as it involves more than the mere suppliance of the negation particle. [2]

8.1.7 *Case and mood*

As discussed above, the accusative case inflected on the predicate of *laysa* and *kāna* did not emerge in the English L1 participants, suggesting that perhaps the participants were not developmentally ready for the form in question given the instruction time allowed (six hours a week). Although case was occasionally included in the classroom input, it was not a target of direct instruction—not even once during the year-long observation. Although three participants received additional input with a focused attempt to teach the accusative case of the predicate of *laysa* and *kāna*, the form emerged in none of the participants' Interlanguage systems. [3] However, additional measures indicate that the participants did notice the form but adopted avoidance strategies to not produce it, since they were probably not developmentally ready for the complex form (see Alhawary 1999).

As for the indicative, jussive, and subjunctive mood, only the subjunctive mood inflected on the verb following the negation particle *lan* and the complementizer *ʔan* exhibited emergence in the Interlanguage systems of the participants. The subjunctive mood inflection did not assume a steady emergence pattern, having emerged briefly in only one participant with *lan* and in five participants with *ʔan*. However, the formal classroom input of both contexts differed significantly. The *ʔan* construction and associated mood marking on the verb following it were presented a month earlier—than the future negation with *lan* and its associated mood marking on the verb following it—and was maintained throughout the input. In addition, the single case of emergence of the mood marking on the verb following *lan* occurred in a participant who received the additional computer session input.[4] Thus, unlike the situation with case ending (associated with the predicate of *laysa* and *kāna*), not all the participants avoided producing the subjunctive mood. In fact, some participants readily acquired the subjunctive mood ending and produced it on occasion. Hence, emergence of mood seems to be closely related to the role of input (to be discussed in the next section).

8.2   Other Contributing Acquisition Factors

Based on the present data, in addition to the role of L1 transfer discussed in the previous chapter, two other factors seem to be significant: input and motivation. The role of input is the more evident of the two, as the foregoing discussion suggests.[5] Maintaining a form in input beyond its direct or casual introduction is significant for acquisition beyond occasional occurrences of emergence. This is evident in the acquisition data of negation structures and mood endings. Although they do not have any functional necessity and their use is restricted to linguistic accuracy, mood endings inflected on verbs following *lan* and *ʔan* emerged in some L2ers (as opposed to other mood markings) primarily due to their somewhat sustained presence in the input (see Chapter 6).[6] One would similarly expect that the participants would not have performed as well as they did on nominal gender agreement and verbal agreement, for example, had these forms not been present and maintained in the input throughout (see Table 3.3, Chapter 3). This is equally evident in the data of the Spanish L1 participants who, even though their L1 exhibits verbal agreement that is likely to transfer to L2, seemed to encounter problems with verbal agreement due to the obvious lack of recycling of the form in their textbook (Chapters 4-5).

As for the role of motivation, although it is not apparent anywhere here, it should not be ignored. A full account of Arabic SLA must also take into account the role of motivation and other external factors (for example, age, aptitude, attitude, anxiety, motivation, learning environment, social distance, ethnicity, etc.) that are still not possible to quantify although they do play a role in L2 acquisition (see, Pienemann and Johnston 1987). The role of motivation has been detected in some of the English L1 and French L1 cross-sectional participants (Chapter 3). In fact, the participants who scored 100 percent correct in singular feminine nominal and verbal agreement seemed particularly motivated to learn Arabic, as indicated in an interview with the teachers of the participants who stated that those particular participants seemed more motivated about learning Arabic than their classmates and fellow participants.

8.3   Who Can Benefit from the Findings

8.3.1 *Syllabus construction: scheduling learning objectives*

Knowing acquisition tendencies and emergence patterns helps the textbook writer in more effectively achieving two main objectives, among others: scheduling the learning objectives of forms (for example, what and when) and recycling forms in the input. In particular, forms that are basic, such as nominal agreement, which may be problematic for certain Arabic L2ers (such as English L1 and Japanese L1 learners), should be introduced as early as possible in the input for such learners and should also be recycled continuously in the input for a considerable amount of time.[7] Forms that do not seem to be particularly complex, such as the various negation particles, should also be introduced as soon as their prerequisite forms (that is, in this case, the various relevant tenses) are introduced.[8] As the data reveal, recycling such forms in the input is also necessary for acquisition (not just emergence) of such forms, as evident in the acquisition of the present tense negation with *lā* versus past tense negation with *mā*, where the former was acquired more readily, probably since it was more consistently recycled than the latter (see Tables 6.4-6.7; cf. Table 6.2, Chapter 6). On the other hand, forms that are too complex due to form-function relationships may not be beneficial to introduce and focus on from early on as L2ers may not be developmentally ready to acquire or produce such forms, and as a result L2ers may adopt avoidance strategies to not produce the forms altogether. In this case, instruction time would be wasted and the L2er discouraged. This is true, for example, for case associated with *laysa* and *kāna* constructions. However, once introduced, such forms should receive a substantial amount of recycling in the input and different types of activities to enhance awareness of forms in the input (see Sharwood Smith 1981, 1991).

8.3.2 *Arabic foreign language pedagogy and teacher preparation*

Implications for syllabus design are equally useful for the classroom teacher, especially the novice one. In particular, knowledge of acquisition tendencies and emergence patterns, among other things, equips the teacher with informed expectations in the classroom. In particular, knowing the specific roles of language learning factors such as L1 transfer can prepare the teacher to adopt strategies and design and implement effective techniques for reinforcing textbook input and offering effective feedback and error correction. Thus, by knowing that English and Japanese L2ers of Arabic may encounter problems with, for example, gender agreement well into the third year of learning, the teacher can realize the need to adopt tolerance strategies for learners' errors. These include effective and innovative ways of error correction rather than the direct error correction method that may lead to frustration in both teacher and learner since such errors are most likely to persist in such learners. Additionally, the teacher can understand the need to reinforce classroom input by incorporating additional drills and activities on gender agreement to supplement textbook input that falls short of recycling the form consistently or to raise the learner's consciousness about gender or other features (for more on grammatical consciousness raising and input enhancement, see, for example, Sharwood Smith (1981, 1991)). Finally, knowing that the highest performance is achieved by highly motivated learners, the teacher can also aim for the highest levels of learner success by nourishing and nurturing learners' motivation and maintaining such motivation throughout the different proficiency levels.

8.3.3 *Foreign language proficiency testing*

Similarly, Arabic SLA findings can inform Arabic second language testing in both training novice testers and refining rubrics within proficiency levels. In fact, the rubrics of the levels of the current ACTFL scale (ACTFL 1999) contain general and vague descriptors in referring to grammatical elements, such as the following (cited from ACTFL 1999; see also ACTFL 1989):

Novice High:

- First language may influence ... syntax

Intermediate Low:

- Syntax ... strongly influenced by first language

Intermediate Mid:

- Difficulty manipulating time and aspect
- Inaccuracies in grammar and/or syntax ... but understood by sympathetic interlocutors

Intermediate High:

- With some consistency can narrate and describe in major time frames (past, present, and future)
- Failure to maintain the narration or description syntactically

Advanced Low:

- Ability to narrate and describe in all major time frames
- Control of aspect may be lacking
- Sufficient accuracy ... can be understood by native speakers unaccustomed to dealing with non-natives

Advanced Mid:

- Good control of aspect
- Much accuracy

Advanced High:

- An imperfect grasp of some forms

Superior:

- virtually no pattern of error in the use of basic structures
- sporadic errors, particularly in low-frequency ... and in some complex high-frequency structures

There are at least three main issues with such vague descriptors. First, no specific grammatical structures are identified to help the interviewer determine the level of the interviewee, placing emphasis primarily on functions. Apart from the two terms referring to tense (or "major time frames") and "aspect," no other specific grammatical features are stated. Second, the descriptors seem to treat the notion of "complexity (such as the case for the superior level) and problematic structures as being static and level-specific irrespective of L2 acquisition factors." The tester here is left to decide, based on what seems intuitive from the tester's point of view, what "basic" and what "complex" mean.[9] However, specifying problematic structures based on SLA findings such as those of the present study can help avoid interviewer confusion and misidentifying of the correct level of the interviewee. Thus, beyond Novice High and Intermediate Low levels, rubrics of other levels do not acknowledge the role of L1 transfer, contrary to the data of the present study. Recall that the study shows that due to L1 transfer, English L1 learners (and others learners with similar L1s) of Arabic are likely to find gender agreement in nominal constructions more problematic than learners whose L1s exhibit gender agreement, perhaps even as their proficiency level comes close to Intermediate High or Advanced Low—as they are finishing their third year of language study. Accordingly, current ACTFL rubrics may need to be refined to acknowledge that certain learners, such as English and Japanese speakers, may make more errors than usually expected at such levels. Testers can then be cautioned to take into consideration other rubrics of the level before rushing to judgment in determining the level of the examinee. Third, isolating tense and aspect in Arabic (indicating that L2ers develop control of tense at Advanced Low whereas they develop control of aspect at Advanced Mid) may not be warranted (pending further future research), since tense and aspect seem to be conflated in Arabic and seem to develop along the same developmental path, along with verbal agreement, as indicated in Chapter 4 (for a similar proposal to refine the ACTFL rubrics, see Spinner 2007). These are just some of the areas where Arabic SLA research can contribute significantly to Arabic proficiency testing.[10]

8.4 Summary and Areas of Future Research

The foregoing discussion is meant to give some brief ideas as to how findings of Arabic SLA data can contribute to a range of subfields in Arabic applied linguistics, such as Arabic curriculum design, Arabic foreign language pedagogy, teacher preparation, and Arabic proficiency testing. The present chapter has been written in the spirit of encouraging research in Arabic SLA, as it remains an underinvestigated area in Arabic linguistics. More research needs to be done to continue to contribute to our knowledge of how the Arabic language is acquired by different L1 speakers. More longitudinal studies are needed, especially those that are conducted for longer than one year. More data are also needed of Arabic L2ers at higher proficiency levels (that is, beyond the first three years), including L2ers at the four to six year levels. Finally, such studies should also consider not only the same target forms investigated here but also other inflectional members of the agreement paradigms as well as other structures. Other typological constellations should also be considered, such as Russian and Chinese speakers learning Arabic as an L2 as well as heritage learners.

Notes

Chapter 1. Description of Target Morphosyntactic Structures

[1] This feminine suffix {-a} is exhibited only in the pause form in MSA. The corresponding feminine suffix in CA is {-ah}. The final /h/ consonant seems to have disappeared diachronically. However, when an additional suffix is added, such as case or the dual, then a final consonant {-t} surfaces. This is true for both CA and MSA, as in *ʔinsān-a-t-āni* "two female human beings." This phenomenon is not exhibited in the masculine form, as in *ʔinsān-āni* "two male human beings."

[2] Note that words ending in {-āʔ}, such as *māʔ* "water" and *dāʔ* "disease," are masculine, because the two segment sounds {-āʔ} are part of their trilateral roots and only one consonant would be left if they were dropped.

[3] Note that the equivalent and synonymous terms *kūb* "cup" and *bayt* "house" are treated as masculine.

[4] Some body parts do not end in a feminine ending, yet they are treated as feminine. The general rule is that a body part that has a pair is treated as feminine. For example, *yad* "hand," *qadam* "foot," *sin* "tooth," and *ʕayn* "eye" all behave as feminine words, since each is one of two identical body parts. In contrast, *raʔs* "head," *lisān* "tongue," *ðˤahr* "back," and *batˤn* "abdomen" all behave as masculine (see also Barakāt 1988). There are a few exceptions, such as *ħādʒib* "eyebrow," *manxar* "nostril," and *xadd* "cheek." What is important here is that body parts (as well as color adjectives) are usually either presented late in the curriculum (for example, Brustad et al. 1995b:334, 339) or, if presented earlier in the curriculum, the gender marking and the underlying rule are not presented. For this reason, gender of body parts (and color adjectives) are understandably not included in the research findings presented in this book.

[5] It should be noted that in CA, when adjectives belonging to such patterns are used as nouns and when the gender of the referent is not possible to ascertain from context, then the rule is to supply the feminine {-a} suffix, as in *raʔaytu dʒarīħ-a* "I saw a wounded female" (Al-Ghalayyīnī 2000:101).

[6] Not producing nunation and case markings does not constitute a major deviation from the target form. However, not knowing or producing such markings may have the repercussion of causing more seriously deviant forms to be produced. This is evident, for example, when a noun is attached to a pronominal suffix. In this case, the exact case marking should be produced to avoid producing deviant forms, for example, of the type (a)-(c) below (marked by an asterisk), which are usually produced by L2ers who have not acquired the case marking rules:

> (a)   * *fī bayt-u-hu*
>   in house.s.m-nom-his
>   "in his house"
>
> (b)   * *fī bayt-a-hu*
>   in house.s.m-acc-his
>   "in his house"
>
> (c)   *fī bayt-i-hi*
>   in house.s.m-gen-his
>   "in his house"

[7] Except in constructions where a pronoun occurs as the subject, as in (d), where both constituent elements are definite, and in emphatic uses where the predicate/comment occurs in the definite and a pronoun suffix surfaces preceding it, as in example (e) below.

> (d)   *hāðā   ʔustāð-ī*
>   this.s.m   teacher-my
>   "This is my teacher."
>
> (e)   *hāðā   huwa   ʔal-ʔustāð-u*
>   this.s.m   he   the-teacher.s.m-nom
>   "This is *the* teacher."

[8] The parentheses here indicate that case and mood markings are not produced as is generally attested (in casual and semiformal MSA) without disrupting the meaning, especially since case does not carry crucial meaning in this context.

[9] *Kāna* should be glossed "he was," since Arabic does not exhibit an infinitival form. The third person singular is the form conventionally selected in lieu of an infinitival form as a term of reference (in Western descriptive and instructional works), since it is the shortest inflected form.

[10] See note 8 above.

[11] The final vowel {-*a*} of the plural number-case suffix is usually dropped as is always the case in formal CA and MSA pause speech.

[12] For example, in CA and MSA a possessive equational construction can also be negated by use of *mā*, which is not inflected for gender, person, or number, as in sentences (f)-(g).

(f)   *mā*   *ʕinda-hu*   *sayyār-a(t-u-n)*
      not   at-his   car-s.f-nom-indef
      "He does not have a car."

(g)   *mā*   *ʕinda-hā*   *sayyār-a(t-u-n)*
      not   at-her   car-s.f-nom-indef
      "She does not have a car."

Invariably, *laysa* can be used similarly with respect to agreement and case, as in sentences (h)-(i).

(h)   *lays-a*   *ʕinda-hu*   *sayyār-a(t-u-n)*
      not-3.s.m   at-his   car-s.f-nom-indef
      "He does not have a car."

(i)   *lays-a*   *ʕinda-hā*   *sayyār-a(t-u-n)*
      not-3.s.m   at-her   car-s.f-nom-indef
      "She does not have a car."

[13] *Laysa* should be glossed "he was not," since it conjugates as a verb. Hence, traditional Arab grammarians treat it as a verb.

[14] See note 8 above.

[15] It might be argued that Arabic verbs are better characterized as exhibiting perfective and imperfective aspect stems, roughly corresponding to past and present tense, respectively. However, Fassi Fehri (1993) argues against such a view and instead proposes that a proper characterization of Arabic is one that takes both into account, with Arabic exhibiting "a dual tense-aspect" verbal inflectional system (1993:146). This book is not concerned here with any such debates of tense versus aspect; the two terms are used interchangeably.

[16] In strict SVO and VSO word orders, case and mood may not be produced, including in casual and semiformal MSA usage. Hence, case and mood markings are included within parentheses. Case, in particular, becomes significant and indispensable when the object precedes the subject for emphasis. This infrequent structure, mostly exhibited in CA, is not investigated here.

[17] It is to be noted here that in Classical Arabic when *mā* is used to negate the perfective it has an emphatic meaning (see Sībawayhi:537). However, MSA speakers do not seem to recognize this usage and they seem to use it interchangeably with *lam*. Similarly, negating

equational sentences (with *mā*) that do not exhibit a possessive meaning such as sentence (60) above occurs rarely in MSA and occurs mainly in CA (see also note 12).

Chapter 2. Existing Arabic SLA Research

[1] More than three decades later and long after the limitations of Contrastive and Error Analysis studies have been pointed out in the literature, Elsheikh Abdalla (2005), within the same framework, examined L2 Arabic errors in Malay speakers' written compositions. Errors identified belonged to two main categories: definite article errors (a total of 591, comprising 53 percent of the errors) and preposition errors (a total of 525, comprising 47 percent of the errors). The errors were further subcategorized into omission, addition, and wrong selection errors. An attempt to examine whether or not the participants were more likely to commit either of the two main categories of errors was made, resulting in non-significant difference between the two. The author concluded by speculating on the sources of errors.

[2] It is to be noted that Nielsen's (1997) findings to do with definiteness in *ʔidˤāfa* (or noun-noun apposition) construction are problematic from a PT perspective. According to PT, the definite article involves a complex form-function relationship, as definiteness also interacts with syntax, being a morphosyntactic feature rather than a mere bound morpheme. Expectedly, the definiteness feature in *ʔidˤāfa* phrases is more likely to emerge at a late stage, since it entails an additional learning task in figuring out the interaction it involves with the syntax. Hence, such a structure involves a complex form-function relationship, which entails additional learning tasks not accounted for by PT.

[3] For a discussion of these structures, see Chapter 8.

[4] The assigning of the participants into "beginning" and "intermediate" in Mansouri's (2000) study seems to be problematic. Mansouri states that the participants were "outpacing the curriculum by learning structures before they are taught" (2000:208); in particular, one of the two "intermediate" participants ("learner 3") is stated to have unexpectedly "almost fully acquired most of the structures" of the study (2000:213). However, based on the sample utterances (included in Appendix E, Mansouri 2000:242), one of the two participants states that the other "intermediate" participant studied Arabic for three years *and a half*, not three years. This may very well explain the difference in performance between the two "intermediate" participants, one of whom seems to be at the advanced level. Similarly, if the "beginning" participants were indeed "outpacing their curriculum," as Mansouri reports, they may well have been at the intermediate rather than the beginning level, or they may have had additional previous exposure to the target structures. Inclusion of participants with zero background in Arabic to be longitudinally (rather than semi-longitudinally/cross-sectionally) observed (as in Nielsen 1997 and

Alhawary 1999, 2003) would not have only helped to produce more conclusive data but would have also been ideal for pinpointing the stages of acquisition where so much to do with the notion of emergence is at stake.

⁵ Mansouri characterizes his data elicited through both tasks as "spontaneous" and "natural" (e.g., Mansouri 2000:123, 207). However, a task such as the oral transformation task described, where the participants are made aware of events/utterances with agents in the first person singular, for example, and are asked to re-narrate those events/utterances with agents in the third person singular, dual, and plural, elicits anything but spontaneous or natural data.

⁶ Findings of other structures are discussed in this section below.

⁷ It is not clear what is meant by "exhibiting signs of emergence," since the notion behind introducing any type of criterion is to conclude as to whether or not the criterion is reached. It seems that Mansouri introduces the notion of sub-stages so as to conclude that the findings are in support of PT and that these are interpreted as mere sub-stages wherever the criterion is not met. However, by so doing PT would be rendered unfalsifiable. Hence, "+/-" should indicate here lack of emergence (i.e., criterion is not reached) and in this case the proper implications of the data become more evident: the findings provide counterevidence to PT's hypothesized speech-processing predictions.

⁸ In fact, part of the problem is that Mansouri claims that: "the equivalent of the English [to go out] or [to eat] would be … xaradʒa "He went out" and ʔakal-tu "I ate"" (Mansouri 2000:25). However, contrary to this nonfactual claim, Arabic does not exhibit any infinitival form. A similar nonfactual claim made by Mansouri (2000) about morphological features is that case in Arabic is "obligatory" (Mansouri 2000:121-123), which would be true only in the context of a VOS word order.

⁹ Mansouri does not provide the motivation for analyzing word order of equational (verbless) sentences vs. that of SVO. Mansouri assumes that word order of equational sentences is a stage 1 form, involving "phrasal" procedures and nothing else, while SVO word order is a stage 2 form, involving "inter-phrasal" procedures (Mansouri 2000:120, Table 17; 193, Table 34). Contrary to this assumption, however, equational sentences require inter-phrasal procedures in that while the subject constituent phrase is definite, the predicate constituent phrase is usually indefinite unless the structure is *marked* (for emphasis purposes), in which case a pronoun (free morpheme) is inserted in between the two constituents (as in *hāðā huwa ʔal-ʔustāð* "This is *the* teacher") in addition to exchange of grammatical agreement requirements in number and gender between the two constituent phrases. Moreover, there is a more complicated interaction with definiteness that entails an additional operation (in terms of PT) if the subject happens to be indefinite. In this case, the order of the two constituents needs to be converted (*tˤālib fī ʔal-sˤaff

"A student is in the class" → *fī ʔal-sˤaff tˤālib* "In the class is a student"). This interaction puts equational sentences at a stage that requires more (not fewer) processing pre-requites than those of canonical SVO word order. Moreover, Mansouri does not seem to be aware of this fact and he seems to dismiss inversion as uncommon in Arabic unlike in German (Mansouri 2000:220).

[10] Western European language concepts and structures seem to be unnecessarily super-imposed on Arabic here. Needless to say, generally speaking, there are no constraints governing adverb placement in Arabic on a par with those in English, German, and others.

[11] Mansouri identifies Pienemann's stage 1 (lemma/word access) as stage 0, which explains the difference by one in the numbering of structures between the two systems. Hence phrasal agreement is a stage 3 (rather than stage 2) structure, S-V agreement is a stage 4 (rather than stage 3) structure, etc.

[12] Mansouri also reports that regular plural, analyzed as a stage 2 structure, was acquired accordingly; dual number, analyzed as a stage 3 structure, was acquired accordingly; and irregular plural, analyzed as a stage 4 structure, was acquired accordingly. However, Mansouri does not provide the motivation for analyzing the stages of the structures in the way he did. For example, it is not clear why the dual is a stage 3 form and regular plural is a stage 2 form, even though the dual follows a watertight rule (and should be a stage 2 form accordingly), whereas regular plural does not. In fact, there is no a priori way for the learners of the study (given their levels) to tease apart regular plural from irregular plural. Hence, the conclusion regarding the acquisition of the dual and the plural forms is problematic. Furthermore, the fact that the dual was acquired after regular and irregular plural (Mansouri 2000:163) provides counterevidence to PT's prediction, if the dual number is analyzed correctly as a stage 2 form.

Argued differently, such analyses and results seem to be rather an artifact of Mansouri's own study due perhaps to both the small size of his data samples and/or due to presentation and focus of the instructional input (giving rise to induced errors). Mansouri reports low occurrence and accuracy rates for the dual (Mansouri 2000: 136, 146, 149, and 156) which in fact may be due to instructional focus and lack of presence in input. The dual marking is often not emphasized and is not frequently recycled as other forms and is usually presented later than other forms in Arabic L2 textbooks. In fact, this is exactly the case with the input which the participants received, as Mansouri reports that regular plural was introduced in Unit 1 (and onward with interrupted recycling) and the dual was presented in Units 4/5 (with no indication of later recycling). Therefore, Mansouri's claim with respect to the stages of the dual and regular plural seems theoretically illogical and methodologically flawed. Hence, the analysis of regular and dual structures as well as the assignment of the acquisition stages (2 and 3, respectively) are, here too, based on unsound assumptions and inaccurate analysis of the target structures.

[13] It is to be noted here that the findings reported in Table 27 (Mansouri 2000:161) as well as the hypothesized predictions listed in Table 17 (Mansouri 2000:120) do not match those findings nor the numbers of the hypothesized stages listed in Table 30 (Mansouri 2000:169), especially with respect to these structures (i.e., SVO word order, negation, VSO, and subordination) (see also Tables 20-26 in Mansouri 2000:136, 142, 146, 149, 154, 156, and 158, respectively). Similar inconsistencies can be observed between Table 28 (Mansouri 2000:163) and Table 31 (Mansouri 2000:174) (see also Tables 20-26 in Mansouri 2000:136, 142, 146, 149, 154, 156, and 158, respectively).

[14] Abu Radwan (2002) does not give examples of actual sentences used but states that he followed Taman (1993) in "constructing the test and devising the computation procedure" (Abu Radwan 2002:195). Hence, the sample sentences provided here are cited from Taman (1993).

[15] The discrepancy in the findings between the two studies might be due to the backgrounds of the native speakers used in both studies. Taman (1993) states that the participants were 100 Egyptians, who were undergraduate students at Alexandria University, and who were studying for their B.A. in Arabic. However, Abu Radwan (2002) does not provide any information about the background of the native speakers used in his study other than their number.

[16] This perhaps explains the low score of the control participants on complex resumptives (as shown in Box 2.9) as some of them seem to be aware that resumptive pronouns are not obligatory.

Chapter 3. The Acquisition of Gender Agreement

[1] Zero or null subject instances were not considered for identification of emergence of S-V agreement in the participants' IL systems. However, the production and findings of zero subjects are in line with explicit and pronominal subject contexts (for zero subject context data, see Alhawary 1999:126-135). It is also to be noted here that although Arabic is a pro-drop/null subject language, the input comprising the instructional materials consists almost exclusively of non-zero subject structures. This is similarly borne out by the production data of the participants. Almost all the instances that are produced by the participants occur in coordinate structures, as in (j) below.

(j) *Pal-walad   ya-šrab*   *wa   ya-Pkul   wa   ya-ktub*
     the-boy.**s.m** **3.s.m**-drink.imperf and   **3.s.m**-eat.imperf and **3.s.m**-write.imperf
     "The boy is drinking and eating and writing."

The remaining few tokens (in zero subject contexts) of the participants' output occur when the participants cannot recall the lexical noun of the subject and substitute for it by pointing or referring to the picture of the referent.

[2] It is to be noted here that S-V agreement of plural masculine (not reported on here) was found to emerge at the same time as S-V agreement of singular masculine and feminine (see Alhawary 1999). Due to the limited number of tokens produced by the participants, it could not be determined whether N-A agreement of plural masculine emerged.

[3] Of course, such use is not necessarily target-like but sheds light on the underlying L2 representation of the IL systems of the participants, including hypotheses which the participants form about the target forms.

[4] It is not possible to speculate on the extent of the productive use of the masculine gender feature on adjectives following feminine head nouns, since the masculine gender marking is a zero morpheme {-0} and no possible productive pattern was found. Similarly, it is not possible to speculate on the productive use of verbal agreement in non-contexts, since there is no infinitival verb form and the participants simply used verb forms inflected for other agreement, although most of the verbal agreement errors were: 1) use of third person singular feminine agreement inflection for third person singular masculine and 2) use of third person singular masculine agreement inflection for third person singular feminine. Examples of produced verbal agreement mismatches, are illustrated in (k)-(m) below.

(k) IL: *hiya ya-sˤħū
            she   **3.s.m**-wake up
     TL: hiya **ta-sˤħū**
            she   **3.s.f**-wake up
            "She wakes up."
            (Japanese L1: Group 2)

(l) IL: *huwa **ta-qraʔa**   ʔal-kitāb
            he   **3.s.f**-read   the-book
     TL: huwa ya-qraʔʔal-kitāb
            he   **3.s.m**-read   the-book
            "He reads the book."
            (English L1: Group 1)

(m) IL: *hiya ðahab-**tu**
            she   went-**1.s**
     TL: hiya ðahab-**at**
            she   went-**3.s.f**
            "She went."
            (Japanese L1: Group 1)

[5] Such tokens, unlike those with rule application of the feminine suffix {-*a*} following masculine adjectives, are coded as correct rule application (even though they are not target-like), since we would expect feminine head nouns to be followed by adjectives inflected for feminine gender.

[6] The context of such tokens is a picture identification task where the participant was required to identify the person with a full sentence. The assumption here, following Bley-Vroman (1983), is to accept this token as exhibiting correct rule application of the form in question and avoid the major pitfall of the "comparative fallacy" which would otherwise result in a misleading assessment of the systematicity of the learner's IL system (i.e., by comparing the learner's production directly with the target language rather than analyzing it as part of the IL system, which is a system by itself).

[7] It is to be noted that other related forms such as equational (verbless) sentence structure involving pronominal (and lexical) subjects are present in the input from early on, including the first 11 units focusing on the phonology and scripts of the Arabic language.

[8] The four textbooks follow somewhat different approaches and formats for teaching the phonology and script of the Arabic language. Abboud et al. (1983) focuses mainly on these components at the word level and presents them at the beginning of the book (part 1) within ten preliminary lessons. Brustad et al. (1995a) presents the phonology and script of the Arabic language mainly at the word level and includes phrases and expressions, all of which are contained within ten units in an independent book. Badawi et al. (1983) and Deheuvels (2003) do not focus solely on the phonology and script, as Abboud et al. (1983) and Brustad et al. (1995a) do, but present the phonology and script as part of other language aspects. Badawi et al. (1983) introduces sentences and questions together with the phonology and script (at the word level) within 11 preliminary units at the beginning of the book. Deheuvels (2003) introduces short dialogues, together with the phonology and script, all of which are contained in the 15 main lessons of the book.

Chapter 4. The Acquisition of Tense/Aspect and Verbal Agreement

[1] As noted in Chapter 1 (note 15), the book is not concerned with any such debates of tense vs. aspect. For ease of reference, the two terms *tense* and *aspect* are interchangeably used here, with the former relied on more so than the latter.

[2] For the past tense narrative tasks, recall that the participants were requested to narrate the planned vacation activities (on a calendar) carried out by each character during his or her vacation (which each took the previous month for a period of ten days) day by day. Thus, the starter *ba ʕda riħlati-hi* "after his trip ..." occurs within the past tense (i.e., *After his trip, last month, ...*) context.

[3] For the present tense narrative tasks, recall that the participants were requested to describe the daily routines/activities of each of the characters at different times of the day from the morning to the evening. Thus, the starter *fī ʔal-sˤabāħ* "In the morning ..." occurs clearly in the habitual, present tense (i.e., *In the morning, of everyday*, ...) context.

Chapter 5. The Acquisition of Null Subjects

[1] These are the same participants discussed in the previous chapter (Chapter 4).

[2] Due to shared knowledge between the interviewee and interviewer as the instruction about performing the task is introduced, even producing an overt subject (a pronoun or NP) with the first event may not be necessary. Hence, not all the control participants produced an overt subject at the beginning of the each of the four tasks.

[3] For the pair-wise comparison, given two dependent variables, alpha is set at .025 divided by 4 (i.e., .006).

Chapter 6. The Acquisition of Negation, Mood, and Case

[1] As explained in Chapter 1, in a VSO word order, the verb agrees with the subject only in person and gender but not in number. Thus, in a VSO order the verb for third person masculine singular would be identical to that for third person masculine plural.

[2] The parentheses indicate that use of mood and case are optional and usually dropped in informal and semi-formal spoken Arabic.

[3] These three participants were used as a control group in the original study (see Alhawary 1999).

[4] For full details and contents of the four computer lessons which focused on all aspects of the target forms, including the functional uses of each of the five negation constructions, past copular verb, and case and mood endings associated with them, see Alhawary 1999: 236-270).

[5] In addition, the following token of the indicative mood was produced by Beth (Interview 8) in non-context: *ʔal-layla lā ʔurīd ʔan ʔaʕmal-u** → *ʔan ʔaʕmal-a* "Tonight, I don't want to work."

[6] The negation construction with *mā* does not require morphological mood inflection, since *mā* occurs with the imperfective/past form of the verb.

[7] Note that other verbal agreement and mood inflections were introduced in the input only towards the end of the period of the observation, including the dual, second and third person plural feminine.

[8] The input of the computer sessions also focused directly on the nominative case affixed on the subject of *kāna* and *laysa* in order to convey a balanced impression that each form has a grammatical ending. The data on nominative case yielded the same finding as that on the accusative case (see Alhawary 1999).

Chapter 7. Theoretical Implications

[1] For a brief account of LFG and how it fits into PT, see Pienemann (1998:93-98); for a comprehensive account of LFG, see Bresnan (1982).

[2] In essence, this claim resembles Krashen's (1977, 1985) concept of optimal input stated within the Input Hypothesis (IH), positing that the L2er will make progress if the level of the input is at i+1. The difference between PT and IH is that the former attempts to identify the make up and nature of this optimal input in a principled fashion.

[3] There seems to be an ambiguity as to whether or not formal instruction can be demonstrated to be beneficial, affecting the falsifiability of claim (2) (see Krashen 1993). In addition, it is not clear from the model how the notion of "functional need" can be controlled for in order to test the hypothesis.

[4] LFG is adopted by Pienemann (1998) as a notational framework for PT.

[5] Moreover, Nielsen (1997) tested PT independently based on longitudinal data from two Danish L1 speakers learning Arabic as an L2 and using the same emergence criterion (see Chapter 2). Recall that the results revealed that while neither S-V nor N-A agreement emerged in learner B's Interlanguage system, both forms emerged at the same time in learner A's Interlanguage system (in recording 4); thus, at least on account of the latter emergence schedule of the two structures, Nielsen's study provides counterevidence to PT claims. The two structures did not occur in two different stages, as PT would predict.

[6] Recall also that suppliance of the complementizer *ʔan* itself emerged in all of the Interlanguage systems of the participants (see Tables 6.12-6.13, Chapter 6).

[7] For other counterevidence to PT based on French and Spanish data, see Dewaele and Véronique (2001) and Farley and McCollam (2004), respectively.

[8] Of course there are probably other factors contributing to the acquisition findings here, such as input frequency. Indeed, *?an* construction together with the subjunctive mood on the verb following it were introduced in the formal classroom input (i.e., textbooks) earlier and are more frequently present than *kāna/laysa* construction and their associated case markings (see Table 6.2, Chapter 6; see also Brustad et al. 1995, 1995b).

[9] Thus, claim (2) is less seriously challenged here, since, as noted in note 8 above, *kāna/laysa* construction and their associated case markings were introduced later in the textbooks of the participants (Brustad et al. 1995, 1995b). The additional computer session input received by some of the participants (see Table 6.3, Chapter 6) was only part of an experimental study and was neither made part of the classroom input (by the classroom teacher) nor was it reinforced in the classroom by the teacher. Hence, it must be stated that this finding is not conclusive. It would be useful to observe in a future study participants who are exposed to additional target structures that are also part of the formal classroom input. Such formal classroom input should also include the enforcement of teaching case and mood from the beginning to see the full extent of the effectiveness of early exposure to such forms. Anecdotally, on various occasions during the author's own experience of teaching and based on occasional discussions with other teachers using the same textbook (which focuses primarily on the functional aspects of the language), students expressed discomfort and even questioned the usefulness of learning or producing case and mood markings. An additional factor to control for in future research is the nature of the orthographic system of the Arabic language. Case and mood markings are written separately in Arabic script and are usually not provided in texts in magazines and newspapers.

[10] It may not be plausible to claim that a single factor such as speech processing prerequisites can explain L2 grammatical development, nor of course L1 transfer alone. In fact, Lui (1991), Tarone and Lui (1995) and Tarone (2007) argue that social contexts can influence SLA to the extent of forcing a stage to be skipped, contrary to PT predictions. Longitudinal data from English L2 acquisition from a five year old child show that the child skipped a stage 3 structure (WHX-front without inversion: "Why you do that?") and produced structures at stages 4-6, including pseudo inversion ("Where's the monkey?"), aux-2nd ("What are you doing?"), and question tag ("You don't like green, are you?"). The child later produced the stage 3 structure. The study was based on Pienemann and Johnston's (1987) framework, a precursor of PT.

[11] Vainikka and Young-Scholten (1998) further claim that the trigger for functional projection in L1 may not be the same in L2. Following Newport (1990), they propose that morphological processing capacity in L2 undergoes a quantitative shift due to critical period effect, hence the developmental differences between L1 and L2 acquisition.

[12] Cf. researchers who rather argue for limited or no UG access and instead appeal for universal cognitive principles or constraints accessed by L2 learners (e.g., Meisel 1983, 1991; Clahsen 1984; Clahsen and Muysken 1986, 1989; Felix 1985; Bley-Vroman 1989, 1990; and Schachter 1989).

[13] In attributing parametric variation to strength of functional features, standard Minimalist assumption is adopted here. On this account, due to rich nominal agreement features, both Arabic and French are analyzed with the functional feature strength set to [+strong] while functional feature strength in English is set to [-strong].

[14] Note with respect to S-V agreement, French, like English, does not exhibit gender verbal agreement, except in past participial forms within compound verb tenses, passive voice, and pronominal verbs.

[15] Additionally, perhaps demonstrative gender agreement is slightly less problematic than N-A gender agreement, since only one part of the former structure involves a small class of demonstratives (initially instructional materials include only two: *hāðā* and *hāðihi* forms) whereas the latter involves two parts that belong to large classes of nouns and adjectives.

[16] See note 14 above.

[17] The old wisdom originating prior to the Principles and Parameter framework that word order is much more salient than an inflectional feature may have contributed to the participants' noticing and acquiring the strong inflection feature that licenses N raising from early on (see Corder 1978, Slobin 1973).

[18] Of course, the contents of such supposed algorithms are overly simplified here, since the dual and broken plural, for example, are not included. The input (both of the formal classroom and the computer sessions) did not contain dual and broken forms as the predicate of *kāna* and *laysa*.

[19] Note that feature strength in Spanish is assumed to be set to [+strong], although Spanish verbal agreement equivalent to that of the target structures in Arabic (third person singular masculine and third person singular feminine) does not involve gender; yet verbal agreement is not morphologically impoverished as is the case in English where feature strength is assumed to be set to [-strong].

[20] Indeed this may be likely, since usually the notions of root and vocalic melody/pattern are not introduced in the input from early on. Arabic L2ers at an early stage are not ready yet to be exposed to these aspects of the Arabic language.

[21] In addition, recall that the study relies on production data rather than on grammaticality judgment tasks in assessing the participants' use of null subjects—a methodology relied on in many of the studies on the issue. This methodology has been criticized for its many limitations (e.g., Ellis 1990, 1991; Lantolf 1990; Goss et al. 1994).

[22] Recall also, as discussed in the previous section, that there is a qualitative difference in the formal input of the three groups of participants. The textbooks used by the Spanish L1 (Al-Khalifa 1999, 2002), the Japanese L1 (Brustad et al. 1995a, 1995b; Badawi el al. 1983, 1992), and the English L1 (Abboud et al. 1983, 1997) participants all focus on form from early on; however, only the textbooks used by the English L1 and Japanese L1 participants recycle verbal agreement rigorously throughout, whereas the textbook used by the Spanish L1 hardly recycles verbal agreement.

[23] A similar observation related to the notion of salience and word order is reported above (Chapter 3; see also Alhawary 2005) where the English L1 (together with the French L1 and Japanese L1) participants learning Arabic as an L2 achieved a near perfect mastery of Arabic noun-adjective word order from the earliest stage of acquisition even though the order in their L1 is, in fact, the opposite: adjective-noun.

Chapter 8. Pedagogical and Applied Implications

[1] Admittedly, there is a good deal of generalization here. However, this may prove useful for the novice teacher in providing a sense of what to expect in a classroom containing L2ers belonging to all or any of the L1s investigated here.

[2] Emergence of *mā* before *lam* seems to be due in part to instructional effect, since the L2ers were introduced first to *mā* and only later to *lam*; the L2ers may have already gotten used to *mā* and therefore switching to *lam* may not have been an easy option. Of course, one would expect negation with *lam* to be more complex than that with *mā*, since *lam* is used with the imperfective stem of the verb and *mā* is simply used with the perfective stem.

[3] The three participants also received additional input with a focused attempt to teach the nominative case of the subject of *laysa* and *kāna*. The nominative did not emerge in any of the participants' Interlanguage systems either (see Alhawary 1999).

[4] As discussed in Chapter 6, it should be noted that emergence tendencies of mood and case endings, based on the longitudinal data, could be attributed to the context of the proficiency-oriented textbook (Brustad et al. 1995a, 1995b), which constituted the formal classroom input of the participants, where the introduction of case and mood endings is delayed until towards the end of the first year and generally not enforced on a par with the other more basic and functional aspects of the forms in question. Similarly, even with

respect to the accusative case of *kāna* and *laysa*, direct exposure was part of an experimental component outside of the classroom input and, therefore, the additional input did not have the advantage of being reinforced by the classroom instructor.

[5] Indeed, the role of input frequency is acknowledged in the SLA literature, especially with respect to morpheme order acquisition. Larsen-Freeman and Long (1991:91) go as far as stating that, among the factors of acquisition of morpheme order, "only input frequency has much empirical support to date." Most recently and based on meta analysis of a number of morpheme order studies, Goldschneider and DeKeyser (2001) found input frequency to be one of five factors (including perceptual salience, morphological regularity, semantic complexity, syntactic category, and frequency in input) that account for variance in the data. Goldschneider and DeKeyser conclude that "a considerable portion of the order of acquisition of grammatical functors by ESL learners ... can be predicted by the five factors" (2001:37).

[6] As it was also stated above (note 9, Chapter 7), these findings to do with case and mood endings should be interpreted with caution. It would be useful to observe, in a future study, participants who are exposed to these target forms as part of the formal classroom input. The additional input which the participants received (during eight-week sessions for two months) was not part of the classroom input and therefore was not reinforced by the teacher in the classroom. Additionally, the textbook used by the participants (Brustad et al. 1995b) does not focus on mood and case until towards the end of the textbook, focusing primarily instead on the functional aspects of the language. Anecdotally, on various occasions during the author's own experience of teaching and based on occasional discussions with other teachers using the same textbook, students expressed discomfort and even questioned the usefulness of learning or producing case and mood markings. Hence, it is not clear how the findings would have turned out had case and mood endings been focused on and enforced.

[7] This recommended scheduling happens to be the same as the one implemented by Brustad et al. (1995a, 1995b) textbook—used by the English L1 longitudinal participants—whose decision accordingly is validated based on the research findings. This similarly validates the scheduling in Abboud et al. (1983), used by the English L1 cross-sectional participants.

[8] As discussed above, the negation construction with *lam* seems to require more attention and recycling than other negation constructions.

[9] This raises even more concern, as there is no consensus nor clear indication in the SLA literature as to what constitutes "complexity."

[10] For suggestions about further implications and interfaces between SLA and language testing research, see Bachman and Cohen (1998).

Glossary

aphasic data: data collected from patients with acquired language disorders, whether partial or total, due to a stroke or brain injuries.

case: a grammatical category/ending attached at the end of nouns and adjectives; in Arabic, depending on the syntactic position of the forms it is attached to, case can be one of three types: nominative, accusative, and genitive.

clitic: a pronoun behaving as a bound morpheme, attached at the end of a verb or a complementizer.

coding: a process following data collection but preceding data analysis that involves parsing or marking utterances according to parts of speech, use, function, etc.

comparative fallacy: a misleading method of analysis where L2 learners' utterances are compared directly with target language use irrespective of their Interlanguage use; such a method leads to misleading assessment of the systematicity of the learner's Interlanguage as a system by itself.

Contrastive Analysis: refers to the earliest SLA research studies between the 1940s and 1960s which espoused a behaviorist view of language learning; identifying learner's errors, predicted on the basis of differences between L1 and L2, was important to avoid bad "habit formation."

cross-sectional data: data collected from learners belonging to different proficiency levels or different stages of exposure to the target language, usually during one or two sessions; cross-sectional data is usually used due to time constraints, where collecting data longitudinally from the same learner/s over an extended period of time is not possible; see also **longitudinal data**.

elicitation tasks: activities that participants of a study are requested to interact with (by means of talking about, describing, narrating, commenting on, etc.) in order to obtain from them production data that relate to the target forms; participants are usually not made aware of the exact issues or forms the researcher is investigating to avoid confounding the research variables.

Error Analysis: refers to studies that appeared with the advent of nativist and cognitive views of language learning as a process of "rule formation;" the main preoccupation was categorizing and speculating on the sources of learners' errors, resulting in providing a partial account of L2 performance to the exclusion of L2 correct production; that is, focusing on the failures and excluding the successes of the L2 learner.

feature checking: a mechanism crucial for syntactic operations by which features shared by elements are eliminated; failures of features to be checked and subsequently eliminated will cause the syntactic derivation/operation to crash.

features: grammatical properties that can be phonological, semantic, syntactic, or morphosyntactic and are usually associated with the binary values [+] and [-].

feature strength: in generative syntactic theory, a feature is assumed to be strong [+strong] or weak [-strong] to motivate overt movement (that is, in the syntax) or covert movement (that is, in Logical Form), respectively.

fossilization: an L2 proficiency level or state where learning reaches a level distinct from that of the target language and fails to approximate to it any further.

functional categories: one of two main types of elements in the lexicon (the other type being **lexical categories**), such as Complementizer (C or COM), Determiner (D or DET), and Inflection (I or INFL), associated with grammatical properties.

functional projection: an expansion of a functional/grammatical rather than lexical element into a phrasal constituent, such as CP (Complementizer Phrase) being a projection of a complementizer and IP (Inflectional Phrase) being a projection of inflection.

grammaticality judgment tasks: tests (usually written) in the form of multiple choice questions, where participants are requested to identify the grammatical or ungrammatical structures.

hypocoristic data: data containing diminutive terms and nicknames.

INFL: a functional category that stands for "Inflection" and is associated with the grammatical information of person, number, and tense; see **functional categories**.

inflection: refers to an affix/ending that conveys grammatical information, such as past or present tense, person, number, etc.

Interlanguage: L2 learner language viewed as a natural language subject to systematic development towards approximation of the target language or towards a fossilized, non-target-like state; see also **fossilization**.

lexical categories: one of two main types of elements in the lexicon (the other type being **functional categories**), such as Noun (N), Verb (V), Adjective (A), and Preposition (P), that convey descriptive, semantic content.

Lexical Functional Grammar: a theory of grammar that, unlike Chomsky's Government and Binding and other earlier versions of Generative syntactic theory, gives a primary role to the lexicon over the syntax, where each sentence structure consists of two components generated by phrase structure rules: constituent structure and functional structure; the latter includes grammatical relations/functions, such as subject, object, and predicate, treated as primitive concepts with one surface structure (that is, no deep structure is invoked).

licensing: an abstract property that allows a **parameter** to be set to [-] or [+] value.

longitudinal data: data collected from learners periodically over an extended period of time.

L1 transfer: the influence of the native language (L1) on the second/foreign language (L2).

Monitor Model: developed by Krashen in the 1980s, the model is comprised of the acquisition-learning hypothesis, the monitor hypothesis, the natural order hypothesis, the input hypothesis, and the affective filter hypothesis; in particular, a distinction is made between acquisition and learning; the former occurs in a naturalistic setting (with the focus on communication) such as child L1 acquisition and the latter occurs through formal instruction (where the focus is on rules and formal accuracy) and whereas acquisition exhibits spontaneous language production, learning exhibits conscious production with the L2 system acting as a monitor/editor and does not become acquisition.

mood: a grammatical category/ending attached at the end of verbs; in Arabic, depending on the syntactic position of verbs and their occurrence with certain particles, mood can be one of three types: indicative, subjunctive, and jussive.

null subject: refers to the subject position (in some languages) as empty or exhibiting a *small pro* (pronoun) that has no phonetic content (that is, no subject is present) with the features of the subject being recoverable from the contexts and/or inflections on the verb.

null subject parameter: a **Universal Grammar** principle that can be set [+null], permitting null subjects in a language, or [-null], not allowing null subjects.

overt pronoun: a pronoun that has a phonetic content in the subject position, contrasting with an empty pronoun (*small pro*) in the same position; see also **null subject**.

overt subject: a lexical or pronoun subject contrasting with an empty pronoun (*small pro*) in the same position; see also **null subject**.

parameter: in Generative theory, a variant principle that is set to a neutral or unmarked value in the core of Universal Grammar (UG) and later, upon exposure to input of a specific language, the parameter is set to the value permitted in the language; for example, the **null subject parameter**.

principle: in Generative theory, an invariant principle that is universally invariant across all language or allows little variation; for example, the Projection Principle, Subjacency, etc.

Principles and Parameters: a concept that constitutes the backbone of the different versions of Generative theory since its inception to the present, referring to innate, universal core grammar available to all humans, consisting of a finite set of principles and parameters; see **principle** and **parameter**.

pro drop: see **null subject**.

pro drop parameter: see **null subject parameter**.

projection: see **functional projection**.

pronoun clitic: see **clitic**.

recycling: in foreign language teaching pedagogy, refers to re-using vocabulary or forms in subsequent lessons, drills, and activities beyond its initial introduction.

restructuring: in first and second language acquisition, a change in the underlying representation of rule/s brought about upon noticing in the input some evidence that indicates the hypothesized representation is not valid.

traditional Arabic grammar: the grammar of Arabic, including the various syntactic, morphological, phonological, semantic, pragmatic, prosodic, and rhetorical aspects of the Arabic language, as codified and formulated by traditional Arab and Muslim grammarians, especially during the formative period from the end of the seventh century (after the rise of Islam) to the tenth century and based on fieldwork by traditional linguists collecting naturally occurring data from tribes of the Arabian peninsula; this resulted in a huge scholarly output of thousands of books and treatises some of which have not survived; the earliest extant and most authoritative work is that of Sībawayhi (765-796 C.E.).

ultimate attainment: the end state or adult target state of language acquisition, especially with respect to first language acquisition and due to a critical period effect that some consider to occur around the age of puberty and others around the age of five; although the commonly held view is that L1 speakers usually reach such a state, it is controversial whether L2 learners can reach a state similar to that of L1.

Universal Grammar: see **Principles** and **Parameters**.

U-shaped behavior: an acquisition tendency, especially in L1 acquisition, where the child starts by using forms correctly as the child hears them in the input (that is, as monomorphemic chunks), goes through a stage where he/she is aware of the rules and starts applying them, resulting in noticeable overgeneralization errors (for example, *He goed), and then starts to apply rules conservatively upon more exposure to input/positive evidence and to adjust to the target form; this process is usually referred to as **re-structuring**.

References

Abboud, Peter, Aman Attieh, Ernest N. McCarus, and Raji M. Rammuny. 1997. *Intermediate Modern Standard Arabic*. Ann Arbor, MI: Center for Middle Eastern and North African Studies, University of Michigan.

Abboud, Peter, Zaki N. Abdel-Malek, Najm A. Bezirgan, Wallace M. Erwin, Mounah A. Khouri, Ernest N. McCarus, Raji M. Rammuny, and George N. Saad. 1983. *Elementary Modern Standard Arabic* Vol.1. Cambridge, MA: Cambridge University Press.

Abd El-Jawad, Hassan and Issam Abu-Salim. 1987. "Slips of the Tongue in Arabic and their Theoretical Implications." *Language Sciences* 9(2):145-171.

Abu Radwan, Adel. 2002. "Sentence Processing Strategies: An application of the Competition Model to Arabic." *Perspectives on Arabic Linguistics XIII-XIV* ed. by Dilworth Parkinson and Elabbas Benmamoun, 185-209. Amsterdam, The Netherlands: John Benjamins.

ACTFL (American Council on the Teaching of Foreign Languages). 1999. *ACTFL Proficiency Guidelines: Speaking.* [http://www.actfl.org/i4a/pages/index.cfm?pageid=3325]

ACTFL (American Council on the Teaching of Foreign Languages). 1989. *ACTFL Arabic Proficiency Guidelines. Foreign Language Annals* 22:373-392.

Al-Ani, Salman H. 1972-1973. "Features of Interference in the Teaching of Arabic Composition." *An-Nashra* V-VI:3-13.

Al-Buainain, Haifa. 1991. "Universality of Language Acquisition Processes in a Study of the IL of a Group of Students of Arabic." *International Review of Applied Linguistics* 93/94:25-69.

Al-Buainain, Haifa. 1986. *Second Language Acquisition of Arabic: The development of negation and interrogation among learners in the UK*. Ph.D. dissertation, University of Edinburgh. Qatar: Dār Al-Thaqafa (1987).

Al-Ghalayyīnī, Al-Sheikh Muṣṭafā. 2000. *Jāmi' Al-Durūs Al-'Arabiyya*. Sidon, Lebanon: Al-Maktaba Al-'Aṣriyya.

Alhawary, Mohammad T. 2007a. "The Split-INFL Hypothesis: Findings from English and Japanese L2 learners of Arabic." *Perspectives on Arabic Linguistics XX* ed. by Mustafa Mughazy, 135-152. Amsterdam, The Netherlands: John Benjamins.

Alhawary, Mohammad T. 2007b. "Null Subjects Use by English and Spanish Learners of Arabic as an L2." *Perspectives on Arabic Linguistics XIX* ed. by Elabbas Benmamoun, 217-245. Amsterdam, The Netherlands: John Benjamins.

Alhawary, Mohammad T. 2005. "L2 Acquisition of Arabic Morphosyntactic Features: Temporary or permanent impairment?" *Perspectives on Arabic Linguistics XVII-XVIII* ed. by Mohammad T. Alhawary and Elabbas Benmamoun, 273-311. Amsterdam, The Netherlands: John Benjamins.

Alhawary, Mohammad T. 2003. "Processability Theory: Counter-evidence from Arabic second language acquisition data." *Al-ᶜArabiyya* 36:107-166.

Alhawary, Mohammad T. 2002. "Role of L1 Transfer in L2 Acquisition of Inflectional Morphology." *Perspectives on Arabic Linguistics XIII-XIV* ed. by Dilworth Parkinson and Elabbas Benmamoun, 219-248. Amsterdam, The Netherlands: John Benjamins.

Alhawary, Mohammad T. 1999. *Testing Pocessability and Effectiveness of Computer-assisted Language Instruction: A longitudinal study of Arabic as a foreign/ second language.* Ph.D. dissertation, Georgetown University.

Al-Hulwānī, Muhammad Khayr. 1972. *Al-Wāḍiḥ fī Al-Naḥw wa Al-Ṣarf.* Aleppo, Syria: Al-Maktaba Al-ʿaṣriyya.

Alkhalifa, Waleed Saleh. 2002. *Curso Práctico de Lengua Árabe II.* Madrid, Spain: Editorial Ibersaf.

Alkhalifa, Waleed Saleh. 1999. *Curso Práctico de Lengua Árabe I.* Madrid, Spain: Dār Alwah.

Anderson, Roger W. 1978. "An Implicational Model for Second Language Research." *Language Learning* 28:221-282.

Bachman, Lyle F. and Andrew D. Cohen. 1998. *Interfaces Between Second Language Acquisition and Language Testing Research.* Cambridge, MA: Cambridge University Press.

Badawi, Elsaid Muhammad, Muhammad H. Abdullatif, and Mahmoud Al-Batal. 1992. *Al-Kitāb Al-Asāsī Part II.* Tunisia: Al-Munaththama Al-ʿArabiyya Li-Al-Tarbiyya wa Al-Thaqāfa wa Al-ʿUlūm.

Badawi, Elsaid Muhammad and Fathi Ali Yunis. 1983. *Al-Kitāb Al-Asāsī Part I.* Tunisia: Al-Munaththama Al-ʿArabiyya Li-Al-Tarbiyya wa Al-Thaqāfa wa Al-ʿUlūm.

Badry, Fatima. 2005. "Acquisition of Arabic Word Formation: A multi path approach." *Perspectives on Arabic Linguistics XVII-XVIII* ed. by Mohammad T. Alhawary and Elabbas Benmamoun, 242-271. Amsterdam, The Netherlands: John Benjamins.

Bahns, Jens. 1981. "On Acquisitional Criteria." *International Review of Applied Linguistics* 21:57-68.

Bailey, Nathalie, Carolyn Madden, and Stephen Krashen. 1974. "Is There a 'Natural Sequence' in Adult Second Language Learning?" *Language Learning* 24:235-243.

Barakāt, Ibrāhīm I. 1988. *Al-Taʾnīth fī Al-Lugha Al-ʿArabiyya.* Al-Manṣūra, Egypt: Dār Al-Wafāʾ.

Bates, Elizabeth and Brian MacWhinney. 1987. "Competition, Variation, and Language Learning." *Mechanisms of Language Acquisition* ed. by Brian MacWhinney, 157-193. Hillsdale, NJ: Lawrence Erlbaum.

Beard, Robert. 1995. *Lexeme-Morpheme Base Morphology*. Albany, NY: State University of New York Press.

Beck, Maria-Luise. 1998. "L2 Acquisition and Obligatory Head Movement: English speaking learners of German and the local impairment hypothesis." *Studies in Second Language Acquisition* 20:311-348.

Beck, Maria-Luise. 1997. "Regular Verbs, Part Tense, and Frequency: Tracking down one potential source of NS/NNS syntactic competence differences." *Second Language Research* 13:93-115.

Benmamoun, Elabbas. 1999. "Arabic Morphology: The central role of the imperfective." *Lingua* 108:175-201.

Berg, Thomas and Hassan Abd El-Jawad. 1996. "The Unfolding of Suprasegmental Representations: A crosslinguistic perspective." *Journal of Linguistics* 32:291-324.

Berman, Ruth A. 1999. "Children's Innovative Verbs versus Nouns: Structured elicitations and spontaneous coinages." *Methods in Studying Language Production* ed. by Lise Menn and Nan Bernstein Ratner, 69-93. Mahwah, NJ: Lawrence Erlbaum.

Berman, Ruth A. 1985. "The Acquisition of Hebrew." *The Crosslinguistic Study of Language Acquisition* Vol.1 ed. by Dan I. Slobin, 255-371. Hillsdale, NJ: Lawrence Erlbaum.

Bialystok, Ellen. 1990. *Communication Strategies*. Oxford, UK: Blackwell.

Bishop, Dorothy V. M. and Laurence B. Leonard. 2000. *Speech and Language Impairment in Children: Causes, characteristics, intervention, and outcome*. East Sussex, England: Psychology Press.

Bley-Vroman, R. 1990. "The Logical Problem of Foreign Language Learning." *Linguistic Analysis* 20 (1-2):3-49.

Bley-Vroman, R. 1989. "What is the Logical Problem of Foreign Language Learning." *Linguistic Perspectives on Second Language Acquisition* ed. by Susan Gass and Jacquelyn Schachter, 41-68. Cambridge, UK: Cambridge University Press.

Bley-Vroman, R. 1983. "The Comparative Fallacy in Interlanguage Studies: The case of systematicity." *Language Learning* 33:1-17.

Bolotin, Naomi. 1996a. "Resetting Parameters in Acquiring Arabic." *Perspectives on Arabic Linguistics IX* ed. by Mushira Eid and Dilworth Parkinson, 166-178. Amsterdam, The Netherlands: John Benjamins.

Bolotin, Naomi. 1996b. "Arabic Speakers' Resetting of Parameters." *Perspectives on Arabic Linguistics VIII* ed. by Mushira Eid, 135-155. Amsterdam, The Netherlands: John Benjamins.

Bresnan, Joan. 1982. *The Mental Representation of Grammatical Relations*. Cambridge, MA: MIT Press.

Brown, H. Douglas. 1980. *Principles of Language Teaching and Learning*. Englewood Cliffs, NJ: Prentice Hall.

Brown, Roger. 1973. *A First Language: The early stages*. Cambridge, MA: Harvard University Press.

Brustad, Kristen, Mahmoud Al-Batal, and Abbas Al-Tonsi. 1995a. *Alif Baa: Introduction to Arabic letters and sounds*. Washington, DC: Georgetown University Press.

Brustad, Kristen, Mahmoud Al-Batal, and Abbas Al-Tonsi. 1995b. *Al-Kitaab fii Ta^callum Al-^cArabiyya*. Washington, DC: Georgetown University Press.

Burt, Marina and Heidi Dulay. 1980. "On Acquisition Orders." *Second Language Development* ed. by Sascha Felix, 265-327. Tubingen, Germany: Gunter Narr.

Burton, Eric and Lois Maharg. 1995. *Going Places 1*. London, UK: Longman.

Cancino, Herlinda, Ellen J. Rosansky, and John H. Schumann. "The Acquisition of English Negatives and Interrogatives by Native Spanish Speakers." *Second Language Acquisition: A book of readings* ed. by Evelyn Hatch, 207-230. Rowley, MA: Newbury House.

Cazden, Courtney, Herlinda Cancino, Ellen Rosansky, and John Schumann. 1975. *Second Language Acquisition Sequences in Children, Adolescents and Adults*. Final report submitted to the National Institute of Education, Washington, DC.

Chomsky, Noam. 2001. "Beyond Explanatory Adequacy." *Occasional Papers in Linguistics* 20:1-28. Cambridge, MA: MIT Press.

Chomsky, Noam. 1999. "Derivation by Phase." *Occasional Papers in Linguistics* 18:1-43. Cambridge, MA: MIT Press. [Reprinted in *Ken Hale: A life in language* ed. by Michael Kenstowicz, 1-52. Cambridge, MA: MIT Press.]

Chomsky, Noam. 1998. "Minimalist Inquiries: The framework." *Occasional Papers in Linguistics* 15:1-14. Cambridge, MA: MIT Press.

Chomsky, Noam. 1995. "Categories and Transformations." *The Minimalist Program*, 219-394. Cambridge, MA: MIT Press.

Chomsky, Noam. 1993. "A Minimalist Program for Linguistic Theory." *The View from Building 20* ed. by Ken Hale and Samuel J. Keyser, 1-52. Cambridge, MA: MIT Press.

Chomsky, Noam. 1991. "Some Notes on Economy of Derivation and Representation." *Principles and Parameters in Comparative Syntax* ed. by Robert Freidin, 417-454. Cambridge, MA: MIT Press.

Clahsen, Harald. 1984. "The Acquisition of German Word Order: A test case for cognitive approaches to second language acquisition." *Second Language* ed. by Roger Anderson, 219-242. Rowley, MA: Newbury House.

Clahsen, Harald and Pieter Muysken. 1989. "The UG Paradox in L2 Acquisition." *Second Language Research* 2:1-29.

Clahsen, Harald and Pieter Muysken. 1986. "The Availability of Universal Grammar to Adult and Child Learners: A study of the acquisition of German word order." *Second Language Research* 5:93-119.

Corder, S. Pit. 1978. "Simple Codes and the Source of the Second Language Learner's Initial Heuristic Hypothesis." *Studies in Second Language Acquisition* 1(1):1-10.

Davis, Stuart and Bushra A. Zawaydeh. 2001. "Arabic Hypocoristics and the Status of the Consonantal Root." *Linguistic Inquiry* 32:512-520.

De Garavito, Joyce Bruhn and Lydia White. 2002. "The Second Language Acquisition of Spanish DPs: The status of grammatical features." *The Acquisition of Spanish*

Morphosyntax ed. by Ana Teresa Pérez-Leroux and Juana Munoz Liceras, 153-178. Dordrecht, The Netherlands: Kluwer Academic Publishers.

Deheuvels, Luc-Willy. 2003. *Manuel d'Arabe Moderne* Vol. 1, 2nd Edition. Paris, France: Asiathèque.

Deheuvels, Luc-Willy. 2002. *Manuel d'Arabe Moderne* Vol. 2, 2nd Edition. Paris, France: Asiathèque.

Dewaele, Jean-Marc and Daniel Véronique. 2001. "Gender Assignment and Gender Agreement in Advanced French Interlanguage: A cross-sectional study." *Bilingualism: Language and Cognition* 4:275-297.

Ellis, Rod. 1991. "Grammaticality Judgments and Second Language Acquisition." *Studies in Second Language Acquisition* 13:161-186.

Ellis, Rod. 1990. "Grammaticality Judgments and Learner Variability." *Variability in Second Language Acquisition: Proceedings of the tenth meeting of the second language research forum* ed. by Hartmut Burmeister and Patricia L. Rounds, 25-60. Eugene, OR: Department of Linguistics, University of Oregon.

Elsheikh Abdalla, Adil. 2005. "An Error Analysis of Malay Students' Written Arabic." *Investigating Arabic: Current parameters in analysis and learning* ed. by Alaa Elgibali, 133-155. Leiden, The Netherlands: Brill.

Eubank, Lynn. 1996. "Negation in Early German-English Interlanguage: More valueless features in the L2 initial state." *Second Language Research* 12(4):73-106.

Eubank, Lynn. 1993/4. "On the Transfer of Pragmatic Values in L2 Development." *Language Acquisition* 3:183-208.

Eubank, Lynn. 1992. "Verb Movement, Agreement, and Tense in L2 Acquisition." *The Acquisition of Verb Placement* ed. by Jurgen Meisel, 225-244. Dordrecht, The Netherlands: Kluwer Academic Publishers.

Eubank, Lynn and Maria-Luise Beck. 1998. "OI-Like Effects in Adult L2 Acquisition." *Proceedings of the 22nd Annual Boston University Conference on Language Development Vol. 1* ed. by Annabel Greenhill, Mary Hughes, Heather Littlefield, and Hugh Walsh, 189-200. Somerville, MA: Cascadilla Press.

Eubank, Lynn, Janine Bischof, April Huffstutler, Patricia Leek, and Clint West. 1997. "'Tom Eats Slowly Cooked Eggs': Thematic verb raising in L2 knowledge." *Language Acquisition* 6:3.171-199.

Faerch, Claus and Gabriele Kasper. 1983. *Strategies in Interlanguage Communication*. London, UK: Longman.

Fakhri, Ahmed. 1984. "The Use of Communicative Strategies in Narrative Discourse: A case study of Moroccan Arabic as a second language." *Language Learning* 34(3):15-37.

Farley, Andrew P. and Kristina McCollam. 2004. "Learner Readiness and L2 Production in Spanish: Processability Theory on trail." *Estudios de Lingüística Aplicade* 40:47-69.

Fassi Fehri, Abdelkader. 1993. *Issues in the Structure of Arabic Clauses and Words*. Dordrecht, The Netherlands: Kluwer Academic Publishers.

Felix, Sascha W. 1985. "More Evidence on Competing Cognitive Systems." *Second Language Research* 1:47-72.

Frisch, Stephan and Bushra A. Zawaydeh. 2001. "The Psychological Reality of OCP-place in Arabic." *Language* 77:91-106.

Gass, Susan and Larry Selinker. 1994. *Second Language Acquisition*. Hillsdale, NJ: Lawrence Erlbaum.

Goldschneider, Jennifer M. and Robert M. DeKeyser. 2001. "Explaining the 'Natural Order of L2 Morpheme Acquisition' in English: A meta-analysis of multiple determinants." *Language Learning* 51(1):1-50.

Goss, Nancy, Zhang Ying-Hua, and James Lantolf. 1994. "Two Heads Better Than One: Assessing mental activities in L2 grammatical judgments." *Research Methodology in Second Language Acquisition* ed. by Elaine E. Tarone, Susan M. Gass, and Andrew D. Cohen, 263-286. Mahwah, NJ: Erlbaum.

Griffin, William Earl. 2003. "The Split-INFL Hypothesis and AgrsP in Universal Grammar." *The Role of Agreement in Natural Language: TLS 5 proceedings* ed. by William E. Griffin, 13-24. Texas Linguistics Forum 53.

Harris, James. 1991. "The Exponence of gender in Spanish." *Linguistics Inquiry* 22:27-62.

Hawkins, Roger. 2001. *Second Language Syntax*. Malden, MA: Blackwell.

Hawkins, Roger. 1998. "The Inaccessibility of Formal Features of Functional Categories in Second Language Acquisition." Paper presented at the Pacific Second Language Research Forum, Tokyo, Japan, March 1998.

Hawkins, Roger and Yuet-Hung Chan. 1997. "The Partial Availability of Universal Grammar in Second Language Acquisition: The 'Failed Functional Features Hypothesis.'" *Second Language Research* 13(3):187-226.

Huebner, Thom. 1979. "Order of Acquisition vs. Dynamic Paradigm: A comparison of method in interlanguage research." *TESOL Quarterly* 13:21-28.

Hulk, Aafke. 1991. "Parameter Setting and the Acquisition of Word Order in L2 French." *Second Language Research* 7:1-34.

Kempen, Gerald and Edward Hoenkamp. 1987. "An Incremental Procedural Grammar for Sentence Formulation." *Cognitive Science* 11:201-258.

Klein, Wolfgang. 1991. "SLA Theory: Prolegomena to a theory of language acquisition and implications for theoretical linguistics." *Crosscurrents in Second Language Acquisition and Linguistic Theory* ed. by Thom Huebner and Charles Ferguson, 169-194. Amsterdam, The Netherlands: John Benjamins.

Krashen, Stephen. 2003. *Explorations in Language Acquisition and Use*. Portsmouth, NH: Heinemann.

Krashen, Stephen. 1993. "The Effect of Formal Grammar Teaching: Still peripheral." *TESOL Quarterly* 27:722-25.

Krashen, Stephen. 1985. *The Input Hypothesis: Issues and implications*. London, UK: Longman.

Krashen, Stephen. 1977. "Some Issues Relating to the Monitor Model." *On TESOL '77 Teaching and Learning English as a Second Language: Trends in research and practice* ed. by Carlos Alfredo Yorio, Ruth H. Crymes, and H. Douglas Brown, 144-158. Washington, DC: TESOL.

Langendoen, D. Terence. 1970. "The Accessability of Deep Structures." *Readings in English Transformational Grammar* ed. by Roderick A. Jacobs and Peter S. Rosenbaum, 99-106. Waltham, MA: Ginn.

Lantolf, James. 1990. "Resetting the Null Subject Parameter in Second Language Acquisition." *Variability in Second Language Acquisition: Proceedings of the tenth meeting of the second language research forum* ed. by Hartmut Burmeister and Patricia L. Rounds, 429-452. Eugene, OR: Department of Linguistics, University of Oregon.

Lardiere, Donna. 2000. "Mapping Features to Forms in Second Language Acquisition." *Second Language Acquisition and Linguistic Theory* ed. by John Archibald, 102-129. Oxford, UK: Blackwell.

Lardiere, Donna. 1998. "Case and Tense in the 'Fossilized' Steady State." *Second Language Research* 14:1-26.

Larsen-Freeman, Diane E. 1975. "The Acquisition of Grammatical Morphemes by Adult ESL Learners." *TESOL Quarterly* 9:409-430.

Larsen-Freeman, Diane E. and Michael H. Long. 1991. *An Introduction to Second Language Acquisition Research.* New York: Longman.

Levelt, Willem J. M. 1989. *Speaking: From intention to articulation.* Cambridge, MA: MIT Press.

Liceras, Juana M., Denyse Maxwell, Biana Laguardia, Zara Fernández, and Raquel Fernández. 1997. "A Longitudinal Study of Spanish Non-native Grammars: Beyond parameters." *Contemporary Perspectives on the Acquisition of Spanish, Volume 1: Developing grammars* ed. by Ana Teresa Pérez-Leroux and William R. Glass, 99-132. Somerville, MA: Cascadilla Press.

Lui, Guo-qiang. 1991. *Interaction and Second Language Acquisition: A case study of a Chinese child's acquisition of English as a second language.* Ph.D. dissertation, La Trobe University, Melbourne, Australia.

MacWhinney, Brian and Elizabeth Bates. 1989. *The Crosslinguistic Study of Sentence Processing.* Cambridge: Cambridge University Press.

Majma' Al-Lugha Al-'Arabiyya. 1984. *Majmū'at Al-Qarārāt Al-'Ilmiyya fī Xamīna 'Aman.* Cairo, Egypt.

Mansouri, Fethi. 2005. "Agreement Morphology in Arabic as a Second Language: Typological features and their processing implications." *Cross-linguistic Aspects of Processability Theory* ed. by Manfred Pienemann, 117-153. Amsterdam, The Netherlands: John Benjamins.

Mansouri, Fethi. 2000. *Grammatical Markedness and Information Processing in the Acquisition of Arabic L2.* Munich, Germany: Lincom Europa.

McCarthy, John J. 1981. "A Prosodic Theory of Nonconcactenative Morphology." *Linguistic Inquiry* 12:373-418.

Meisel, Jurgen. 1994. "Getting FAT: Finiteness, agreement and tense in early grammars." *Bilingual First Language Acquisition: French and German grammatical development* ed. by Jurgen Meisel, 89-129. Amsterdam, The Netherlands: John Benjamins.

Meisel, Jurgen. 1991. "Principles of Universal Grammar and Strategies of Language Use: On some similarities and differences between first and second language acquisition." *Point-counterpoint: Universal Grammar in the second language* ed. by Lynn Eubank, 231-271. Amsterdam, The Netherlands: John Benjamins.

Meisel, Jurgen. 1983. "Strategies of Second Language Acquisition: More than one kind of simplification." *Pidginization and Creolization as Second Language Acquisition* ed. by Roger W. Anderson, Rowley, MA: Newbury House.

Meisel, Jurgen, Harald Clahsen, and Manfred Pienemann. 1981. "On Determining Developmental Stages in Natural Second Language Acquisition." *Studies in Second Language Acquisition* 3:109-135.

Molinsky, Steven J. and Bill Bliss. 1996. *ExpressWays*. Upper Saddle River, NJ: Prentice Hall Regents.

Newport, Elissa. 1990. "Maturational Constraints on Language Learning." *Cognitive Science* 14:11-28.

Nielsen, Helle Lykke. 1997. "On Acquisition Order of Agreement Procedures in Arabic Learner Language." *Al-ᶜArabiyya* 30:49-93.

O'Grady, William, John Archibald, Mark Aronoff, and Janie Rees-Miller. 2001. *Contemporary Linguistics*. Boston, MA: Bedford.

O'Malley, J. Michael and Anna Uhl Chamot. 1990. *Learning Strategies in Second Language Acquisition*. Cambridge, UK: Cambridge University Press.

Oxford, Rebecca and Andrew Cohen. 1992. "Language Learning Strategies: Crucial issues of concept and classification." *Language Learning* 3:1-35.

Pienemann, Manfred. 1998. *Language Processing and Second Language Development: Processability Theory*. Amsterdam, The Netherlands: John Benjamins.

Pienemann, Manfred. 1992. "Teachability Theory." Unpublished MS. Sydney, Australia: Language Acquisition Research Center, University of Sydney.

Pienemann, Manfred and Gisela Håkansson. 1999. "A Unified Approach toward the Development of Swedish as L2. " *Studies in Second Language Acquisition* 21:383-420.

Pienemann, Manfred and Malcolm Johnston. 1987. "Factors Influencing the Development of Language Proficiency." *Applying Second Language Acquisition Research* ed. by David Nunan, 45-141. Adelaide, Australia: National Curriculum Research Centre, Adult Migrant Educational Program.

Poeppel, David and Kenneth Wexler. 1993. "The Full Competence Hypothesis of Clause Structure in Early German." *Language* 69:1-33.

Pollock, Jean-Yves. 1989. "Verb Movement, Universal Grammar, and the Structure of IP." *Linguistic Inquiry* 20:364-424.

Prévost, Philippe and Lydia White. 2000. "Missing Surface Inflection or Impairment in Second Language Acquisition? Evidence from tense and agreement." *Second Language Research* 16(2):103-133.

Prunet, Jean Francois, Renee Beland, and Ali Idrissi. 2000. "The Mental Representation of Semitic Words." *Linguistic Inquiry* 31:609-648.

Rammuny, Raji M. 1976. "Statistical Study of Errors Made by American Students in Written Arabic." *Al-ᶜArabiyya* 9:75-94.

Ratcliffe, Robert. R. 1997. "Prosodic Templates in a Word Based Morphological Analysis of Arabic." *Perspectives on Arabic Linguistics X* ed. by Mushira Eid and Robert. Ratcliffe, 147-171. Amsterdam, The Netherlands: John Benjamins.

Richards, Jack C. 1974. *Error Analysis: Perspectives on second language acquisition.* London, UK: Longman.

Sasaki, Yoshinori. 1994. "Paths of Processing Strategy Transfers in Learning Japanese and English as Foreign Languages: A Competition Model approach." *Studies in Second Language Acquisition* 16:43-72.

Sauter, Kim. 2002. *Transfer and Access to Universal Grammar in Adult Second Language Acquisition.* Ph.D. dissertation, University of Groningen, The Netherlands.

Ṣaydāwī, Yusuf. 1999. *Al-Kafāf.* Damascus, Syria: Dār Al-Fikr.

Schachter, Jacquelyn. 1989. "Testing a Proposed Universal." *Linguistic Perspectives on Second Language Acquisition* ed. by Susan Gass and Jacquelyn Schachter, 73-88. Cambridge, UK: Cambridge University Press.

Schumann, John. 1979. "The Acquisition of English Negation by Speakers of Spanish: A review of the literature." *The Acquisition and Use of Spanish and English as First and Second Languages* ed. by Roger W. Anderson, 3-32. Washington, DC: TESOL.

Schwartz, Bonnie D. 1998. "On Two Hypotheses of 'Transfer' in L2A: Minimal Trees and absolute L1 influence." *The Generative Study of Second Language Acquisition* ed. by Suzanne Flynn, Gita Martohardjiono, and Wayne O'Neil, 35-59. Mahwah, NJ: Lawrence Erlbaum.

Schwartz, Bonnie D. and Rex A. Sprouse. 1996. "L2 Cognitive States and the Full Transfer/Full Access Model." *Second Language Research* 12:40-72.

Schwartz, Bonnie D. and Rex A. Sprouse. 1994. "Word Order and Nominative Case in Non-native Language Acquisition: A longitudinal study of (L1 Turkish) German interlanguage." *Language Acquisition Studies in Generative Grammar: Papers in honor of Kenneth Wexler from the 1991 GLOW Workshops* ed. by Tuen Hoekstra and Bonnie D. Schwarts, 317-68. Amsterdam, The Netherlands: John Benjamins.

Sharwood Smith, Michael. 1991. "Speaking to Many Different Minds: On the relevance of different types of language information for the L2 learner." *Second Language Research* 7:118-32.

Sharwood Smith, Michael. 1981. "Consciousness Raising and the Second Language Learner." *Applied Linguistics* 2:158-68.

Sībawayhi, Abū Bishr 'Amr. 1990. *Al-Kitāb.* Beirut, Lebanon: Mu'ssasat Al-A'lamī.

Slobin, Dan I. 1973. "Cognitive Prerequisites for the Development of Grammar." *Studies of Child Language Development* ed. by Charles A. Ferguson and Dan I. Slobin, 175-208. New York, NY: Holt, Rinehart and Winston.

Sorace, Antonella. 2003. "Near-Nativeness." *The Handbook of Second Language Acquisition* ed. by Catherine J. Doughty and Michael Long, 130-151. Oxford, UK: Blackwell.

Spinner, Patti A. 2007. *Placement Testing and Morphosyntactic Development in Second Language Learners of English*. Ph.D. dissertation, University of Pittsburgh.

Stenson, Nancy. 1974. "Induced Errors." *New Frontiers in Second Language Learning* ed. by John Schumann and Nancy Stenson, 54-70. Rowley, MA: Newbury House.

Taman, Hassan A. 1993. "The Utilization of Syntactic, Semantic, and Pragmatic Cues in the Assignment of Subject Role in Arabic." *Applied Psycholinguistics* 14:299-317.

Tarone, Elaine. 2007. "A Sociolinguistic Perspective on Interaction in SLA." Paper presented at the 30th Annual AAAL Conference, Costa Mesa, CA, April 2007.

Tarone, Elaine. 1980. "Communication Strategies, Foreign Talk, and Repair in Interlanguage." *Language Learning* 20:417-431.

Tarone, Elaine. 1977. "Conscious Communication Strategies in Interlanguage: A progress report." *On TESOL '77 Teaching and Learning English as a Second Language: Trends in research and practice* ed. by Carlos Alfredo Yorio, Ruth H. Crymes, and H. Douglas Brown, 194-203. Washington, DC: TESOL.

Tarone, Elaine and Guo-qiang Lui. 1995. "Situational Context, Variation, and Second Language Acquisition Theory." *Principles and Practice in Applied Linguistics: Studies in honour of H. G. Widdowson* ed. by Guy Cook and Barbara Seidlhofer, 107-124. Oxford, UK: Oxford University Press.

Vainikka, Anne and Martha Young-Scholten. 1998. "The Initial State in the L2 Acquisition of Phrase Structure." *The Generative Study of Second Language Acquisition* ed. by Suzanne Flynn, Gita Martohardjiono, and Wayne O'neil, 17-34. Mahwah, NJ: Lawrence Erlbaum.

Vainikka, Anne and Martha Young-Scholten. 1996. "Gradual Development of L2 Phrase Structure." *Second Language Research* 12:7-39.

Vainikka, Anne and Martha Young-Scholten. 1994. "Direct Access to X'-Theory: Evidence from Korean and Turkish adults learning German." *Language Acquisition Studies in Generative Grammar: Papers in honor of Kenneth Wexler from the 1991 GLOW Workshops* ed. by Tuen Hoekstra and Bonnie D. Schwartz, 265-316. Amsterdam, The Netherlands: John Benjamins.

White, Lydia. 2003. *Second Language Acquisition and Universal Grammar*. Cambridge, UK: Cambridge University Press.

White, Lydia. 1989. *Universal Grammar and Second Language Acquisition*. Amsterdam, The Netherlands: John Benjamins.

Wode, Henning. 1978. "The L1 vs. L2 Acquisition of English Negation." *Working Papers on Bilingualism* 15:37-57.

Zobl, Helmut. 1984. "Cross Language Generalizations and the Contrastive Dimension of the IL Hypothesis." *Interlanguage* ed. by Alan Davies, Clive Criper, and Anthony Howatt, 79-97. Edinburgh, UK: Edinburgh University Press.

Zobl, Helmut and Juana Liceras. 1994. "Review Article: Functional categories and acquisition orders." *Language Learning* 44:159-180.

Index